LETTERS TO PAULA

David Ben-Gurion Letters to Paula

Translated from the Hebrew by
AUBREY HODES

UNIVERSITY OF PITTSBURGH PRESS

First published in Hebrew
in Israel, 1968

First published in Great Britain
in 1971 by Vallentine, Mitchell
& Co. Ltd., 18, Cursitor Street,
London E.C.4.

ISBN 0 8229 1102 7

Library of Congress Catalog Card Number 72-164702

Manufactured in Great Britain

ACKNOWLEDGEMENTS

Grateful acknowledgement is made to
the following for their kind assistance
and permission to use the photographs
included in this book: Mr Joseph Fraenkel,
the Jewish Agency, the Gluck Archives,
The Wiener Library, the *Jewish Chronicle* Archives.

CONTENTS

All the letters in this book were
written to Ben-Gurion's wife Paula,
except where the name of one or
other of their children is given
at the head of the letter.

The sign + after a name indicates
that brief biographical details of
that person may be found in the
glossary.

PREFACE

These letters to my late wife Paula* and the children were written during three different periods. Part I contains letters written during my service in the Jewish Legion, from May 30, 1918 to July 25, 1919. Part II covers the period from September 1923 to 1935, when I travelled abroad on Zionist business, even though most of my time was taken up by matters concerning the *Histadrut* trade union and the *Yishuv*, the Jewish community in Palestine: Paula knew about and felt involved in these activities, so it is natural that the letters of this period should deal largely with Zionist affairs. Part III consists of letters to Paula and my children (Geula, Amos and Renana): they were written after the Zionist Congress in Lucerne in September 1935, when I became totally involved in the affairs of the Zionist movement in Palestine and abroad, and go up to March 16, 1939 — when the British Mandatory Government's talks with the Jews and Arabs in London (the 'London Conference') ended, and with them, in effect, the Mandate itself: this date marked the beginning of the real and prolonged struggle for the establishment of a Jewish State. And finally, there is the letter I wrote to my family after my father died in 1942.

The first section contains scarcely any historical material, apart from my first-hand description of life in the Jewish Legion in Canada, Britain and Egypt. The main thread running through these letters is a reaction to the pangs of loneliness of a young, pregnant woman who shortly after her marriage in America was left alone — because her husband was a Zionist, and the implementation of Zionism was more important to him than anything else. At that time, Zionist matters themselves were completely foreign to the young woman, and only because she listened to her husband's speeches did she begin to take some interest in the problems of the Zionist movement, which remained strange to her and incomprehensible for a long while. True enough, her husband told her clearly before they were married that if he could return to the Land of Israel (from which he had been

*Paula Ben-Gurion died in 1968.

IX

expelled by the Turks in 1915) he would do so at the earliest opportunity and that she would have to come with him in the full knowledge that she was going to a primitive country, which had no electricity or cars, and in which their house would be lit only by oil lamps, and where it was almost impossible to obtain domestic help. And she knew also that as the American Government had agreed to establish a Jewish Legion in the United States, which would serve in the British Army on the Palestinian front, her husband would volunteer immediately for the Legion and she would have to come to Palestine after the war was over. She agreed to this — but this agreement, to which she consented because she had no alternative, did not save her from her lonely ordeal. And these letters of mine were in effect only my participation in her suffering, which had to be borne on her own.

The third section contains a great deal of material on the four years of progress and failures, difficulties and successes, exultant hopes and bitter disappointments, which marked the four years between the 19th Zionist Congress in Lucerne in 1935 and the outbreak of World War II.

DAVID BEN-GURION

LETTERS 1918 – 1919

It's now 4 p.m., and this is the first free moment I've had since six this morning, when, after reaching Fall River at dawn, we left the boat. We marched from the boat to the synagogue, where Magen David Adom* had breakfast waiting for us. Then by train to Boston, which we reached at eleven. We marched through the streets of Boston for over an hour, accompanied by music and flags, and cheered by a large crowd.

At noon we held a public meeting. I spoke, and so did other Legionnaires. The meeting finished at two o'clock. Three young men in the crowd joined the Legion on the spot. Then they arranged a first-rate lunch for us, after which we were photographed. Now we're off duty, so I am writing you this note.

We're leaving Boston at seven-thirty tonight, and tomorrow morning at eleven we will reach Saint John in Canada. I had great difficulty finding a place to sleep on the train. We had second-class tickets, and these didn't entitle us to sleeping berths. The Legionnaires from Philadelphia were the only ones with first-class tickets, and one of them gave me his ticket.

From St. John we'll travel by ship to Windsor, and when we get there I'll be able to write to you in greater detail. I'm rather tired now, from the marching and also from the speeches, both mine and the other people's

Congratulations on your new apartment. I'm sorry I couldn't see what you've done to it. Regards to your new neighbour and all our friends and acquaintances.

*The American Zionist Medical Unit, later named the Hadassah Medical Organization.

1

At last I'm here — and I'm writing this card to you sitting on the ground, in a military tent, in other words in the camp. We arrived here at eleven, and our boys, wearing uniform, were waiting for us next to the railway station, with British and Jewish flags. They've already given me a number, and now I'm a soldier of His Majesty the King, though I won't get my uniform for a few days.

Ben-Zvi+ is a real soldier already. His face is tanned from the sun, and I can hardly recognize him. All of us are in an open field. The grass has a good smell, and I would heartily recommend to everyone that they spend a few months here together with us.

Today, in honour of the Sabbath, we have the day off. Tomorrow is Sunday, so we'll be free again. Soon we'll be given blankets and each of us will get his tent ready for inspection.

There are about 400 Legionnaires here, and we'll probably stay two or three weeks. Please, my dearest, send me Jewish papers and also the *New York Times.*

My address is:

Private D. Ben-Gurion, No. 3831, Platoon 11,
Windsor N.S. Canada. Jewish Legion.

Windsor
June 1, 1918.

My first day in camp has been so rich in experiences and fresh impressions that I hardly know where to begin. I feel drunk with my new life. Everything here is better, more pleasant and more interesting than I thought it would be or expected. I am only sorry that you are not with me and that you can't feel what I feel.

I would advise everyone to leave the suffocating cities and the boring villages and to come here for a while to enjoy the life in the camp. True enough, there is an iron military discipline here. Yet for some reason I feel myself much freer and less inhibited than I have ever done before. I don't know what will happen in the future. But at the moment I am almost intoxicated with my new life and the new conditions, and the only thing that worries me and takes me out of this fresh atmosphere is you and my thoughts about you.

I want to describe our way of life to you and how we spend our time both in camp and off duty. I'll do this in detail in my next few letters. But today I want to tell you about the journey from New York to Windsor.

The whole trip was passed in singing — you can imagine this for yourself. Most of the boys in our group were pleasant young fellows, full of life and good company. I was amazed they didn't get tired, during three days of travelling, and never stopping singing, dancing, playing jokes and pranks and then singing again. In all the towns we went through — Fall River, Boston, Newport, Portsmouth, Bangor and Saint John — we were received with great enthusiasm. At Portland, which we reached on Friday night at eleven, a tremendous crowd was waiting for us with flags and music. The moment I came out of the carriage, and the crowd saw me, they lifted me up and shouted 'Hurray!', and when I managed with difficulty to free myself, they caught hold of me again and carried me high above the heads of the hundreds of people who had gathered next to the railway station. I was forced to speak, even though I was very tired and tremendously moved by the wonderful welcome.

An even warmer reception awaited us that same night, at four in the morning, in the town of Bangor. Despite the late hour the entire Jewish community came to meet us, waving flags and singing. I sat in the Pullman, not far from the other Legionnaires, and the crowd from Bangor, which had been waiting all night, asked for me and tried to find me — but couldn't. As if in a dream I heard the sound of the music, but the gifts and presents that were still there the next morning — heaps of chocolates, cakes, cigarettes and flowers — proved to me that the Legionnaires' praise of the Bangor Jewish community was not exaggerated.

We spent the night in the small town of Truro, not far from Windsor. There we stayed in the hotel. We had to leave

Truro at 6.40 a.m., and we begged the hotel proprietor to wake us promptly at five. And of course he promised to do so. But he didn't wake us until half-past six, and we jumped out of bed as if we had been stung. We were dressed within ten minutes and just about managed to reach the train in time. We got there literally at the last minute. Three of the boys missed the train and had to stay in Truro.

We reached Windsor at ten. At the railway station a number of Legion members were waiting for us, wearing their uniforms. From the train we marched in military formation, and the local Legion welcomed us with cheers and applause, but without any singing. Ben-Zvi was among those waiting.

They wrote our names down and took us for a medical examination. Then they took us to the tents where we will sleep. Meanwhile the local Legionnaires went to pray in the synagogue, as they do every Saturday. Ben-Zvi went along with them. After the service the Legionnaires came running to see the new recruits, and from all sides they came to shake my hand. The whole camp knew I was coming, and they waited for me impatiently.

My darling, write to me in detail about everything that interests you and me. You are the only thing I miss, and I won't find anything as precious as you in the whole world, not even in the Land of Israel. Write to me as often as I write to you. Love me as I love you, and think of me as I think of you.

Windsor
June 3, 1918.

This is my third day in camp, and every day is better than the one before. I'm still not wearing uniform, but I've already begun doing basic training. Today I was vaccinated against smallpox and also given an injection against typhus, and because of this I probably won't train tomorrow. But I already feel I am a soldier.

The first full day in camp — Saturday — was spent in meeting people and arranging various formalities. As it was the Sabbath all the boys were let off training, and they came along to shake hands with me.

I've already told you that my first impression of life here was enthusiastic. I was a little apprehensive about sleeping in a tent for the first time and on the ground. But it was all right. Each of us has been given four thick blankets. You spread two out on the floor and wrap yourself in the other two, with something placed under your head as a pillow. Many people use a kind of rubber cushion for this, which can be blown up and kept in a shirt pocket when not in use. It is convenient and a good thing to have. So I've bought one, for one and a half dollars. The first night it was a bit cold, but on the second night I felt fine and slept soundly. It's easier to sleep on the ground than I thought it would be, and although I have to wake up at half-past five, I feel I've had a good night's sleep. That's what I've been most afraid of — getting up so early in the morning. But I need not have worried. Not only do I not mind having to wake up so early, but, on the contrary, find it extremely pleasant to wake up with the sun and to wash on the grass in the cool air of early morning. If at home I never liked getting up early in the morning, then you must have been 'to blame' for this!

I wish you could see how quickly I shave and shower every morning and how I wash my shirts and handkerchiefs, which dry quickly in the burning sun over here. The first night it rained, but luckily not a drop came into my tent. Otherwise it's been fine and warm since I've been here.

On Sundays, also, there is no training, but we were kept busy all day until four in the afternoon. At noon the sergeant-major held an inspection, and we had to tidy up our tents and clean around them and stand next to our kit. After the inspection I was given an order to take the tents down so that the sun could dry the ground under them. This kept us busy until four. Then we held a general assembly of all the Legionnaires in the Town Hall. This was to welcome the new Legionnaires. Ben-Zvi greeted us on behalf of the 'old-timers', while I replied on behalf of the newcomers. Then they chose four additional members for the committee which represents all the Legionnaires. The ones chosen were Frankel, Santop, someone from Philadelphia and me. This meeting lasted a long time and so yesterday I could only write you a postcard.

5

I slept much better the second night, and at half-past five I was already up and waiting. Today I had my first training session. This began at eight. First we had two hours of physical training (PT for short), which was first-rate. I'm sure that in a month's time I'll be much healthier and stronger because of these exercises. Ben-Zvi, for example, looks like another man. After 10 o'clock we usually do military drill. But today we didn't have any because it's King George's birthday. Instead they took us to the hospital — a large tent in our camp — and vaccinated us. This didn't take long — and then we were free for the rest of the day.

The food here isn't bad, although of course it's not outstanding. For breakfast they give us white bread and coffee. At lunch-time we have soup, meat (a good helping), bread, and coffee or tea. At about five in the evening we have bread again, with butter, and coffee or tea.

After dinner we usually go to town, where we stroll along the streets or visit the YMCA. Most of the boys in the camp are non-Jews. But when our whole crowd goes into the YMCA you would think it was a Jewish wedding or a farewell banquet. The boys dance and make merry, sing Jewish songs and behave as if they were in the 'old country' and not in Canada. The non-Jews sit silently and look on in amazement — and I suppose also in annoyance — at these wild dances and noisy songs in a strange language. It is as if it is the non-Jews who are in the Galut* here . . . But just before ten o'clock we all hurry back to the camp and get ready for bed. Until half-past ten the camp buzzes like a beehive. But it soon quietens down when the lights go off, as a thousand young men fall into a deep sleep.

I'm now waiting impatiently for your letter. I beseech you, my dearest, write to me in detail about yourself as I have written to you, and as often as I have written to you. I keep your picture next to me. I feel every drop of love and longing in your heart, my darling. And I know and feel what you are going through. I promise you it will not be in vain. I will make you happy. I know that you are suffering now because of me; but I believe that I and my ideals will compensate you in the course of time.

*The Jewish Diaspora, or dispersion.

6

We are still in civilian clothes. But I'm making progress in my army training. Today we had a special parade in honour of our commander-in-chief, who called us together and asked us how we felt here and what we thought could be done to improve things and make us more comfortable. He summoned the members of the committee — including Ben-Zvi and myself — and asked us for suggestions. This is the first time I've seen an army commander officially recognize a committee elected by the men he commands. In general, the people at headquarters have an excellent attitude towards us, and the non-Jewish soldiers here envy us and complain that we are given special privileges. All our demands about the food, for example, were approved at once.

In a few days time some of the Legionnaires who came here before us, from the Eighth and Ninth platoons, are leaving. Ben-Zvi and I are not among those who will be sent, although we are trying to persuade them to make an exception and let us go now. It's possible that they will agree to this. Our sergeant-major promised to release us, and now it's up to the captain. We should know in a day or two. If I'm going — I'll send you a cable. I send you my warmest kisses, my dearest one.

Today I received your letter of June 10 and the three photographs. During the last few days, while I was waiting for a letter from you, I was confused and worried. But today I feel easier in my mind. The letters you've written to London won't get lost. But I don't know when I'll be there. About a week ago they called more than 400 Legionnaires and told them to prepare for the journey abroad. But the next day this was changed, and about 100 men were removed from the list. I was one of these 100, and I remained here. Ben-Zvi went. All of us were convinced that they were being

7

sent straight to England. But three days ago I had a phone call from Halifax. It was Ben-Zvi. He said that he and a few others were staying in Halifax, and they didn't know when they would sail for England. Two days ago I had a talk with our captain, and from what he said I gathered that if a ship is available they'll send all those who are still in Halifax, and also the 100 men from Windsor who were on the original list. If this is correct, I'll travel together with Ben-Zvi. But I have no idea when this will be.

You said in your last letter that you want to come here, my dearest Paula. I would like to see you just as much as you would like to see me. But to my sorrow this is quite impossible. First, it would involve considerable expense, and second, I could leave here any day, and if you come here you might no longer find me. We must wait, my dearest, and must be patient. My heart is with you, and will be with you as long as it beats.

I am sending you four photographs of me. As you'll see, they're not very good. I don't know why, but I look like a boy of fourteen or fifteen. I remember that I looked like this fifteen years ago.

Several days ago the sergeant sent for me and said that the sergeant-major wished to promote me to corporal. I didn't want it. I explained to the sergeant that I am the representative of the company in Windsor, that the men here have elected me to the committee, and that as a private I had greater authority than I would have if I became a corporal. The sergeant replied that he understood this.

But yesterday evening, out of the blue, they published an order announcing that I had been made a corporal. I have not agreed to take this post, and unless they force me to accept it because of military discipline, I won't do so. Meanwhile the camp is buzzing with the story of the promotion and my refusal.

I have now completely adjusted to the new conditions here, and feel like a veteran. My health is first-rate. I'm tanned, and the skin on my face has peeled off. I'm certainly much healthier than I was before, because of the daily marching and training and the open-air life. I would feel very happy here if I didn't long for you so much.

8

I get the *Tog** every day: but apart from this — nothing at all. I asked you to send me the *New York Times* and *Hatoren***, and also a fountain pen. The pen I brought with me isn't working properly and I can't use it. So I have to borrow other people's pens. If you can, please send me a good fountain pen with the sixth group of Legionnaires. Please send me also the *Tzukunft**** for June. You needn't worry about my insurance policy, as all we'll have to do is to pay $250 within thirty days after I leave here.

Regards to everyone, especially Riasa, Peggy**** and Mrs Gutman. Why don't you ask one of your woman friends to stay over with you when Peggy has to work at night?

Ask Moshvitzki or Lev how the translation of our book *The Land of Israel***** is progressing, and how the book is selling?

Did Kaufman collect the three parcels of my writings which I left with you? Yes, it would be a good idea if you could write to me every day. I haven't been able to write to you during the last two days, as I was on guard duty and couldn't leave my post. I was released only at 6.30 p.m. Keep well, and if you feel like it read Graetz's *History of the Jews.*

Windsor
June 14, 1918.

Today I received your letter of June 11. You think, my dearest, that if I loved you more I would not have volunteered for the Legion. I see you don't know very much about me! I don't know if there is in all the world a man who could love a woman more than I love you, now that you have taken upon yourself the heaviest burden a woman can accept for the sake of the man she loves. If great, deep love can bring happiness — then, dear Paula, you should be the

*A Yiddish daily newspaper.
**A Hebrew weekly newspaper published in New York.
***Yiddish socialist monthly journal, founded in New York, 1890.
****A friend of Paula's.
*****A 477-page volume by Ben-Gurion and Ben-Zvi, published in New York 1918 (by Alpha Press Inc.) under the auspices of the Poalei Zion Palestine Committee. It was being translated into English.

9

happiest of women. I will redeem you from your present suffering. I cannot console you now in your sorrow and longing. I know what a price you are paying, with your youthful happiness, for the sake of my ideal. This price is high, terribly high, and I don't know whether I can repay you as you deserve. But this is the cruelty of a deep love. On the other hand, if I had stayed with you now, I would not be worthy of the child you will bear me, and all our life together would be ordinary, petty and pointless. *This* is not the kind of life I want to live with you: not as cheap, small and empty as this.

Look after your health and build up your body and spirit. For a great, glorious and happy future awaits you.

Windsor
June 15, 1918.

I have received your two letters written on June 12. Many thanks for writing so often. The best and happiest moment of the day is when I am given a letter in your handwriting. Then I want to fall down at your feet and ask your forgiveness, I want to embrace you and press you to my bosom, so that you can feel how my heart is beating. I want to cry in your arms and kiss you, to show my longing for you, which grows greater from day to day, and with my love heal and soothe the pain I have made you suffer. But you are so far away, and I can only see you in the photograph I carry in my uniform, a photograph which is precious and sacred for me.

Sacred: this is the only word, my dear Paula, which expresses sufficiently strongly what you mean to me in my life. I loved you even before we were married, and you know it, although I did not tell you this. My love for you grew greater after our wedding, because I discovered that you were more beautiful and had a finer nature than I had ever anticipated. Now this is something more than love. You are sacred to me, the suffering angel who hovers about me without my being able to see it, to which my soul is drawn — because what you have done for my sake is far greater, immeasurably greater, than what I or anyone else is doing.

And your sacrifice is so tremendous that I sometimes long to take my hat off and bow to your courage, which I shall admire and remember all my life.

When I read your letters I feel everything you feel and suffer. I knew before I left that it would not be easy for you, and sensed what you would have to go through. And yet I left you, my dearest — but not because I don't love you enough. I did what I had to do for you as well. And I promise you, my dear Paula, that the time will come — and it is not so far off — when you yourself will feel this and understand. Then you will realize that the greatest thing I could do for you now was to say goodbye and to volunteer for the Legion, to leave you and your unborn child and to go off to war, because what I have done will make our love holy and prepare the way for our happiness. When I fell in love with you and decided to join our lives together, I didn't want to give you a small, cheap kind of happiness. I have prepared for you the great, holy, human happiness that is bought with suffering and torment. The greatest joy of my life is that I am convinced you were born for this kind of happiness, and that you are spiritually ready to suffer together with me for the sake of a great goal, a fresh and eternal ideal. This is why I love and cherish you so much, and why you are so precious to me. I know that your soul is rich enough and your heart is big enough for the exalted world into which I want to bring you.

I say this not in order to console you, because I know that nothing can console you now. You are suffering too much. You are so lonely and do not know where to turn, you say. But I promise you that you are not alone in your loneliness. I am with you heart and soul. My heart beats together with yours, whatever the distance between us. I will live your life and suffer together with you and hope for a moment of the deepest joy when we will be together again.

Windsor
June 16, 1918.

I've already told you that they wanted to make me

11

a corporal, and why I refused. Yesterday there was a general inspection, and the sergeant-major went on a tour of all the tents to see that they are tidy. When my turn came, the sergeant told the sergeant-major that I was 'the best man in the Jewish Legion,' and added that I had declined to be a corporal because as a private I had greater moral influence in the Legion. The sergeant-major came up to me and said I ought to accept this promotion, because in England they would no longer allow a committee to run the Legion, and the leaders of the company would then be only the officers and non-commissioned officers; thus as a private I would no longer be able to do anything for the Legion. It seems that whether I like it or not I cannot remain a private. At the moment I'm still an ordinary soldier, and over the weekend we are off duty and no promotions are made. But by next week I'll probably be a corporal.

I've already received my first pay packet as a soldier. On Friday evening we were all paid for the first two weeks we spent in camp. We got 50 cents a day, and they say we'll receive another 10 cents a day in London for all the time we've been here. In England itself we'll be paid only 36 cents a day. So I received $7.50 for the two weeks. During this time I spent nearly $15. But my greatest expenses were during the first week. I'm spending much less now, and 50 cents a day will cover all I need here; I might even have something left. The food is satisfactory, and has improved lately due to the efforts of our committee, of which I am chairman. The sergeant-major takes us very seriously, and in effect fulfils all our requests. We have a special kosher kitchen, and our own ritual slaughterer and butcher and special cooks, and our committee looks after all this as well.

Yesterday the sergeant-major called the committee of the Legion to his room, together with the Jewish non-commissioned officers, and among other things complained that I had refused the rank of corporal. He seems to think that I have refused to accept any responsibility for the Legion's affairs. We explained the real reason to him. But eventually I was forced to accept this promotion, and from now on I will be busier, and what with my other duties as chairman of the Legion committee I'll have my hands full.

Write to me about your impressions of the Magen David Adom conference. There are many married soldiers here, who have left their wives virtually without any support, and they are anxious to know whether the conference decided anything about helping the Legionnaires' families.

Has Miss Szold+ paid you yet for my article?

Windsor
June 17, 1918.

I've already written to explain why I couldn't write for two days. I am not a free man: I'm a soldier. And a soldier can't always do what he would like. Up till now we have had to go into town, to the YMCA, if we wanted to write letters. But we can go to town only after training, which means after 4 p.m. Sometimes, however, they give us CB (confined to barracks) and then we can't leave the camp; sometimes there is a special job which keeps us busy the whole day, and occasionally at night. Last week this happened to me twice, when I had to do guard duty.

Now we've improvised a library and a place to write letters in the camp itself. So we no longer need to go to the YMCA, and in fact I'm writing you this letter from our 'library'. It is a large tent, with a few tables and a cupboard for books. From now on I'll be able to write to you every day, as long as we're here.

Ben-Zvi wrote to me from Halifax. He sends his regards to you, and asks whether you received his photograph. I also sent you four pictures of myself — one together with Ben-Zvi. Have you received them?

Please ask the Poalei Zion* office why they don't send me their journal, *Yiddische Kemfer?*

Windsor
June 18, 1918.

Today, for the first time, I received the *New York Times,*

*Poalei Zion ('Workers of Zion') the Socialist Zionist Party.

the one for June 15. I also received all the Jewish papers from New York that you sent me.

I am very busy these days. Our committee is undertaking a vigorous cultural programme among the Legionnaires, and I have to handle most of it. The drill and training are also more strenuous now. From tomorrow I have to take part in a special course for NCOs, which will take up another two hours of my time every day. I've made good progress in my military training, and if our instructors were better we could reach a higher standard. Unfortunately, the man who trains our platoon doesn't know much more about it than I do, and the result is that I have to go over the same thing almost every day, and I'm getting tired of it.

My skin has already peeled off twice because of the strong sun. I'm as sunburnt as if I've lived in the open all my life. The defect in my eyesight has gone completely, as if I never had it. If I knew you were as healthy as me, I would be happy. The exercises we do every morning from eight to ten strengthen the muscles and the whole body. So you don't have to worry about my health.

Windsor
June 20, 1918.

I have become a student again. But this time I am being given lessons not in school or university but underneath the blue skies, sitting on the green grass in an open field — more accurately, lying on the grass. This is a special course for NCOs. We sprawl on the grass and write down in our notebooks what they tell us — about our duties, the various ranks, systems of training and so on. Today I attended one of these sessions for the first time, and I enjoyed it, as I did a special training drill, with a first-rate instructor. We can learn in a short time what privates take months to pick up.

Today I had a second vaccination, and so I'll have another day off from training. The vaccination makes one feel weak the first day. Last time I had a temperature for 24 hours. In another four or five days I'll have a third vaccination.

I didn't get any papers today. But I did get the fountain

14

pen you sent me. And I'm writing this letter with it. I'll take good care of this pen, because it's a present from you. I'll keep it until you come to Palestine, or until I come to America to fetch you. Many thanks for sending me such an excellent pen. How much did you pay for it?

I'm waiting for your letter. Today I can write to you earlier than usual, because of the vaccination.

How are you? Can you feel Yariv?*

P.S. When you write to me from now on put 'Cpl.' before my name instead of 'Pte.' — the way I've done it on the back of the envelope.

Windsor
June 21, 1918.

Today I received the *Tog* with the report of the Magen David Adom conference, the *Times,* the *Evening Post,* the Hebrew and Yiddish papers you sent me, and also your two letters of the 17th and 18th. I hardly know how to thank you. You even remembered to send me the *Evening Post,* although I didn't ask you to, because you know that I used to enjoy reading it in New York. I could not wish to have a finer symbol of your love for me. If only you knew how much I think about you during the quiet nights in my tent, and how burning my longing is for you — because of all the people in the world you are the most precious to me. I've explained to you why I couldn't write to you for two days. But apart from this, I write to you every single day. My own girl — don't you know that in moments of loneliness and sadness your love for me is the deepest and most soothing consolation, and that I have never felt for any other person the warm love I feel when I think of you . . .

I am the kind of person who when he loves once, loves for always and with all the fire and strength of his being. Our future together cannot be foreseen today. But I am certain we will love one another, whatever happens.

*If their child was a boy, Ben-Gurion wanted him to be called Yariv.

15

The new boys who arrived here on Thursday gave me regards from you. They told me you have been elected to the executive of Magen David Adom. The *Tog* had a report of the conference, but it was sketchy and didn't say much. As you yourself took part in this conference, you could have written in much greater detail about the things that interest me. I particularly want to know what the new executive is going to do for the families of our Legionnaires.

Today marks my third week in the camp. It feels as if I've been here for years. I'm already a soldier in every way, and much healthier and stronger than I was before. I wish I could pass some of my health on to you.

I want to ask you something. One of my comrades here, the Legionnaire Avraham Weiss, has a wife in New York, in difficult circumstances. The Magen David Adom office promised to help her, but she complains that she has not received any assistance from them. Now that you're a member of the executive, could you try to see that something is done for her? Weiss is one of the best men in the Legion, and is very active in our committee. His wife is certainly entitled to the utmost assistance that Magen David Adom can give her. Let me know whether anything is being done for her.

Today being Sunday, we are free, and because of the rain that fell all night we were also let off the usual morning roll call, which takes place on Sunday as well. All the same, I've had one of the busiest days in my life. We held a meeting of all the Legionnaires, which lasted for over four hours and was very stormy. I was the chairman. The main discussion was about Magen David Adom and its attitude to the Legionnaires, and especially to the families of the married Legionnaires. Many vehement complaints and accusations were levelled against Magen David Adom, which promised to help the wives but in many cases has given no help at all. Some of the men were very bitter. Others who had heard about the recent conference related discouraging news about disputes between the New York branch and branches in other cities, and about inefficiency in the Magen David Adom office. The temperature of the meeting often reached boiling point, and I had a difficult time trying to keep order.

Eventually the meeting adopted a series of resolutions which I proposed, calling upon the Jewish public, and in particular Magen David Adom, to organize the appropriate assistance that the Legionnaires' families should receive, not as charity, but as a duty which the Jewish people owes to their sons who have taken up arms in order to redeem them.

Let me know what your organization is doing to help the wives of our men, who must not be allowed to feel that they are being given charity.

Windsor
June 24, 1918.

You ask if I need anything, and say that you will send it to me. I assure you, my dear Paula, that I am not short of anything, except one thing which I cannot have: and that is you yourself. Nothing else can fill this vacuum. But apart from wanting to be with you I need nothing. You already send me the newspapers, which I am now receiving regularly, and you don't need to send anything else.

Tomorrow I'll send you another three photographs. About the payment for the article I wrote for Henrietta Szold: the best thing would be to phone Hadassah* and ask Miss Szold's secretary or Miss Szold herself to send you the cheque as soon as possible.

*The Women's Zionist Organization of America, founded in 1912 by Henrietta Szold.

You need not apologize to me for telling me about your loneliness and suffering. Aren't you part of me, and aren't I part of you? Isn't your pain mine as well? You know how I love you and how tenderly I feel towards you. But there is something else, great and holy, which in my eyes comes before everything else, and which has made me leave you temporarily. You know what it is. The day will come when you will see the vision I see and will feel it instinctively, as I do. You must believe me when I say that I did what I had to do knowing what a price you would have to pay for my action and how much you would suffer. God in heaven knows *how much your suffering costs me and how dear and beloved you are to me!*

You complain in your letter that my letters have become shorter. The truth is that I have very little spare time nowadays. There are days when I find it almost impossible to find a free half-hour to sit down and write to you. I get up at half-past five. At five forty-five we have roll-call. Then I have to wash and shave — every soldier has to shave every day — make my bed, clean the tent and have breakfast. At eight there is another roll-call, and then we do training until twelve. After the morning drill we are free until one forty-five. But this is lunch-time, and we have to wait in line for about half an hour until our turn comes. This happens at every meal. From two to four we have more training. Then we have our dinner, until five. This is when we collect our mail. The soldier on duty calls out the names of the men who have received letters, and this takes about twenty minutes. From six to eight I have to attend the special courses for NCOs. By nine it is getting dark already, and we have to prepare for bed.

As you can see, I have only an hour or two to myself all day, apart from Saturday and Sunday. There is just time for my public duties and for a little reading. In addition I have a special job to do: anyone who has a complaint, or thinks he has been ill-treated, comes to me. If anyone wants some information about the Legion, he comes to me. Add to this

18

three sessions with the committee, and you'll see what sort of day I have. I used to go to town occasionally, before I became a corporal. But now I haven't put a foot out of camp for a week.

Windsor
June 26, 1918.

Yesterday I sent you three photographs taken in Boston. I look very bad in them. I must have been tired from marching and from talking all day. Since then I've become a completely different man. I only wish you could see me. It grieves me that the same thing has not happened to you during the last few weeks. You have certainly not become stronger since we parted.

Forgive me for writing such a short letter this time. In just a few minutes the committee is meeting. I am also supposed to meet some of the newcomers.

Windsor
June 27, 1918.

I have the impression that we shan't be here much longer. Today I was given a third vaccination, and I won't need any more. This morning the major told us about the new draft. In any event, we'll still be here on July 1, which will be a day of competitions, games, a concert and a procession. We are working very hard on the preparations for this day. But after July 1 at least some of us will be leaving; whether it will be Halifax or England we don't know. Ben-Zvi has already left for England. There aren't more than 50 Legionnaires left in Halifax. So some people think we'll be sent there. But no one knows anything definite.

Windsor
June 28, 1918.

I am sending you the article about the book *The Land of Israel* and its authors (Y. Ben-Zvi and D. Ben-Gurion), which appeared in *Kundas* on June 21. Please stick it in the little book I gave you. Some time ago I also sent you a cutting of Yoel Entin's article about me. Did you receive it, and have you stuck it in the book?

We all expect to leave here soon. For the moment write to me at this address. When I send you a telegram telling you to write to me c/o [J.] Pomerantz, the secretary of Poalei Zion in London, you will know I have left Windsor.

Windsor
June 29, 1918.

Thank you for your telegram, which reassured me somewhat, although I am worried by the state of your health. I note that you are unable to go outside the house, although you didn't say anything about this in your previous letter. Last night was the worst I've spent since coming here. I lay awake thinking about you and unable even to close my eyes. Are you seeing Dr Ellsberg? I'm writing to him about you and also about the money the Zionist Federation owes me for articles. The reason for the delay is probably because they are busy with the Zionist Convention. In any case, I will remind them. By the time you receive this letter Miss Szold will be in New York, and you can talk to her direct. Please let me know what happens.

There are various rumours about our travel plans. Some people say we will be leaving soon, others say we will stay here another two weeks. I haven't heard anything concrete.

I must hurry off to a meeting. Tomorrow we will hold a memorial meeting to Herzl+, and as usual I have to do most of the work.

Yitzhak Ben-Zvi (left) and David Ben-Gurion (centre) with Yisrael Shochat, Commander of the corps (Hashomer) formed in 1909 to defend Jewish settlements.

Ben-Gurion with his bride, Paula Monbaz. They were married in New York on December 5, 1917.

Moshe Shertok (later Sharett) in the officer's uniform of the Turkish Army, 1917.

Henrietta Szold, founder of Hadassa, the Women's Zionist Organization of America.

Ben-Gurion and Jabotinsky, members of the British army's Jewish Legion during World War I.

Members of the editorial board of the Poalei Zion journal Ha'ahdut ('The Unity'), founded in 1910. From left to right: Yitzhak Ben-Zvi, Yaakov Zerubavel, Ben-Gurion, Rachel Yannait (later Ben-Zvi's wife).

Today being Sunday, the mail is not distributed and I am deprived of the pleasure of a letter from you. The soldier on duty did tell me that there are two letters for me. But I can't get them until tomorrow afternoon: and I want them more than ever, as I am worried about your health.

Yesterday should have been 'Pay Day'. But as luck would have it they postponed it, and so I couldn't send you any money. I ask you again, my dear Paula, not to try to save money and to call a doctor to give you a proper examination. You must be and must remain healthy — this is more important than anything else.

Today was the memorial meeting for Dr Herzl. It is fourteen years since the death of the great leader of the Jewish people and the father of political Zionism. The entire Jewish Legion marched to the opera house in Windsor, where we held the commemoration. I was the chairman, and spoke about Herzl's personality and his historic undertaking. It was an impressive gathering. At the end I called for contributions to a special fund for planting a forest in Herzl's name, and within five minutes we had collected $150. I have seldom witnessed such enthusiasm. A hat was placed on the stage, and dollars and five-dollar pieces were thrown into it joyfully and with such fervour that everyone present in the hall was moved almost to tears.

The main topic of conversation in camp now is when we will be leaving for overseas. Most people think we will stay here for about another week. You can write to me at Windsor until I cable to say that we have gone. Please write my address exactly as I write it on the back of the envelope. The number of the platoon is unnecessary, as I am no longer in it.

P.S. Could you please send a photograph showing the two of us to, A. Reubeni, Jerusalem, Palestine? This is Ben-Zvi's brother. He asked me for a photograph of you and me. I have one copy of this picture, which I always carry with me. And I am sure you have several copies of it.

21

Windsor
June 30, 1918.

Your two last letters alarmed me, and I am greatly concerned about your health. I have just sent you a telegram and asked you to cable me immediately and tell me how you are. I will have no peace of mind until I get your answer. Tell me in detail what happened, how and where you fell and how you are feeling, who is looking after you and who is staying with you. Dear Paula, I am going to ask you to do something — if not for your own sake, then for my sake and the sake of your unborn child: get a first-rate doctor to see you every day, and don't try to save a few dollars on something so important. I'll send you all the money you need. You don't know how much I shall suffer if you try to avoid spending money and your health suffers as a result. Tomorrow I will send you $20. I have the greatest confidence in our happy future. I firmly believe that the day is not far off when we will meet again, not two of us any more but three, all in good health and pleased to be together. But you must look after yourself until then. You must watch your health carefully, because on it depends the future and happiness of three people.

Windsor
July 1, 1918.

I've just been handed four letters from you, written on June 27 and 28, and it made me happier to read them. This time you are no longer writing in a pessimistic mood. I was glad to hear what the doctor told you. You have no idea how worried I was, and how relieved I am to hear the good news about the child, and even more relieved that you feel much better. I love our unborn child very much, but you are even more precious to me.

In general, it's been a day of good news. First your welcome letters, and then we learned that we will leave here very soon. Later on today I will cable you if this report about our departure is correct. When you get my cable about

Pomerantz, write to me care of him.

Today we are having a parade in honour of July 1, which is Canada's National Day. The Jewish flag is flying together with the flags of Canada, England and Australia. At first they didn't fly the Jewish flag, and our boys were going to refuse to take part in the parade. I went to the major and demanded that the Jewish flag be displayed as well, and at once he gave the order to fly the blue-and-white flag.

Windsor
July 2, 1918.

Yesterday I thought that we would no longer be here today. But I was wrong. I might have to stay another day, or even longer. We probably won't know when we are leaving until the last moment. On the other hand, I was pleased I was still in camp today. We received about ten copies of the *Jewish News* for our library, and the whole camp wanted to see the picture of Mrs Ben-Gurion. You have no idea how famous you are over here. It is an excellent picture of you, and it gave me much pleasure to see my wife in the paper . . . But my popularity here makes things difficult as well. Almost nothing happens in camp which is not brought to me. One man asks my advice, another wants information, a third just feels like talking to someone, and what all this means is that I scarcely have an hour a day to myself. In this camp there are all the types to be found among the Jewish people, from the most lofty-minded idealists and the highly educated to coarse and evil-minded individuals, born criminals: one can hear things which can only be heard in the underworld and the lowest strata of society. There are also intrigues and insults, and some of the Legionnaires seem to respect nothing, neither God nor Satan. What is strange is that the only person in camp whom they respect and will listen to is yours truly.

There is one fellow here who has been in camp for only ten days but who who has already been in the military jail twice. He is not afraid of anything, and boasts that he has been in Sing-Sing and that no one can control him when he gets into a fight. But one word from me and this fellow calms

23

down and sits quiet as a lamb. Because of this they come to me every moment of the day with a complaint or a request, until I wish sometimes that I was just an ordinary soldier and that no one would bother me. But when I saw how the boys looked at your picture today, with such interest and sympathy, then after all, I was pleased to be popular in camp.

I think I've already written to you about Ben-Zvi's journey. He left a week ago, on Tuesday. I hope I'll see him soon. It's clear that we won't stay here much longer, so it's not worth sending anything. In any case, there's nothing I'm short of. If someone wrote that the Legionnaires need sheets, then I can tell you this is not true. We have enough sheets. The sweaters they've given us are first-class — strong and warm. I haven't had to wear mine yet.

Windsor
July 3, 1918.

As you can see, I am still here, and I'm starting to fear that I'll be here longer than I thought two days ago. It is not certain when we will leave, and we might remain here another week or even longer. On the other hand, it's quite possible that we'll move tomorrow or the day after. I'll cable you only when I know definitely. In any event, if you don't receive any letters from me two days running, this means we're already on our way.

Today a group of about twenty-five Legionnaires arrived from New York. Several of them brought regards from you. But I haven't really had a chance to talk to them yet, and will do so later.

I would advise you to go to the village, to Goldschmidt. That would be good for you. You need the country air, and you can arrange for your letters to be sent on to you from New York. I'll probably be leaving here soon, so in any case you won't be receiving letters from me for four weeks. There is no chance of my remaining in Canada until the child is born, in another two months. It's most unlikely that they'll keep us here such a long time.

Again you ask me whether I need anything. I promise you

24

once more that I need and miss only two things: Eretz Yisrael* and you. Nothing else. And I believe I will have both these things in the near future.

> *Windsor*
> *July 4, 1918.*

What I predicted yesterday has happened. All talk about our going abroad has receded into the background. People are saying that we will not serve overseas. What this means is that for the moment we are staying here indefinitely. And after this anti-climax I find it almost impossible to carry out the normal routine. Today we did all the usual things automatically, and it was incredibly boring. The only thing that grips us now is — when will we eventually be called up? And so we wait from morning to night, from night to morning. Today seemed even longer than usual. For the first time we had heavy rain, and so we couldn't do any drill. At nine in the morning they did take us into the fields, but they had to bring us back almost at once, as the ground was so wet. So we were forced to spend the whole day in the tent and to waste our time. It is still raining, so the same thing will probably happen tomorrow as well.

What did Miss Szold say to you about the payment for my article? And what about the ones published by the Zionist Federation?

In his letter to me Nissim Bechar** says he sent you a Hebrew textbook. Are you studying Hebrew now? If not, I beseech you, Paulitschka, study the language.

Last Will and Testament of D. Ben-Gurion
July 4, 1918

This is the will and testament which I bequeath to my household before going with the Jewish Legion to fight in Palestine for the redemption of our land. If I should have any accident en route, or if I should fall on the field of battle, I

---

*The Land of Israel (Palestine).

**A Sephardi Jew, born in Palestine and educated in France, Bechar became principal of a boys' school in Jerusalem run by the Alliance Israélite Universelle.

request my relatives and friends, wherever they may be, to carry out my last wishes, as follows:

1. I wish my beloved wife Pnina (Paula) Monbaz Ben-Gurion and my dear father Avigdor Grin to be the guardians and educators of my unborn child, who will be born to me by my wife Pnina Monbaz Ben-Gurion, and I desire that they will raise and educate this child according to the following wishes:

2. I want my child to be named Yariv, if it is a boy, and Geula, if it is a girl.

3. I wish and command that my child be brought to the Land of Israel at the earliest opportunity and educated there in the Jewish schools, and that until conditions allow the child to be brought to our country, he or she will be taught Hebrew before learning any other language, and that my wife Pnina will talk Hebrew with her child, and for this purpose I request my wife to learn Hebrew.

4. I leave all my property and capital, my writings and copyright in these writings, all I have at present and will have in future, to my child who will be born from my dear wife Pnina Monbaz Ben-Gurion, and until the child reaches maturity my wife and my father shall be the custodians of the child's inheritance.

5. I wish and command that the sum of $2,500 which my heirs will receive after my death from the New York Life Insurance Co. be placed in trustworthy hands or in the Hebrew Bank in Palestine, until my child grows up. However, if the other financial means are not sufficient to educate my child, part or all of this money should be taken, if and when necessary, in order to educate the child, as I have instructed above.

6. If my father does not live long after my death, which heaven forbid, or if he be gathered to his fathers before my child reaches maturity, my brother Avraham ben Avigdor Grin will take his place as guardian of my child.

7. If my child should die, heaven forbid, or should be still-born, I wish and command that my property shall be divided in the following manner:

a. My beloved wife Pnina Ben-Gurion shall receive as her portion $2,000 from the insurance money which shall

26

be paid, as above.

b. My dear father Avigdor Grin shall receive the sum of $500, and I request him to use this money to travel to the Land of Israel and to see the length and breadth of it, for at least once in his life.

c. All my books in New York, Constantinople, Jerusalem and elsewhere shall be handed to the National Library in Jerusalem, as the gift of David and Paula Ben-Gurion.

d. All the income from my articles, books and other writings shall be placed in a special fund, whose purpose will be the publication of original articles, books and research on the Land of Israel in the Hebrew language.

e. If my wife should not live long after my death, heaven forbid, I wish and command that the sum of $2,000 which I bequeathed to her be divided into two equal parts: the one half, namely $1,000, shall be handed to the Central Committee of the Poalei Zion Party in Palestine for the publication of literature by and about workers in Palestine, in Hebrew; and the other half, also of $1,000, shall be deposited in the special fund referred to in Clause (d) above, whose purpose is the publication of original literature on the Land of Israel, in Hebrew.

f. Should my father Avigdor Grin not live long after my death, heaven forbid, I wish and command that the sum of $500 which I bequeathed him be given to my brother Avraham Grin, in order that he may travel to the Land of Israel.

g. I hand the legacy which came to me after the death of my dear mother, may her memory be blessed, to my brother Avraham Grin.

All these aforesaid things shall come to pass only if my child dies or comes into the world still-born.

8. I wish and command that the executors of my literary estate shall be the following comrades and friends: Yitzhak Ben-Zvi, who is called Avner; Yehuda Kaufman, who is called Yehuda Even-Shmuel; Dr N. Syrkin; and another comrade, to be nominated by the Central Committee of the Poalei Zion Party in Palestine. Two of the four comrades mentioned above shall be entitled to decide and to act on every matter

27

concerning my writings, if it will be impossible for all four or even for three of them to be in Palestine at the same time. But the two who take these decisions must be in the Land of Israel when they do so.

9. I want my literary executors to publish everything among my writings which they consider worthy of publication in the form of a book or an anthology and to translate the articles written by me in Yiddish into the Hebrew language. If I shall be unable myself to edit the book *The Land of Israel* in Hebrew, I request that the translation of this book shall be undertaken by Y. Ben-Zvi and Y. Kaufman.

10. If after my death or at the time that my will shall be executed no fund for the publication of original Hebrew writing on the Land of Israel shall exist, I instruct my literary executors to set up such a fund from the monies I have set aside for this purpose. If such a fund shall already exist by this time, these monies shall be handed over to it, on condition that my executors have the right to express an opinion on the expenditure of these sums.

11. I hereby appoint my dear father Avigdor Grin as the custodian of the legacy I leave to my child, and my brother Avraham Grin to be his deputy, until my child grows to maturity. I further appoint my friend Dr Shmuel Ellsberg, of New York (279 Broadway, New York), to carry out the content of this will and to hand over the management of my estate to my father or my brother at the earliest opportunity.

This last will and testament has been written and signed by me in my own hand, in the camp of the Jewish Legion in Windsor, Nova Scotia, Canada, on Thursday, July 4, in the first year of the British Government's declaration of freedom.*

David Ben-Gurion

N.B. A will and testament similar to this in content has been made by me in English, in accordance with the demands of the law in the United States, on May 28, 1918, in the city of

*The reference is to the Balfour Declaration of November 2, 1917, which promised the Jewish people a National Home in Palestine.

New York, and signed by me and by two witnesses — Yoseph Halperin (140 Rivington Street, New York), and Daniel Persky+ (201 E. Broadway, New York).

One copy of the English will and testament is in the hands of the official executor, Dr S. Ellsberg. Another copy is in the hands of my wife, and I have the third copy.

The life insurance policy is held by my wife, who is now living in New York, in Brooklyn (Mrs D. Ben-Gurion, 188 Penn Street, Brooklyn, New York, U.S.A.).

Windsor
July 6, 1918.

The moment I finished guard duty I hurried off to town so that I could write to you. Again there are reports that we will be leaving here in another two days. Officially, however, we have been told nothing. But people who are in the know say that our major received a telegram telling him we have to move. This time it seems like the real thing, and yet I hesitate to believe it, after the let-down we had last time. But this new rumour might be correct. I hope so, because I am so impatient that everything bores me even more than before. I had planned a whole series of cultural activities among the Legionnaires. But since the bitter joke of our 'departure' began, I've had to stop all these programmes, and the public and social life here has more or less come to a standstill.

Your latest letters have cheered me up, although I have the feeling that you are putting things in a brighter light than they are in reality, so that I should not worry. And although I am grateful to you for this noble sentiment, which does you credit, I would ask you to write accurately about yourself, giving me the good things and the bad. I want to be your partner and soulmate in everything, in joy and in sorrow, in suffering and in happiness, in loneliness and in longing. However far I might be from you geographically, I want to be close, very close, to you, so that I can feel your breathing and be at one with you. And do not fear, dear Paula, that by telling me the truth you will cause me too much worry and anxiety. I am not perhaps very strong physically, but
29

spiritually I can stand anything, and nothing can break me. So tell me everything that happens to you, and how you are carrying this heavy burden I have made you bear.

I am returning Miss Szold's letter. And I'm certain that you'll soon receive the money for the article. I've sent my old clothes on to Palestine, as we do with all the Legionnaires' civilian clothing. I no longer have the Legion badge which I used to carry in New York, as I lost it in Boston on the way to the camp.

Windsor
July 9, 1918.

This will be my last letter from Windsor. We are definitely leaving here tomorrow morning at eight. We've already said goodbye to our people in the camp office and been photographed with them. I'll send you the photographs. The major wrote me a letter, and I enclose a copy. I've sent another copy to the Legion headquarters, for publication in the press.

Today an order was issued making me a full corporal. Now I have to put another ribbon on my sleeve. Until now I've been a lance-corporal.

I am very busy today. Apart from arranging my own affairs before leaving here, I have to see about the Legionnaires who are staying. So I can't write you a very long letter.

I sent Goldberg a Hebrew article for his journal. After it is published he will send you the money for it. Once I am in London I'll send an article to *Hatoren,* and they'll also pay you directly. Don't write any more letters to me at Windsor. And don't send any more papers there. If you need anything ask Dr Ellsberg, Goldberg and Nissim Bechar. I know that they will do all they can for you, as if you were their sister. Be brave, and love me. I love you, love you with all my might, dear Paula, and all my life will be yours.

(The date of the next letter and its
opening paragraph are missing. It
was probably written soon after
Ben-Gurion arrived at the camp in
Plymouth, England.)

. . . Apparently we'll be here another month, possibly
longer.

The camp we are staying in is not far from the beautiful
port of Plymouth, which is about forty-five minutes away by
foot. The place we are in is called Egg Buckland. It is one of
the most marvellous places I have ever seen. When I went out
into the fields at dawn for the first time and gazed at the
view around our tents, I was intoxicated by the charming
scene. Somehow I didn't imagine I would ever see a
panorama like this in England. Green mountains and valleys
covered with silk, fertile fields and the shadows of nearby
forests.

The only flag flying in our camp is the blue-and-white flag
of the Jewish people. When the flag is lowered in the evening
the whole camp stands still and motionless, as if cast in
bronze, until the flag has been properly lowered by the senior
officer in camp, a lieutenant-colonel, who is Jewish, and a
warm Jew at that. He has great respect for the Legionnaires
from the United States who have volunteered to fight for a
Jewish Palestine under the British flag. The Sabbath is
observed here, and on that day we are let off all training,
apart from marching to the synagogue together with all the
officers, headed by the colonel.

The routine here is similar to that at Windsor. We get up at
six. Breakfast is between seven and eight. At eight-thirty our
real work begins, and this runs through until twelve when we
have a break until one-thirty, which is lunch-time. The food
here, incidentally, is better than at Windsor, and the helpings
are more generous too. From one-thirty to four there is more
training and drilling. Dinner is at five, and afterwards we are
free for the rest of the evening. Many of the men go into
Plymouth, which is a large and attractive city. But everyone
has to be in camp by half-past nine and by ten we are asleep.

On our second day in camp the colonel invited me to his

31

quarters and discussed various questions concerning the Legion. He showed me the emblem of the Royal Fusiliers of which we form part. The colonel wants us to be a special unit in every way, and in addition to the Shield of David which we wear on our sleeve we will also carry a distinct Jewish emblem on our caps. I told him I thought the emblem on our caps was the most important thing at present. He agreed with me, and promised to try to obtain permission for this from the Government. He also told me that we will soon go to Egypt.

All in all, the life here is more interesting and fuller than in Windsor, although the training at Plymouth is definitely more strenuous.

I received your letter of July 12 and was very pleased to hear that you've received the money from Miss Szold and that at least you won't be short of money. I am sorry that from now on neither you nor I can hear from one another as frequently as before. If I didn't have your picture with me I wouldn't be able to allay my longings. Now at least I have something to look at, and in the lonely hours I gaze for a long time at the face which is so dear to me.

I am busier with training now than I have ever been, and I am also closer to the Land of Israel. But at the same time my longing for you grows greater every day. When I think about the future there is only one picture I see in my mind's eye, and that is the picture of our meeting — may it come soon . .

London
August 6, 1918.

I arrived in London yesterday together with a group of several hundred Legionnaires, all of us on leave. Previous groups were given ten days, but we have been allowed only six, as we'll probably leave for Egypt soon. We'll be here until Saturday (August 10). It is holiday time in London, and many of the people I wanted to see are in the country, so I won't be able to talk to them.

I spent the whole of yesterday sightseeing. I went to the

famous Tower of London, the historic fortress prison within whose walls many bloody events in British history took place. I visited Parliament during a session, when the Minister Bonar Law* was speaking. I saw the King's palace from outside (the public is not allowed inside) and other important places. Today I'm going to the famous British Museum. Tomorrow I have a meeting with Nahum Sokolow+ and with the secretary of the Zionist Office. I've already written to you that the British Zionists want to translate and publish my book on Eretz Yisrael. They have arranged two mass meetings for me, on Thursday and on Friday evening, and they wanted to arrange a meeting for tomorrow evening as well. But I refused to address this third meeting, as I wanted to have an evening to myself. After two months of army life it's a real pleasure to feel that you can do as you please, without orders or commands, and that you can go to bed and get up whenever you please, can eat whatever you like and when you feel like it, at your leisure.

> London
> *August 7, 1918.*

I'm sending you some pictures of the grandest sights in the world's largest city. This is the large park in which they hold meetings and rallies. You will also see the King's palace, with the beautiful new monument to Queen Victoria, the splendid building of the oldest Parliament in the world, and the historic Tower of London which I visited on my first day in this city. I wish you could have been with me for these six days . . . But I hope that one day I'll be able to show you all these places, when I come to fetch you and our baby and take you to Palestine.

---

*Andrew Bonar Law (1858-1923): Leader of Conservative Party, 1911-21; Prime Minister or Britain, 1922-23.

I hoped to receive a letter from you before leaving Cairo. But in vain. Like an orthodox Jew who waits each day for the Messiah, I waited every day for your letter. Today I return to camp without a word from you, my dearest. And you have so many important things to tell me. You are undergoing difficulties, moments of joy, suffering and ecstasy — and all by yourself, without me. A new world is about to open for you, which will change your life for ever. You will have a great burden to carry, a pleasant one but heavy all the same. And I am far away, and can take part in your happiness and responsibilities only from afar, though with all the warmth of my love for you both.

I am leaving soon. But it seems to me that I'm getting closer to you all the time. Great changes are taking place now which will bring us together much sooner than I had imagined until recently. Already one country is free, and the great liberated and independent morrow for our people is dawning over the hills of Judea and Galilee. The birth of our child is taking place at a happy moment, when our land has been redeemed. The glory of this moment will light its entire life.

Please write to me, Paula. Tell me how both of you are, whether you have a new apartment and how you are managing. How are your Hebrew lessons coming along? Did you receive the payment for the article I sent to Goldberg?
P.S. Please send me the Arabic-French dictionary, the one with the red cover.

My dearest treasure,

I cannot tell you in words — at least not in written, dead

*The Feast of Tabernacles (a Harvest Festival).

words — what I have gone through since receiving your telegram. For many weeks I have waited impatiently and anxiously for this happy news. I waited for it before it came, and the delay worried and alarmed me and kept me awake during the long nights. Now at last it has come. On the day after Yom Kippur* (September 17) they handed me a sealed telegram, and my heart shuddered with joy. A few short words: but what a powerful message it brought me, and how happy it has made me.

But this happiness is mingled with sadness. And my dearest wish at the moment is to leap over the distant oceans separating us and to be in the quiet room where the two of you are lying, the two most precious to me, and to bend over you quietly and embrace you both. But this is a vain dream. I am far away from you, and no matter how much my heart is torn I cannot change this. I know this must mar your joy and double your sorrow at this moment of pain and happiness. But, dear Paula, this is the way it had to be. Our suffering will not be in vain. Our first child comes into the world at a tragic and holy moment in time, and from this experience of ours a great future will grow and a bright light will shine over the life of this baby.

Cairo
October 2, 1918.

I never imagined a time like this. Day after day I have been waiting for word from you, as a thirsty man walking in the desert longs for a drop of water. As fate had it, both of us were in hospital at the same time. Now I am completely back to my full strength, and tomorrow or the day after I will leave the hospital. I haven't told you about this until now, as I didn't want to upset you. But now it's all over and I'm all right again, so I can tell you about it.

Several days after we arrived in Egypt I came down with dysentery and was forced to go into hospital. This was four weeks ago. They gave me injections and I soon recovered. But

*The Day of Atonement.

because I had to go on a strict diet for eighteen days, I was rather weak. Now I am healthy and as strong as before. Because of the daily injections I had it was difficult for me to write. I received your telegram while lying in bed. Today I was able to stroll about outside from two to seven in the afternoon. At seven I have to return to the hospital. And yesterday the doctor told me the good news that I'll be able to leave tomorrow or the day after tomorrow.

Dear Paula, are you angry with me for not staying with you at a time like this? This is torture, for me and even more for you, I know. But I also know that I have never been so intimately close to you as now. There is a real closeness — the closeness of the great spirit which never dies, the eternal union of souls, which no force in this world can overcome. And our souls — I feel this today with tremendous force — are so intertwined that I feel one soul loves in both of us. And whatever the physical distance between us, I feel we are so close to one another that we are never apart.

What does our baby look like? Tell me everything about her. Did you have a hard time? Have you found a more comfortable apartment? I am waiting eagerly for a photograph showing you and our new treasure together.

The time goes so slowly . . .

By now you will have heard the good news of the last few days*. I hope this means I'll be able to see you much earlier than I previously thought possible. I hope to be with you next summer, if not before then.

Kiss Geula for me.

*Cairo
October 2, 1918.*

On Saturday (that is, in two days' time) I shall leave the hospital and return to camp. I am fully recovered already, and wish you were as healthy as I am now. When the sergeant-major told me that at long last I was being released, I felt as if I was being let out of jail. This gives you some idea of

*The British Army's advances in Northern Palestine, which pointed to a Turkish defeat.

how much I hated lying in hospital and the enforced idleness. The only thing I could do was read. I haven't read novels in European languages for years, because I haven't the patience to read stories in any language except Hebrew. But when I'm compelled to lie in bed like this, I'll read even the most boring books.

Among other books I read a most interesting one, the great work of the French writer Romain Rolland: *Jean-Christophe*. This is a novel in ten volumes which created a great impression in Europe and won its author the Nobel Prize for literature. It describes the life of a German musician from his childhood to his death. It is more than a story: it is the history of an entire generation and a critical analysis of all aspects of social life in Germany and particularly in France. The whole book breathes a great love of humanity. It is really a very great work, and I would very much like you to read it. It has been translated into all the European languages (and will soon appear in Hebrew), so you will be able to find it in English.

Several days ago I sent you a copy of *Palestine*, which contained a review of my book. Note that the reviewer pays special attention to Parts 3 and 5. Those are the parts I wrote (as well as Part 1).

Here in Cairo I saw a French paper which is publishing translations from my anthology, *Yizkor**, and also from my book *The Land of Israel*. People who have come from Eretz Yisrael told me the book has created a great impression there.

There are about a thousand Legionnaires here from Palestine — among them many friends of mine.

I am waiting impatiently to hear how you are and how Geula is getting on. Are both of you missing the father who is so far away?

Please send me the Arabic-French dictionary which I asked for in a recent letter. I need it urgently, and cannot get one here. How are your Hebrew lessons progressing? And when are you going to write me a letter in Hebrew?

The Allies are advancing, and by the time this letter

*In Memoriam: An anthology honouring watchmen and workers who died in Palestine, edited by Ben-Gurion and A. Hashin and published in Yiddish in the United States in 1917.

reaches you greater and more important revolutions may have taken place. You have no reason to worry about me, my dear Paula. Everything will be all right, and even better than you yourself would wish. At present I can't write to you in detail, for obvious reasons. But your mind can be at rest. The day is not far off when we will be together again and — I believe — will stay together for the rest of our lives.

Tell el-Kebir
November 18, 1918.

'Today, they gave me your letter of September 30. And when I read what is happening to you, and how lonely and helpless you are, I felt as if a sharp knife had been plunged into a hidden wound. It is terrible, dear Paula. I knew you were suffering, and I cannot do anything to help you at present. I see from afar how, in the sad and lonely nights, you shed tears over our young angel. And in vain I hold out my hands to embrace you and comfort you. Then a very heavy weight rests on my heart, and all I can do is to send my warmest, burning love to you and our dear treasure. More I cannot do.

The worst months are behind us, luckily. The time for our reunion has not yet come, but it is no longer far away. The war is already over, and I hope contact between the various countries will soon return to normal. Then we might be able to meet. I would naturally like you to come here as speedily as possible. But I don't know whether Geula could stand up to such a long sea voyage. I don't think I will be able to leave my duties here this winter. But in the spring I will be able to travel to Europe, and then I will come to America as well. Until then we must both be patient, Paula dear. We will not be separated for longer than this.

Tell el-Kebir
November 20, 1918.

Today, I received the first letter you sent me — at last. You

38

can't imagine with what joy I recognized your handwriting on the envelope, which was dated September 25. Together with the letter I received your cable of November 12.

During the last month I've been so anxious about you and Geula that I haven't been able to sleep at night. I waited for your letter, but in vain. A month ago I sent you a telegram. But there was no reply. I didn't know what to think. Terrible thoughts came into my mind. I imagined the very worst. How happy I am now that all my fears were groundless! I see that each of us was afraid for the other. But all's well that ends well. There is peace in the world, and you can see for yourself that I am alive and well and that I belong to you, body and soul, even more than before.

I am still in uniform, and I am still a soldier. A week ago I was in Palestine. Ben-Zvi and I were given ten days' leave. With the gun over my shoulder and a bundle of luggage, I returned, after three years and eight months in exile, to Tel Aviv (Jaffa), from which Ben-Zvi and I had been expelled 'never to return', according to the order issued by Jamal Pasha*, who sent Turkish soldiers to see we left the country. When we protested against our deportation, Jamal Pasha replied: 'You will never come back to Palestine. There is no place here for you.'

To friends who accompanied us to the ship I said: 'We'll see who remains in this country, Jamal Pasha or us.' And now less than four years have gone by, and there is no trace of Jamal Pasha and his government in this country, apart from the tens of thousands of Turkish prisoners of war captured by the Allies, and looked after by the Jewish troops who have come here to drive Jamal out of our country. I never dreamed I would have such a marvellous return to Eretz Yisrael.

To my sorrow, I couldn't stay there long. The ten days passed in a flash, and then I was compelled to return to the desert in Egypt, where our company is stationed. For the last two months we have been in charge of the Turkish and German prisoners brought here from Palestine. This duty has now been taken over by the Indian troops, and we have resumed our training. But I might soon travel to Palestine for

*Turkish Commander-in-Chief in Syria.

a longer stay. The Zionist Commission* has asked Ben-Zvi and me to come to Palestine for a month, and they have asked Headquarters to give us a travel permit.

Extremely important work lies ahead of us, and I am drawing up plans for our activities in the very near future. I'll still be in the army for another six months, it seems, if unexpected events don't force us to shed our uniforms before then. Next summer, if not earlier, I will apparently have to be in Europe, from where I will travel to the United States. Write and tell me when you think our baby daughter will be able to make the long and difficult journey from New York to Jaffa. I would very much like to go with Geula and you to see my father in Poland. You can't imagine how joyfully my father would receive the news that I'm married and the father of a child. To my great sorrow I do not know what is happening in the town where I was born, as I have not heard anything from there for over three years. But now I intend to try to contact my family, and perhaps, with the end of hostilities, my letter will get through.

Please send me my good suit, as I may need it in the near future. Also the notebooks in which I have stuck my published articles. Send everything to this address:

D. Ben-Gurion, c/o E. Blumenfeld, Jaffa, Tel Aviv, Palestine.

Jaffa
December 28, 1918.

I am writing to you both from our home, our old and new home, on the green shores of the Mediterranean Sea. We have left the sands of the desert in Egypt and are encamped in the orange groves of Judea, near the Jewish settlements. The Zionist Committee has claimed me for thirty days, and so I am now in Jaffa. Several days ago we inaugurated a preliminary conference to discuss the formation of a Jewish Assembly for Palestine.

*The Commission appointed by the British Government and sent to Palestine in 1918 to advise the British Military Authorities there on the implementation of the Balfour Declaration.

I represented the Jewish Legion at the conference. It lasted for five days, and I was kept busy day and night. Apart from the regular sittings, there were special sessions with the labour faction. The main problem at the conference was how to formulate our national demands at the Peace Conference in Paris, and I had a lot to say on this subject. The conference adopted a proposal of mine, calling for the election of a three-man committee to clarify our political demands. The three members chosen were the agricultural expert Ettinger+ (who is an authority on settlement questions), Z. Jabotinsky+ and myself.

Now that the conference is over, I am busy with the elections to the new Assembly. The party has asked Ben-Zvi and me to draw up a pamphlet on the current social, political and economic problems. The party also selected me as its delegate to the Peace Conference; but as things stand it is impossible for me to travel. The recent conference was supposed to elect a delegation of three people to represent the Yishuv* at the Peace Conference. But they did not accept our demand that one of these three should come from the labour movement. So my journey depends on the possibility of leaving Palestine at present, which is not easy. But we will ask the Zionist Commission to arrange a special visa for us.

Two days ago we had a celebration: Ben-Zvi got married. You see I'm not the only one who can be so foolish . . . His wife is Rachel Yannait. I've told you about her several times. And there is a picture of her in my album. Until an hour before the wedding we knew nothing about it. There was a routine meeting of the party's Central Committee, and afterwards Ben-Zvi invited me to Rachel's house for a glass of wine. We all felt somehow that there was more to it than this. And true enough, when I arrived at the house I found Ben-Zvi looking rather embarrassed, and I realized what was going on. The wedding was held at the house of the veteran Hebrew writer A.S. Rabinowitz, who comes from the same town as Ben-Zvi. There were about ten friends present, and the ceremony was a fully religious one, correct in every detail. In short, our Ben-Zvi arranged the whole thing. I'm afraid that

*The Jewish Community of Palestine.

41

I'm a little to blame. A bad example is contagious, you know . . .

Jaffa
January 16, 1919.

After a long interval I received three letters from you yesterday. I have been very worried about you and our baby, as I had heard that there is an epidemic of Spanish 'flu in America. I would have cabled you, but it's impossible to do so from here. Now that I have your letters, it feels as if a heavy stone has been lifted from my heart. But now I want more than your letters and the news of the baby. I want both of you to be here with me. I don't know yet how this can be arranged under present conditions: whether you'll receive exit visas from the United States, when there are cargo boats from New York to Jaffa, and whether you'll be allowed to enter Palestine now. I heard that a second delegation of Hadassah* women is coming here. Perhaps you could join this delegation. In a few days time I'll see (E.W.) Lewin-Epstein, the Hadassah representative, about this possibility. He is in Jaffa at present. At the moment this would seem to be the only possible way, since I doubt very much whether ordinary passengers will be allowed to travel from the United States to Palestine.

In any event, I will do everything within my power to bring you over here as soon as possible. At the moment I cannot say anything definite. I don't know where I myself will be in the next four or six months. If I come to Europe I shall also come to America, and then the three of us will return together.

Last week the last group of Legionnaires arrived. Among them was Bunim, who gave me regards from you and Geula and brought a photograph of you both, taken while you were still in hospital. Unfortunately, it is a poor picture and I can't make out the child's face. I'm enclosing two copies of a photograph of me, taken in Jaffa this week.

*See footnote on page 17.

I believe you when you say Geula is still too small for the journey. But if you only knew what I have gone through from the day I received your cable about the baby's birth, you would understand why in every letter I remind you to send me a photograph . . . At least a photograph!

Dear Paula, I know what you have to endure in your loneliness, and the heavy burden on you. But you are not entirely alone; you are together with the child — while I am quite alone, all on my own, far from the two people closest and dearest to me in the world. I live only in the hope that it will not be long before we are together again. Remember that I've never seen my daughter.

So please, Paula, send me a picture of her as quickly as you can. Soon Geula will be six months old, and I hope that you can take her to a photographer's studio. Have a good, large picture made, by the best photographer in New York, and don't worry about the cost. I want to have it soon.

For the last three weeks I've been in camp again. But I'll soon be given leave for a longer period. The Zionist Commission demanded that I should be freed for six weeks. I've spent all my time organizing the workers of Palestine and trying to get them to unite. I've already written to you about my efforts to bring all the Jewish workers in Palestine into a single Zionist socialist labour party. This task is almost completed, and in another week we'll hold a general conference of all the labour groups, as well as the Legionnaires from the United States and Argentine, with the aim of founding a united party. After the conference I'll be able to give you more details about my own personal future. The comrades here want me to travel to London and Paris for the Zionist and socialist congresses which will be held soon. But I can't leave here until I finish the work of creating a united organization. Perhaps in a week's time this work will be done.

Jaffa
March 3, 1919.

I received the photographs yesterday, and a new vista of joy and happiness opened before me. I have never seen a finer picture of a child. And I envy you having her close to you.

Today I gave the photographs to a studio here and asked them to make several copies for me. The moment postal communications are resumed, I want to send two pictures to my father. Unfortunately, they are still not accepting letters from Palestine to Poland. Perhaps you are allowed to send letters from America. Here is my father's address — perhaps you can try to send him a picture:

Mr Victor Grin, Plonsk, Warsaw Governorate, Russian Poland.

I received the notebooks with my articles. Thanks very much. I'm very busy over here. Three conferences of workers have just ended, and the union, on which I've been working for the last three months, has been successful, despite all the difficulties. Many people, including some in my own faction, were opposed to the union, and I had to persuade them. The debate lasted two entire days, and I myself spoke for three hours. At the end there was a general conference of all the organized workers, together with the Legionnaires from North and South America. I was the chairman, and I have never seen such stormy discussions. The final session, which had to vote on the resolutions, lasted for twenty hours without a break, and I had to keep control all this time. I wish you had been there to see it. Then you would have been proud not only of your daughter, but also of your husband.

At five in the morning the resolutions were adopted unanimously, after which I announced a break. I was very tired and had to lie down and sleep. The next morning the elections were conducted without me. I was chosen as the sole delegate to the Zionist Congress and the Poalei Zion* conference in London. Now there is a great amount of work ahead of me. Very shortly I have a meeting with the new Executive, and so I must end here.

*See footnote on page 13.

44

The new members of the Zionist Commission have arrived: Dr Friedland, Szold+ and Robinson. Perhaps with their help you will be able to come here. At first I thought I would be in London sooner or later and I would bring you there from New York, and afterwards we would all come back to Palestine together. But now it is clear that I will remain in uniform until all the troops are released, and that I won't be able to leave the country, and so the only way left is for you to come straight from America to Palestine.

(The end of this letter is missing)

Ekron
April 15, 1919.

I am writing from one of the farming settlements, far from Jaffa, from which I fled several days ago. There were so many meetings and conferences there, and they went on for so long, that I didn't have a free moment for you. I have to prepare some articles for an anthology we are planning, and I was forced to find somewhere quiet so that I could concentrate.

My dear Paula, you complain that I don't write to you often enough. I don't always have the opportunity to sit down and write to you. But if you knew how much I wrote to you with my thoughts, without paper and without ink, you would know how much my heart and head are yours! When I read your letters and gaze at the two faces in the photograph, my heart almost bursts from me with longing. I live for the day when all three of us can be together here, in Eretz Yisrael.

Ramleh
May 8, 1919.

Last night I was on guard duty when they brought me four

letters from you. In your last letter, dated April 2, you write that people told you I am already back in civilian life. Dear Paula, if I had been released from the army you would have been the first to know about it, and you would not have had to hear it from others. In any case, you can see for yourself that it is just a rumour and not true. I am still in the Legion and I don't know when I will be released. I can't travel freely, and I can't come to New York at present. The only way is for you to come here. I wrote to London and asked them to obtain a permit for you from the British Government. I've also asked Professor Feinman, one of the leaders of Poalei Zion in the United States, to get you a visa from the American Government.

You are worried that you won't be able to find milk and eggs here. My dear Paula, do you really think I would bring my child here so that she would suffer? I will give you so many eggs and so much milk for her that you'll be able to bathe her in milk, if you'll feel like it! Why do you pay attention to the stories people tell in New York about life in Palestine? I promise you, Paula, that Geula will have everything here that she has in Brooklyn and the Bronx, at least until she wants to go to the Metropolitan Opera.

Jaffa
June 24, 1919.

I've been in Jaffa for the last five days, practising shooting. I'll be here a few days longer, until I've completed the shooting course, and then I'll return to camp. I don't yet know how much longer I'll have to stay in the army. It might be several months. I don't mind at all. The main thing is that you should come here as soon as possible. That will solve all our problems.

You write that you've had another photograph of Geula taken. Why don't you send it to me? Never mind, I'm prepared to do without the copy as long as you send me the original.

46

There is a rumour that all the 'foreigners' in the Legion — in other words, those who are not British citizens — will soon be released. I don't know whether there's any truth in this. I'll let you know when I hear something definite.

I sent a letter to my father, and also the picture of you and Geula, through Stockholm. I hope that this time it will reach him. As you know, I haven't been able to contact him for over three years.

I am living in the expectation of your arrival. This is my personal Messianic dream. The moment you get your permit, cable me. The same applies if you join the Hadassah Medical Unit coming out to do nursing here.

Ramleh
July 25, 1919.

The release of the Legionnaires has begun. This week the first group of 105 left. Next week there will be a larger group. No one from our group, Company 39, has been released yet. But people say it will not be long now — perhaps even next week. All we've been told officially is that non-British subjects are not to stay in the 'army of occupation', and that they will be released after the Peace Treaty is approved. I've seen the official order at the Zionist Commission. But no one knows when or how it will be carried out. We'll have to wait and see.

A group of us are now planning a new quarter in Jaffa. It will be constructed on socialist lines, and named after our late comrade, Ber Borochov+. I am also a member of this group. Until the quarter is built and we are able to live in our own house (which will not be our own property, but where we shall have the right to live), we'll rent a flat.

So in a few weeks' time I might be released from the army. But when will I be freed from my loneliness? If by the time this letter reaches you you haven't been given a permit, ask for one as a *refugee*. After all, you know I was expelled from

47

Palestine by Jamal Pasha in 1915, and on this basis you as my wife should be allowed to return to my home. I'm doing everything possible over here. But unfortunately it all depends on New York.

My military address is:

Pte. D. Ben-Gurion, 5770, A. Coy, 39 R.F. Palestine.

I am a private now, and not a corporal, because I went to Jaffa without a permit and was court-martialled. They took my rank away from me and transferred me to Company 39.

(In November, 1919 Mrs Ben-Gurion and her daughter arrived in Jaffa).

LETTERS 1923-1935

The exhibition* will last another two months, until November 15. I trust my work won't be in vain.

I haven't had a reply from your sister. But your sister-in-law told me that one of your relatives will come to see me in a few days' time.

How are the children?** Please ask David Zakai+ to send me the *Manchester Guardian* from the office. I have no idea what is happening in the world outside Russia.

Greetings to you, Geula, and to you, Amos, from your father in Moscow. Speak to your mother only in Hebrew. Buy yourselves some nice toys.

Moscow
October 26, 1923.

I'm pleased you took the trouble to arrange an immigrant's permit for your sister Fania, and I hope it will come through while I am here. Then she'll be able to come with me. I'm sure you will enjoy having her to stay with us in Jerusalem.

The exhibition closed on the 21st. It was a tremendous success. Generally speaking, my visit to Russia was more worthwhile than we expected beforehand. I have to stay here another two weeks. And during this time Fania's permit might be granted. Unfortunately I won't have time to visit Minsk and to see your relatives there. But at least I'll bring back one of your sisters!

---

*The Agricultural Exhibition. The Histadrut (Labour Federation) took part in it, and Ben-Gurion was its representative.
**By this time Amos, Ben-Gurion's second child and only son, had been born.

Moscow
October 29, 1923.

Today I sent home five parcels containing about sixty books, most of them on trade union questions in Russia and the revolutionary movement. There are also twenty-three volumes for Zakai — the collected works of Chekhov. If any of our friends (Ben-Zvi or Reubeni) borrow a book, please write down its name, so that when I come back I'll be able to trace it.

In another ten days I'll leave here via Germany.

Moscow
November 23, 1923.

I'm very happy to inform you that Fania has received her entry permit for Palestine, and went to Minsk yesterday to arrange her Russian passport. This will take about six weeks, and then she'll leave for Eretz Yisrael immediately, through Constantinople. I have given her money for expenses during the journey.

London
July 29, 1924.

I have been here for a week, and it's by no means certain that I'll go to Russia. The Zionist Actions Committee is still sitting. We are engaged in a difficult struggle to satisfy our demands. We've already obtained £125,000 for agricultural settlement, £8,000 for housing urban workers in Jaffa and Haifa, £30,000 for building operations and £12,000 for the Histadrut health service. I also managed to obtain £3,000 to cover travelling expenses for 500 *halutzim** from Russia. But the political problems still lie ahead.

Tonight there is a mass meeting at which Berl Locker+, Shlomo Kaplansky+ and I are talking, also a Member of the British Parliament.

*Halutz (plural *Halutzim*): A pioneer, especially in agriculture.

The Zionist Commission received by two British officers. Front, left to right: Major E. Walley, B. Yaffe, E. W. Lewin-Epstein, S. D. Levontin, L. Simon, S. Levi, I. Sieff, J. Cowen, C. Weizmann, Major W. Ormsby-Gore. Back: Dr. M.D. Eder, W. Mever, A. Aaronson, M. Roseneck.

Ben-Gurion speaking at the foundation of the first Workers' Sports Centre (Beth Hapoalim), 1924. He was then Secretary of the Histadrut.

The family circle in the early 1920's: Ben-Gurion with Paula, their three
children and Ben-Gurion's father, Avigdor Grin.

Lloyd George, the Prime Minister,
with Winston Churchill, 1916.

Lord Balfour and Dr. Chaim
Weizmann in Tel-Aviv, 1925.

Oxford
August 16, 1924.

Here I am, in this ancient university town, taking part in an international conference on the education of workers. Moshe Shertok (Sharett)+ and I are the delegates from Palestine. In two days' time I'll return to London.

I am waiting for official information from the Government of Palestine about my journey to Russia. At the moment I don't know whether it will be possible to go, and if so, when. Meanwhile there are various conferences in different countries which I have to attend. Write to me at my London address, and the letters will reach me wherever I am.

Ruskin College,
Oxford
August 17, 1924.

The conference continues. There are delegates from twenty-five countries, including Australia, South Africa, Japan and India. There are delegates with black skins (Africans) and yellow skins (Japanese).

Yesterday we talked to some of the delegates from Britain, America and Australia about the labour movement in Palestine. They were extremely impressed and were surprised to hear about our achievements.

I am returning to London tonight. If I find there satisfactory news from Palestine, I shall be able to proceed to Russia in three or four weeks.

London
September 23, 1924.

I was in Berlin for two days, but received a cable from the Zionist office in London saying my presence there was essential. The British Foreign Office has written to the Russian Legation here about me and requested that our entry visas be approved. But so far nothing has happened . . .

I've already sent you a cable: 'Everything fine'. In fact I arrived here a day earlier than I was supposed to. I had an argument with B. I said the journey from Constantinople to Paris took only three days. But he insisted, quoting Cook's, that it took four. And of course Cook's can't be wrong. When I arrived in Constantinople I found out that it's three days, after all.

This morning I arranged the American visa without any difficulty, and the American Consul in Jerusalem had cabled the Embassy earlier. I have a berth in the tourist class. The ship leaves from Cherbourg on the 19th.

All of our friends are in London, apart from Abraham Harzfeld+, who will return in a couple of days. The political outlook seems brighter. But we must wait and see. Today there will be a debate in Parliament. Write to me in New York.

November 23, 1930.

This is our fouth day on the Atlantic Ocean. The skies are cloudy all the time, there is a strong wind and the sea is rough. But I feel perfectly all right. My cabin is in the tourist class. It should hold four passengers. But there are only two of us, and the food is excellent, almost like the first class. This is the best rest I could have dreamed of. On Wednesday we shall arrive in New York.

There is a daily paper printed on the ship, but it has hardly any news of the wide world, and none at all from our country.

Chicago
December 9, 1930.

This afternoon I came here from Rochester. In every city one goes to people think one is visiting only them and not going anywhere else. They don't give one a moment's rest. I'm spending only six hours here, and I've already visited the Hearst offices; then two Yiddish papers, *Vorwaerts* and *Yiddishe Courier*. In every place you are interviewed and photographed. In addition I had to meet the Hadassah ladies — and this meant more speeches, questions and answers. Tonight there will be a rally. I insisted on two hours' rest during the afternoon. But when I returned to the hotel I found a man from the *Chicago Tribune* waiting for me, and a delegation from the American trade union *(American Federation of Labour)*, and a cousin of mine had already discovered my telephone number and was on to me.

I left Cleveland yesterday, and there I had six meetings in a day and a half. In Chicago I shall have five. I am supposed to be in the United States for two and a half weeks. Will I have the strength for it all?

Well, never mind. I'll manage it, even though it *is* a bit too much. But it's hard to say no to comrades. What's the news at home? How is the building of our home in Tel Aviv progressing?

New York
December 18, 1930.

As you see, I am back in New York. In the last ten days I have been to Cleveland, Rochester, Chicago, Montreal and Boston. I gave twenty-two speeches, apart from interviews and discussions with smaller groups. I had to speak two or three times a day, and on one occasion five times in twenty-four hours. In Chicago I gave nine speeches, and afterwards I felt exhausted. But then I went to Montreal, and after a whole day in the train I was able to continue at the same pace.

I returned to New York yesterday, and will stay here for two days. The usual hectic routine. Many people send regards to you.

In Montreal several women said they envy you. I replied that you are not at all proud of me and not impressed by me in the slightest. Did I speak the truth or not?

55

I'll probably leave America next Saturday, the 27th. I am waiting for a cable from Yosef Sprinzak+ about the Zionist Congress. Here in New York they want to postpone it, and if they do I might stay for a little longer.

Here it is cold and snow is falling. Many people ask me about Geula. They remember her when she was a baby.

On the New Amsterdam
January 12, 1931.

I left New York on Friday and will reach London on the 15th. So I'll spend nine days on board ship. I like smaller ships like this: you can rest on them. America tired me out very much, and I don't know whether I'll be able now to make a trip to Poland. I want to come home. But I'll decide this in London. In New York I received a telegram from the Zionist Actions Committee* which didn't make sense to me and I'll have to clarify it in London.

Basle
July 20, 1931.

Well, the 'fair' is over at last. The long, tense, nervous, stormy sessions of the Zionist Congress have ended. Also the short, peaceful and, in fact, boring meetings of the Jewish Agency Council. The public has gone home, and only a few of our comrades are left here in Basle. Tomorrow morning I'm travelling to Bad Gastein in Austria to meet Dr Weizmann+. Berl Katzenelson+, Chaim Arlosoroff+ and Yosef Sprinzak are the other members of the delegation to Weizmann.

After this I might spend three days in Vienna and also visit Czechoslovakia. Then on the 29th I sail from Trieste, and on August 3 I'll be home.

I've attended several Congresses already. But I've never

*The supreme advisory and supervisory body in charge of Zionist Affairs between Zionist Congresses.

been to one as difficult, nerve-racking and critical as this one. It had to face three great and serious problems. We lost on one of these, and won our fight on the other two.

The first question was: Weizmann. Apart from the Revisionists*, there were many General Zionists** who wanted to dismiss Weizmann at all costs. Several months ago I told our comrades that for the good of the party and the good of Weizmann himself he shouldn't stand for the Presidency at this Congress. Unfortunately my words weren't listened to, and the majority decided to insist on Weizmann's candidacy. This led many Zionists to oppose our party and its policies. Our comrades thought it was still possible to ensure a majority for Weizmann. On the heels of all this came a harmful interview given by Weizmann to the Jewish Telegraphic Agency, in which he said it was not essential to have a Jewish majority in Palestine. This ruled him out as President of the Zionist Organization.

But our Weizmannites were blind to all this and still hoped to succeed — and this was a grave error. Instead of Weizmann withdrawing of his own free will and in this way keeping the sympathy and love of most of the Zionist movement, their short-sighted and misguided policy led to Weizmann being voted out in an unfair manner.

The second question was: our policy — or that of the Revisionists. After an arduous and bitter struggle, which took a lot out of me personally, we won this battle and the Congress adopted our policy by a large majority.

The third issue was: the Executive. Would we control the governing body of Zionism, or the Revisionists? You know the result already. An Executive was formed with members from all the parties — excepting the Revisionists. Our party and other parties wanted me to serve on the Executive. I don't know what you thought of the proposal. But my work in the Histadrut and the situation in this body prevented this. I cannot leave the Histadrut now. Berl Katzenelson was also

*Revisionists: Zionist party founded by Jabotinsky, which advocated a Jewish State on both sides of the Jordan and opposed the official Zionist policy towards British mandatory rule. It seceded from the World Zionist Organization in 1935.
**When, early in the 20th-century, socialist and religious parties emerged in the World Zionist Organization, there simultaneously developed a more broad-based faction known as the General Zionists.

57

approached to join the Zionist Executive, but he too refused. Sprinzak and Kaplansky were ready to join the new Executive. But many of our comrades opposed them, and we chose Locker and Arlosoroff instead. Arlosoroff will probably stay in Jerusalem, while Locker will be stationed in London.

On Saturday last I was invited to meet the Prime Minister (Ramsay MacDonald)+ at Chequers. Keep this to yourself, as it's top secret. I flew from Basle to London and spent four hours with MacDonald; and I think I obtained very important assurances from him. I'll give you the details when I return.

Vienna
July 22, 1931.

Together with Berl Katzenelson, Sprinzak and Arlosoroff I'm here for the second day. We are having talks with Weizmann on future activities. Tomorrow I leave here, on my way home.

London
July 24, 1932.

I arrived here this morning. I had to remain in Paris for a few days in order to finish my articles on the crisis in Zionism and the Labour movement, which will be published in *Hapoel Hatzair.* Kaplansky was here, but left for Berlin several days ago. So far I've seen only Berl Locker.

Zalman Rubashov (Shazar)+ is expected tomorrow from New York, and then our meetings will start. The Zionist Actions Committee will begin its deliberations on Thursday morning, and they will last more than a week. Then the Jewish Agency's Administrative Committee will meet. So I'll have to be here for at least two weeks.

Tonight I'll see Weizmann. The Zionist Actions Committee will not be a picnic and we have to prepare for a struggle.

Children, I would like to hear from each of you. Send me

the marks you got at school, and tell me what you are doing during the holidays. What books you are reading and what you do the whole day long. Have you planted grass in the garden in front of the house? And have the flowers we planted come out yet? You too, Renana*, write and tell me if you received my letter and what you are doing.

Warsaw
August 31, 1932.

I've now been in Poland for a week. Two days in Plonsk and five in Warsaw. Meetings and discussions from early morning until late at night without a break, so that my head reels and I can scarcely hear what people are telling me. Today I intend spending in the forest, and tomorrow morning I'll set off for Galicia. I'll have to spend ten to twelve days there, and then I'll come straight home. I think I should be in Tel Aviv by September 20.

In Warsaw I addressed a large rally; it was very successful. The Jewish press in both Polish and Yiddish reported my speech prominently, although not all the reports were accurate.

The situation here is terrible. The poverty gets worse every day. Everyone dreams only of Palestine. I know you have many relatives here, but I haven't come across any.

Memel
April 25, 1933.

This morning I came here from Kovno. Memel used to be part of Germany, but now it belongs to Lithuania. The Jews of Memel, who initially regretted leaving Germany, are now happy that they are no longer under Hitler's rule. There is a good Zionist movement here, and many of the Lithuanian *halutzim* work in it. Tonight I'm addressing a public meeting.

In Kovno I had two large meetings and a series of

*The third of Ben-Gurion's three children.

committee meetings. Everywhere I find the same phenomenon: a large youth movement, huge crowds attending all the meetings (hundreds and sometimes even thousands are forced to leave the hall because they cannot get in). Fantastic interest in Palestine. Tremendous enthusiasm among the young people. Sometimes this makes me afraid. Wherever I go I find youngsters who study my articles and speeches and who know my writings published in the Land of Israel — and I shudder when I think of the great responsibility resting upon these words that I have written. I never anticipated this, I never wanted it and I never aspired to it. But the more I travel and the more I meet the masses and the young people, the more I realize what a great responsibility I bear, and I become afraid. I suspect that from now on it won't be so easy for me to write and speak in the Land of Israel. Tens of thousands of Jewish youth — and the best of the youth — are listening, reading and studying what I say, in all the countries, in all the towns and villages. I never realized this before my present visit, and to be aware of it now is neither easy nor pleasant.

Lemberg
May 22, 1933.

I've just come back from Stanislav, a large town in Eastern Galicia, and yesterday was another day of hard work, although very interesting and I think fruitful. At the train there was a mass reception, with people on bicycles and young people in scout uniform and representatives of various bodies. Immediately after the reception came a conference of twenty-seven towns and villages, which I addressed for one and a half hours. At six in the evening there was a two-hour public meeting in a theatre. It was packed out, and over a thousand people were unable to get seats and had to go home. The Communists tried to create a disturbance in the hall. But the Zionist youth threw them out, and the meeting was quiet and orderly. Many Revisionists came along, but they did not interfere.

In the evening there was a dinner. Speeches and greetings

on behalf of the Jewish community, the General Zionists, the Mizrachi*, teachers, university staff, members of our party and so on — until midnight, when I returned to the hotel tired and worn out.

Tomorrow I'll continue my journey. And for the next five days this will be the pattern, every single day. I don't know whether I'll be able to last out until the elections in mid-July.

A representative of the Polish Government came to see our chairman in Stanislav this morning and congratulated me on my speech. He said that Jabotinsky spoke here two weeks ago. He compared Jabotinsky's speech with mine, and pointed to the difference between us; Jabotinsky has phrases, while I have earnestness . . . I didn't know that the Poles are such experts on speech-making!

Warsaw
May 30, 1933.

I returned yesterday from my visit to Eastern Galicia. It was my most difficult journey to date. Because I could not spare more than ten days, they squeezed enough meetings and work into this short time to last at least a month. If I didn't have to move on to the other places I would have accepted the burden with love. The Zionist movement in Eastern Galicia is large, and the work gave me great spiritual satisfaction. The rallies in places like Stari and Turnopol were well-attended, and people walked four or five hours to reach them, sometimes in pouring rain. The last gathering in Turnopol was particularly impressive. Over 1,200 delegates from the neighbouring towns turned up. When I arrived at the railway station there were thousands of people waiting, and when I walked from the station to the hotel the streets were packed.

Tomorrow I'm going to Bendin, and when I return to Warsaw I'll spend a whole week just resting. I still have twelve more cities to visit. If I leave Galicia sound and healthy, it's a sure sign I'm as strong as iron.

*Religious Zionist Organization. Founded in 1901, the Mizrachi adopts a programme of religious Zionism within the framework of the Zionist Movement.

At last I have a chance to rest for a few days. Yesterday I returned to Warsaw from Bendin, and until next Friday I don't have to travel anywhere. I have to tackle some organizational problems over here.

I've already received from Palestine most of the proofs of my book, *From Class to Nation*. And by the time you receive this letter the whole book may be ready for publication.

The book will be published in Poland in Yiddish. Several of the articles in the book were originally written in Yiddish (in America), and won't need to be translated. But we have to find the original text, which is lying at home. You know the yellow notebooks stored in the right-hand side of my writing desk. There are seven or eight of them. On each one is written 'In the Diaspora', with a number — 1, 2, 3 and so on.

Please give these notebooks to Moshe Lubetkin at the Histadrut, and he will send them to me in Warsaw. I would like the book to appear in Poland before the elections to the Zionist Congress.

There is a mountain of work here now. In addition to all the election meetings and rallies, I have to keep an eye on the organizational side in Poland. We are responsible for 600 towns in Poland alone, and this involves tens of thousands of voters. Then I also have to correspond with our comrades in Galicia, Czechoslovakia, Rumania, Lithuania, Latvia and Estonia, not to mention the constant contact with Palestine.

After the elections I'll take a break. This will be in the second half of July. You must have received the cheque for £10 — payment for an article published in *Haint**. Now I'm enclosing a cheque for $15 from *Morgen Journal,* for the last article I sent them from Warsaw two weeks ago. Since then I haven't written any articles, because I haven't had the time.

*Newspaper published in Warsaw, 1908-1939.

But I hope to write another article for *Haint* this week.

It would be marvellous if you could come to the Congress. You could travel a bit in Europe and rest. And you would find the Congress interesting. Ask Dobkin+ how much it will cost. I'll make an effort to arrange it. But what about the children?

What's new in our suburb? And the garden? Is the lawn in front of the house green? Are the orange trees and strawberries doing well? Do the children help you with the garden?

I hope we can meet at the Congress. It will probably be held in Carlsbad or Brussels*.

Warsaw
June 26, 1933.

After the terrible news of Arlosoroff's death I couldn't write. I couldn't imagine coming home and not finding him there. I heard about the tragedy when I came to Vilna. At three o'clock I left Grodna for Vilna, knowing nothing about the catastrophe. I reached Vilna towards evening. Our comrades there had already received the telegram for me, which contained the news that Arlosoroff had been murdered. But they didn't give it to me. There were hundreds of people to meet me at the train — members of our party and representatives of the Zionist movement in Vilna. The welcome was festive and cordial, as it has been at every place I've visited. We went to the hotel. Our comrades told me that there was a telegram for me, but they had left it at home. We talked about the political situation, the election — as if nothing had happened. The mass meeting was planned for the next day, and from Vilna I was due to travel to Dvinsk, in Latvia. They told me that Melekh Noi-Nisht, who works in the election bureau in Warsaw, had cabled saying I should not proceed to Dvinsk. To this I replied: even if the whole world turns upside down, I will go to Dvinsk, because I've disappointed this town twice already.

We went on talking, and they asked me if I'd heard the

*The Congress was eventually held in Prague.

news from Tel Aviv. What news? I asked. Riots, attacks? What's happened? They said to me: Perhaps the Arabs. I asked: Arabs in Tel Aviv? Instead of replying directly they asked me: Which member of the Zionist Executive lives in Tel Aviv? None, I answered. They all live in Jerusalem. We went on talking, and then someone said: There are worrying reports. I asked: What are they? Now the comrades told me: Something has happened to Arlosoroff. Arlosoroff? What are you talking about? Then they took out the 'misplaced' cable and gave it to me: Arlosoroff had been murdered in Tel Aviv.

My whole world went black, and I fainted. According to the newspapers I read afterwards, I called out 'What!' in Hebrew, although we had been speaking Yiddish all the time. When I became conscious again I rushed to a nearby newspaper office to phone Nisht in Warsaw. But I couldn't find his number. I phoned *Haint*, and Goldberg, the editor, gave me fuller details.

Then the dreadful suspicion came into my mind: Arlosoroff returned to Palestine only three days before his murder. It happened at 10 p.m., near the workers' suburb in which he did not live. The murderer could not have been an Arab. Arlosoroff lived in Jerusalem. Why didn't they kill him in Jerusalem? How did the murderers know what time he would be in Tel Aviv? How could an Arab escape from a place like that at ten o'clock at night? And why Arlosoroff? Someone suggested that it might have been done by Communists. But why? And why in Tel Aviv? The dreadful suspicion would not leave me. I wanted to telephone Tel Aviv. But it is impossible to do this so late at night.

I cabled the Actions Committee of the Histadrut and asked for full information. And I added: No revenge! I told the comrades that I would not remain in Vilna and would not speak at any more meetings, and that I would return to Warsaw immediately.

That same night I returned to Warsaw on an express train. When I parted from our Vilna comrades they told me that before my arrival the police had said there might be an attack on me. True enough, three policemen were stationed at the hotel to protect me. The comrades wanted me to stay in Vilna for another day. But I told them this was out of the question, and that I wouldn't remain there any longer, even if I didn't have to make a speech that night.

The police agents accompanied me to the train, and didn't leave my side until it started.

When I arrived in Warsaw I heard the ugly rumours spread by the Revisionists, claiming that the background to the murder was a love affair. At once I sent an open letter to all the newspapers about this dirty tactic — and the rumours stopped.

During the day we have heard reports of arrests in Palestine. You will know all about this.

On Sunday night I phoned Eliahu Dobkin and told him I wanted to come home. He begged me not to do this, and assured me everything was calm in Palestine. The next morning I received a telegram from Jerusalem saying that I should stay in Poland and carry on with my work. The following Wednesday there was an article in *Der Moment* — a newspaper* to which Jabotinsky contributes — attacking the Labour movement and me in particular, in a scurrilous fashion. I wrote a reply, but the paper refused to publish it.

Warsaw
July 5, 1933.

It is not clear from your last letter what you intend to do with the children, particularly with Renana, if you do come to the Zionist Congress. As I wrote to you earlier, you should not bring her with you, since you will not enjoy your trip to Europe if you do. You would be busy with her all the time, as a child as young as she is can't be left in a strange city.

I might come home after the elections to the Congress. In Poland they are being held on the 23rd. So I could leave here on July 25 or 26, after the results are known.

*Published in Warsaw 1910-1939.

By the time you receive this letter the Zionist Congress will be over. But today we are just beginning our discussions. The main problem will be the composition of the new Executive. The Labour Faction is too big to be left out. But we need a coalition partner, and are dependent on the General Zionists for this. They are divided into two groups: A and B. A is closer to us. They want Weizmann as President, are progressive in thinking and would like to co-operate with us. But, on the other hand, they are weak-willed and do not know what they want. The other group, B, knows exactly what it wants, but in their heart of hearts they are hostile to us, although they try to hide this. The Mizrachi is also split: the minority is close to us, and we could work with them, but the majority is closer to the Revisionists, and conceal their animosity towards us under the cloak of religion. The Revisionist position is known, of course.

There is another small group of fourteen delegates, led by Yitzhak Gruenbaum+. They are our closest friends and allies. But we cannot rely only on them, as this will not give us a majority. So, two weeks before the end of the Congress, the situation is still unclear.

Within our own party the situation is almost as complicated. Who will serve on the new Executive? The greatest difficulty is in filling Arlosoroff's place at the head of the Political Department. No man, as far as I know, *can* take his place. But this position must be filled. Shertok is excellent in this type of work, but he himself and several of our comrades doubt whether he will be able to accept this responsibility.

Locker must remain. This is what almost everyone thinks. Some want Kaplan+ and Berl Katzenelson to enter the Executive; others want Kaplansky, while some favour Sprinzak. One thing has been clear to me all the time — that I am staying at the Histadrut and will not serve on the Executive. I am convinced that I should not leave the Histadrut in its present state. Until now I would have thought this was the general view, and was sure that most of the

Jewish workers would oppose my leaving the Histadrut. But there is increasing pressure on me to do this.

All the other Zionist parties want me in the Executive, to my great surprise. I appear to be the most vigorous opponent of all the other parties. Yet they demand that I move from the Histadrut to the Executive. And so do the comrades in my own party who formerly agreed with me that my place was in the Histadrut. Shertok, for example, makes my nomination for the Executive a condition for his own entry. I have never faced such a difficult personal decision. I feel it is a fateful question. My own awareness of what I ought to do is out of step with what my party wants.

The committee we appointed to decide our representatives on the new Executive have proposed: me, Berl Locker, Kaplan, and Shertok (as Political Secretary). I don't know how the matter will end. The Congress is scheduled to close tomorrow or, at the very latest, the day afterwards. I shall have to stay on for another week for talks on the party, and I hope to leave for Tel Aviv on the 14th.

Prague
September 6, 1933.

Of course by now you will have heard the results of the Congress, which were rather surprising. Even as far as my own position is concerned, I did not expect things to turn out as they have. I have always favoured a broad coalition — everyone apart from the Revisionists — and I worked very hard for this. But it wasn't feasible, mainly because the General Zionist B group insisted on conditions which were too severe and which we could not accept. During the last two days I have come to the conclusion that we should form an Executive with our friends from the General Zionist A group, which is smaller but closer to us. Under these conditions it has become essential for me myself to serve on the Executive.

The difficulty lay in my inability to leave the Histadrut, and so I agreed to enter the Executive on condition that I need not accept responsibility for any specific department, and that I can continue to live in Tel Aviv and to work in the Histadrut as before. I will devote only one or two days a week to the Executive. Most of this time will be spent on political matters, which will be my special concern. In order to do this I'll have to install a telephone in my room at once. But my phone number will be known only to Moshe Shertok and one or two other people, who will be able to phone me whenever they need to.

Yesterday the new Executive met for the first time. It was decided that I should travel to Italy to see Weizmann (who is in Merano), and then to London to negotiate with the Colonial Office an increase in the immigration quota.

I shall arrive in London on September 13 and spend four or five days there before returning to Tel Aviv.

London
September 16, 1933.

I arrived here from Merano on Thursday. Yesterday I spent two hours at the Colonial Office with Professor Brodetsky+ and Yitzhak Gruenbaum, discussing the recent Zionist Congress and immigration. The general tone of the conversation was satisfactory, but there are no concrete results as yet. We will naturally raise this matter when we see the High Commissioner in Jerusalem, and will then take it up in London again.

On Monday morning I shall meet MacDonald+ Junior, with whom I'll be able to discuss the political questions which concern me. I can talk to him freely and in detail, and this will give me some idea whether this government can be relied on for anything concrete.

I'll remain here for four or five days. Apart from meeting the members of the Executive, I have to see various people about German Jewry and the possibility of setting up a fund for our work in Jerusalem and London.

If everything goes as planned, I'll leave Trieste on the 21st. If I'm delayed, then on the 28th, and I'll be in Tel Aviv before the Festival of Succot.

I thought of travelling to Port Said the day after tomorrow, via Marseilles. I already had a train ticket to Marseilles as well as a ticket for the ship. But when I went to arrange an Egyptian visa, it appeared that I'm still on the black list. They sent a telegram to Cairo, but it will take two days to get the reply, so I won't be able to sail from Marseilles, and will go via Trieste on September 27.

I'm already tired of all this travelling and longing to be home again. I'll just have to spend a day or two in Paris. Weizmann is coming here tomorrow, and I have to talk to him about a few things.

It's midnight, and everything is quiet in the High Commissioner's home. But I can't sleep. The two talks I had tonight — one before dinner, and the second afterwards — tired me, and I can't fall asleep. So far I haven't received any reply to what I said. The High Commissioner* listened to me attentively, wrote down what I said, observed that my stand was logical, and promised to think about my remarks — and to give me a reply.

The conversation after dinner was unofficial, and touched on all kinds of subjects.

We'll see what happens tomorrow morning.

I came here yesterday by plane, from Berlin. It took three hours and forty-five minutes — an easy flight. We flew over the sea for about an hour. I arrived here on the Silver Jubilee

*Sir Arthur Wauchope+.

69

of King George V. I've never seen London like this. And I never thought I'd see English people dancing in the streets. I didn't see the King's great procession, as I was busy with meetings. But later on I heard the speeches of greeting from Canada, Australia, Africa and India and eventually the speech of the King himself, on the radio.

I spent three days in Berlin and one and a half days in Danzig. On Saturday morning I flew from Berlin to Danzig, flying back the next night. In Berlin I also took part in the conference of the German Zionist movement.

The ship leaves Southampton tomorrow, and I leave London in the morning.

At yesterday's Executive meeting we discussed my journey to America. Sokolow and Brodetsky want me to return as soon as possible because of the urgent political matters facing us: the Legislative Council*.

*Southampton
May 8, 1935.*

I am writing to you from the ship. The sky is rather cloudy, but I hope the sea will be calm. From here we sail to Cherbourg, in France, and then across the ocean. In seven days' time I'll be in New York.

This week I travelled on every form of transport — on land, in the air and by sea. The most convenient and comfortable of them is of course by 'plane.

I've hardly slept for five nights. In Berlin, Danzig and London I had many meetings. So I am looking forward to resting on the ship for a few days, if the weather allows this.

---

*According to the British Government's proposal, the Legislative Council for Palestine would comprise 28 members. Twelve of these would be elected (eight Moslems, three Jews and one Christian) and eleven appointed (three Moslems, four Jews, two Christians and two representatives of commercial circles), together with five Government officials. The chairman would be a neutral figure from another country. The High Commissioner would have the right of veto, full control of immigration and power to enact legislation without the approval of the Council. The Jews of Palestine rejected this proposal vehemently.

New York
May 15, 1935.

I arrived here last night, and plunged immediately into interviews with journalists and meetings. I'm enclosing the three Jewish newspapers of this morning.

At lunch-time there was a press conference with journalists from both the Yiddish and the English press. I spoke in English on the situation in Palestine and the problems facing Zionism.

On Saturday there'll be a rally in Carnegie Hall.

On Friday I'm seeing Brandeis+ in Washington.

May 22, 1935.

I came here this morning from Milwaukee, and will be here for two days. During the week I've spent in the United States I've already been in Washington, Boston, Milwaukee and Chicago. In Washington and Boston I met Brandeis and Frankfurter+ about political matters. In Milwaukee and Chicago I addressed large public meetings.

The rally at Carnegie Hall in New York went off well. In his speech Dr Stephen Wise+ demanded that I should be the head of the Zionist movement. I don't know at present how long I'll remain in America. I'm waiting for news from Moshe (Shertok) in Jerusalem.

June 1, 1935.

Yesterday I received a telegram from Moshe to return to Palestine at once, because the High Commissioner has decided to make preparations for the Legislative Council and I have to take part in the negotiations (this is secret at the moment). I've been dealing with this question over here, and have fixed my departure from America for June 13. From here I'll go to London, and after spending a few days there I'll return to Tel Aviv through Marseilles and Trieste. So by the end of the month I'll be at home.

71

I've been in Boston, Washington, Chicago, Milwaukee, Detroit and St. Louis, and covered 4,430 miles by 'plane. The most interesting flight was by night from Chicago, when I went over New York and Chicago and saw the lights of these two great cities from a great height. The grandest sight I have ever seen.

I am sorry that I have to leave America in such a hurry, as there is a lot to be done here. The Zionist Socialist Party here, and the Zionist movement as a whole, are in a bad way, and can be improved only by help from the outside. But I must return for the talks in Jerusalem.

June 10, 1935.

It seems that I will leave here in another three days, as I wrote earlier. We haven't been able to postpone the plans for a Legislative Council, and according to the telegrams from London and Jerusalem the negotiations on this question will start soon. I must be in Jerusalem during the discussions with the High Commissioner. There is a slight hope that the new Minster, Malcolm MacDonald (Ramsay's son), will agree to delay the plan for a while, and in this case I would stay here for another ten days. I haven't finished my work here yet. Felix Warburg+ begged me to stay on until d'Avigdor-Goldsmid+, one of the leading non-Zionists, comes from London to discuss the composition of the next Executive. But if I don't hear from London tomorrow that the Legislative Council has been postponed, I'll have to leave at once.

LETTERS 1935-1939

Dear Geula and Amos,

During the Zionist Congress I didn't write to you, because I didn't have a minute to myself. And when the Congress ended I was very tired. During the closing sessions I could hardly stand on my feet, and I felt emotionally and physically exhausted. It will take a few days before I recover my strength, and meanwhile work has to go on — because when the Congress closes the Jewish Agency meets, and between one session and the other there are the usual talks, clashes and other final reminders of the Congress.

Last night there was a meeting of the new Zionist Actions Committee, and it finished its business that same night. Incredible! I was elected a member of the Jewish National Fund's board of directors, so that I can be the Governor of the organization, with the right of veto.

I want to try to explain to all of you what I hoped this Congress would achieve, and what the actual results were.

Lucerne
September 7, 1935.

Dear Geula and Amos,

Again I found myself caught up in meetings and couldn't find a spare moment until today. The day before yesterday the members of the Political Executive (Weizmann, Brodetsky, Moshe and I) decided that I should go to London for two months, until the High Commissioner returns to Palestine.

I might spend another week in Switzerland in order to rest after the Congress, and I hope to finish this letter there.

Now I will tell you what I wanted this Congress to do.

First of all, I thought it important that the question of *implementing* Zionism should be brought before the Congress as fully as possible. I stress the implementation because I don't think we have to discuss the *need* for Zionism any longer. For it has never been so obvious both to the Jewish

75

people and to the entire world that the existence of the Jewish people in the Diaspora has become impossible.

The real question is whether Zionism can solve this problem — in other words, whether the Land of Israel can absorb large masses of Jews, and how this can be done. And so I tried to show not only what could be done, but *how difficult* the task is, and what great internal and external efforts will be needed. This was the main purpose of my speech on the second day of the Congress, which you've probably read in *Davar**.

I faced two problems in making this speech: time and language. I never write a speech out in full, but this time I wrote down for myself the main points. And according to these, the speech would have lasted at least four hours. This is unthinkable at a Zionist Congress, and so I was forced to cut out some key points. Then there was the language. I can talk about something which touches me deeply only if I speak Hebrew. But many of the delegates cannot understand Hebrew. And I thought it important to use a language which as many people as possible understood. So I decided to speak in Yiddish. But it is difficult for me to speak in Yiddish on this subject, as I have to translate my thoughts from Hebrew all the time, and sometimes I can't find the right words. So making this speech was a great ordeal for me. When I finished I was bathed in sweat, right through to my jacket. This fatigue naturally showed itself in my speech. But I think the main purpose was accomplished: the horizons of Zionism have been enlarged in the consciousness of the movement, and the problems of implementing Zionism have been stressed clearly, so that we all know what tremendous efforts will be required.

The second thing I wanted this Congress to achieve was the formation of a coalition, so that internal unity would be strengthened. I wanted to see a front comprising all the parties, apart from the Jewish State Party** (which has all the disadvantages of the Revisionists, without the talents of Jabotinsky).

*Israel's largest daily newspaper, published since 1925 by the Histadrut.
**Formed in 1933 as a breakaway group from the Revisionists. Unlike the latter, it remained within the Zionist Organization.

My third demand was that *the structure of the Zionist Organization should be changed*. When Herzl founded the Zionist movement thirty-eight years ago there were scarcely any parties. Everyone was just *a Zionist*. Today there are parties, and people are expected to join one or other of these parties. But what happens to a Jew who doesn't want to join any specific party and who just wants to be an ordinary Zionist? At the moment he has no place in the Zionist framework. There are many Jews like this, who are ready to agree that the Jewish people have no solution to their problem other than Zionism. But they do not yet understand the differences between the Zionist parties, and cannot decide which one is right.

Now I believe that Zionism could become *a great national movement* which could attract *new masses of the Jewish people*. But they will be attracted by Zionism, not by the parties! So I think we should create an organizational structure which will enable these non-party Jews to belong to the Zionist movement, *without having to belong to any of the parties* if they do not want to.

For this reason I proposed that the Congress should set up in each country a unified Zionist organization, which would include every Zionist, whatever his political outlook; and the various parties and bodies should exist within this organization.

I also demanded that the Congress should give a clear and comprehensive lead to the movement and should chart our path for the future. The Executive chosen at the 18th Congress in Prague paved a new way for Zionism in the spheres of politics, finance, immigration and organization. In our attitudes to the British Government and the Arabs we adopted a new political approach, one of *a great, courageous* Zionism, a Zionism which is *realistic* in its view of the present and *daring and far-seeing* in its vision of the future. I am not certain, dear Geula and Amos, whether you'll be able to understand at present what I mean by this. But when you are both a little older you will certainly understand. And when one day my talks with the High Commissioner are made public the entire people will understand my words, as the few friends who were secretly given the notes of my talks did.

Dear Geula and Amos,

Before telling you what happened at the Congress, I want to give two further reasons why I insisted on a broad coalition.

The one is the need *to accelerate the work of Zionism.* We are facing an unprecedented period of *great possibilities.* During the last two years about 100,000 more Jews have entered Palestine. In 1935 this immigration could perhaps reach 60,000. The draining of the Huleh Lake, north of the Sea of Galilee, must be carried out, and we should (and can) acquire large new areas of land for settlement.

For over a year I've been talking to the High Commissioner about the Negev — a huge tract of land in the south, running from Gaza to Akaba, about eleven million dunams in all. Part of it is desert and useless. But there is also good land in the Negev, and if we can only find water in it a large and almost empty territory (there are only a few Arabs in the Negev) will be opened for mass settlement.

All these possibilities require large resources and great political strength. And they can only be realized if we enlist the support of the entire Zionist movement. If all the parties do not co-operate in the Executive, which runs the movement, we will only waste our energy in internal squabbling, and this will repel many potential supporters. A massive Zionist effort is only possible if we join forces.

Another reason is *the need to avert possible dangers.* At the moment there are not only great possibilities, but also great dangers. It is not unlikely that if the price of oranges in Britain drops, or if we cannot find a market for our growing citrus crop, there could be an economic crisis. The same applies to any slowing-down in the building programme, which could cause unemployment.

We are also facing a possible *political crisis.* The dispute between Italy and Ethiopia is liable to end in war, and if war breaks out in Ethiopia it is impossible to tell where it will end. There is no shortage of gunpowder in the world, and any spark can set off a global conflagration. Hitler is only waiting for a convenient opportunity to recapture the parts of Germany which were taken from it at the end of the World War. First of all he wants to take Austria. And if he has enough arms and thinks France and Italy are weak compared to him, he will shrink from nothing and will enter Vienna and perhaps other countries as well — and then we will face another world war. And even if there isn't an actual war, there will soon be the danger of war. And this danger, this feeling that a world war can break out, can bring about a crisis in Palestine. Then our situation can become very difficult, and only the united strength and efforts of the entire Zionist movement will perhaps be able to overcome these dangers.

Lucerne
September 8, 1935.

Dear Geula and Amos,
Now I am going to tell you what happened at the recent Zionist Congress. I assume you have read *Davar* and know all the 'open' things about the Congress; I will add only the things that haven't been published in the newspapers, and couldn't have been published.

1. The Agenda
The agenda and order of the Congress sessions were laid down many years ago, in the time of Herzl, and their external form has hardly changed at all during all this time, even though conditions have changed. I concluded several years ago that the present way of doing things is no longer appropriate for our time, and I wanted to introduce a new system; but I have been only partly successful.

When I returned from America the Executive met in London, and I proposed that apart from the opening address (by Nahum Sokolow), there should be only one other speech, made by a member of the Executive, who would sum up the work done during the two years since the previous Congress. Until now it was customary for virtually all the members of the Executive to speak on the opening night. These speeches bored the Congress, disturbed its train of thought and made the proceedings intolerably long.

After a general discussion I proposed that there should also be an address on the Executive's plans for the coming two years. The tone of the discussion was favourable to my proposals, i.e. there would be only two speeches apart from Sokolow. But when we came to take practical decisions I saw that the members of the Executive weren't ready to accept this harsh decree. Dr Ruppin+ volunteered to talk on 25 years of settlement, and all of us thought this would be a good thing. They wanted me to talk on the work of the Executive during the last two years. But I didn't think I was the right person for this, because I had not worked on the Executive all the time, had done a lot of travelling and wasn't familiar with some day-to-day matters. So Eliezer Kaplan was chosen instead. Then they proposed that I should talk on the *chances* of implementing Zionism.

First of all, I did not agree with the title of the lecture, and proposed that it should cover 'problems' of Zionism. I also had serious personal reservations about the task which did not make me anxious to be the speaker. But when I came back to Palestine and found that without this address something basic would be missing from the Congress, and that no one else wanted to do it, I gave in.

In my opinion, these two speeches and Ruppin's were enough. But Brodetsky demanded that he be allowed to speak on the political situation. All the members of the Executive in Jerusalem were against a third speech. But out of respect for Brodetsky they refrained from a vote on this question, and left the final decision to the Executive in London. And naturally London decided that Brodetsky should speak, and so we were left with four addresses, apart from Sokolow's.

Once more, then, it was shown how hard it is to change an accepted tradition. Because there are vested interests in every tradition, and these interests manage to preserve themselves even when they are no longer appropriate or effective.

Another proposal, that the new Executive should be elected *before* the Congress, and not after the debate, as is customary, was also not approved.

So we went into the Congress without an agreed platform and without a ready-made Executive.

2. *The Presidency*

For the last four years, since the 17th Congress at Basle, Nahum Sokolow has been President of the World Zionist Organization. Sokolow is a veteran writer, gifted and with an encyclopedic knowledge which makes him perhaps unique in our generation of Jews. He speaks many languages, is an authority on Hebrew literature and is personally acquainted with all the great figures of Jewry and many famous people throughout the world. His Hebrew is rich and mellow, although not clear and penetrating, and he has a remarkable capacity for work. However, he is not a statesman; also he does not fully comprehend the problem of Zionism as it applies to political matters or settlement. In short, he is not a suitable man to be the *political* representative of the Zionist movement and the Jewish people. But as Weizmann was dismissed at the 1931 Congress, no one else was found to take his place, and Sokolow was elected.

In effect, Sokolow was President in name only. He did not handle the political matters, and could not have done so. Whenever he did intervene in these problems he was simply ridiculous. No one took him seriously, and if he had met British statesmen he would not have enhanced the prestige of the Zionist movement. For these reasons we were reluctant to agree that he should continue as President.

And if not Sokolow then the *only* possible President was Weizmann. When I was in New York recently I did hear about a third proposal. Dr Stephen Wise suggested at a large rally in Carnegie Hall that I should be chosen President. This suggestion cropped up in London as well. Harry Sacher+, who was once on the Executive, and Weizmann himself suggested that I should accept the Presidency.

I never took these suggestions seriously for a minute, for three reasons: I am not suitable for the post, our Zionist Socialist Party is not yet ready for the Presidency, and the time has not yet come to replace Weizmann.

Weizmann has several personal drawbacks, apart from the fact that he does not understand the *internal* problems of the Zionist movement. He is volatile and changes mood rapidly.

And he is also liable to make *political* mistakes. But he is a *great man*. There is a holy flame in him. He has a magnificent record. And he has an enormous reputation in the English-speaking world. He is trusted by the British Government, and Britain's trust in us is an important condition for our political success.

For these reasons I favoured Weizmann's return, even though I knew that if he became President again it would place an extra burden on the Executive. For the fact is that many people in the Zionist movement, including some of his own friends, do not trust Weizmann *politically*. It is also not easy to work with Weizmann, as he is accustomed to people taking his word as gospel. We of course will not, and if we do not agree with him, we shall say so clearly and not give up so easily, particularly on political matters. But weighing up all these factors, those in favour of his return to office overrule those against.

So we approached Weizmann some time ago and asked him to come back. This was not easy for him, because of the way the 17th Congress rudely cast him out, leaving him angry and bitter. He has also begun working at the Sieff Institute in Rechovot, and this work is very important. Weizmann was also in touch with chemical companies abroad, with the aim of erecting plants in Palestine. He was supposed to become the head of this chemical company, and the chairmanship of a commercial firm in Palestine wouldn't have been appropriate to the President of the Jewish Agency. There were also family difficulties, and so he hesitated for a long time. He agreed, and then regretted it. Once more he agreed, and again he changed his mind.

One day — I think it was the last Saturday before the end of Congress — he announced that he could not accept the Presidency, but he was ready to be the head of the Political Department, if I would be President of the Zionist Organization. When I told him this was out of the question, he agreed that Sokolow should continue as President, as long as he did not intervene in political matters. All of us were pleased by this proposal of Weizmann's, and accepted it. Some of us felt it would have been better if he had agreed to the Presidency, while others thought it best that he did not become President, because of the internal situation in the movement. But both schools of thought gladly accepted Weizmann's decision (when we thought it was his *final* one) to enter the Executive as the head of the Political Section. (I have just checked my diary, and I find this was not on the Saturday, but on Friday, August 30.)

The moment all the delegates to the Congress heard of Weizmann's agreement they rejoiced, and his prestige rose even higher. His consent to serve on the Executive *under* Sokolow as President displayed considerable moral courage. Even Weizmann's detractors were astonished and conceded that he had acted bravely.

But all our rejoicing was shortlived. Apparently Weizmann's wife couldn't do what Weizmann had done. She announced that she was flatly opposed to Sokolow being President while Weizmann was a member of the Executive, even if he was head of the Political Department.

That same evening (Israel) Sieff asked me to meet him. He used to be Weizmann's private secretary during the World War. Now he is a very wealthy man. He and his two brothers-in-law Sacher and (Simon) Marks have a huge business (inexpensive shops)* which brings them hundreds and thousands of pounds profit every year. All three of them are Zionists and contribute large sums of money to Zionist purposes. People call them 'the family'. All the time they have opposed Weizmann's return to the Presidency. One of the reasons was the Sieff Institute in Rechovot. They have invested about 60,000 Palestine pounds in it, so that Weizmann could run it. If Weizmann returned to the Presidency — so they feared or said — he would neglect the Institute. There were also other reasons for their opposition. Sacher thought that Weizmann's re-election would lead to further rifts in the movement, because many people do not believe in his policies. And because we have to close our ranks now, Sacher thought my own Presidency would arouse more internal trust and unity.

When I met Sieff that evening he said to me: I have come to Lucerne with a special aim — to bring Weizmann back to the Presidency, even though previously I had a different opinion.

*Marks & Spencer.

I have been talking to several members of the British Cabinet and people close to the Cabinet. They told me the world situation is grave. It is possible war may break out (because of the dispute between Italy and Ethiopia). If this happens Palestine would be in the centre of the conflict. The days of 1914-18 would return. Great and historic things would have to be decided. Britain would need us then as she needed us during the World War, and perhaps it will then be possible to achieve a lot.

So it is important that Weizmann should lead us. The English have confidence only in him, and only he could attain these great things for us. No other Jew in England can match him. But Weizmann cannot return to the Presidency now, for various reasons. When the great things happen he will come back, but not now. For this reason Weizmann should be elected *outside the Executive,* as the man directing Zionist politics. Weizmann will appoint the people to help him in his work. He will be responsible to the *entire* Executive, but will not be a *member* of the Executive, and *individual* members of the Executive will not interfere with his work.

Immediately after talking to Sieff I saw Dr Eder+, who used to be in the Zionist Executive himself. He is also a close friend of Weizmann's and a friend of our movement (the Labour wing). I understood from him that Weizmann's wife is firmly opposed to his serving on the Executive while Nahum Sokolow is its President. This is the reason for the new proposal.

I saw Weizmann at once and told him that in my opinion this new proposal is quite out of the question. The Zionist movement as a whole and our own faction would not agree that all political activities should be taken out of the hands of the Executive and given to any one man, even to Weizmann. There are only two alternatives: either the Presidency or membership in the Executive. There is no third possibility. Weizmann replied that he understands my point of view, but he was confused and found it difficult to make up his mind. He said he would give me his reply the following day.

At once I invited some people to my hotel: Berl Katzenelson, Yitzhak Tabenkin*, David Remez+, Zalman

Rubashov, and a few others. I told them all about it and asked them what they thought. Every single one of them agreed with me. It was unthinkable to take political activities out of the Executive's hands, and Weizmann could not possibly become a kind of 'political dictator'. He should be the first among equals and not more than that. We had to take part in political activities, and to play a decisive role.

Tabenkin said it was important that I should direct the political action, even if Weizmann were the formal head of the political section.

The next day we discussed this with our allies from the General Zionists, Group A, and they also agreed with us. Stephen Wise and Judge Julian Mack+ (the latter from the Brandeis group, which is opposed to Weizmann) whom I have previously seen in the United States and tried to convince that Weizmann should return, were pleased by my stand on the new proposal. There was another consultation with Weizmann, and I informed him on behalf of both groups that the new proposal was unacceptable. He had to be either President or a member of the Executive. Weizmann asked for more time to think it over.

The next day two of our comrades, Berl Locker and Kaplan, went to see him. They returned with his reluctant agreement to accept the Presidency. This became known in the late afternoon. At midnight we called a small meeting of the leaders of the Labour wing and Group A, at which Weizmann announced officially that he was ready to accept the nomination for President. This was the 'coronation' party. There were speeches praising Weizmann and congratulating him. One of them was by Stephen Wise, who has always been opposed to Weizmann and a rival of his, and who now promised loyalty and assistance. Then at the end I spoke.

What I said was more or less what I had said at the 17th Congress four years ago, when Weizmann was removed from the Presidency by a majority comprised of the Mizrachi, the Revisionists and the General Zionists, Group B, against the

*A prominent Labour Zionist born in Russia in 1889, he was head of HaKibbutz HaMeuchad.

85

desire of the Labour Faction and General Zionists A, who were then in the minority. I had then been among the minority which opposed the eventual decision, so I am now in a better position to comment on the historic significance of this decision. At the 17th Congress the rift which developed over the years between Weizmann, the leader, and the movement as a collective force attained expression in a vehement, neurotic and unfair way. Weizmann came from the people, from Russian Jewry, and to this day he carries within his heart the folk spirit which prevailed in his small town. But Weizmann emerged as a leader at a decisive moment, during the World War, when his latent political genius came to light.

During the period after the Balfour Declaration, the Jewish people followed blindly after the leader who had attained this great political triumph for the Zionist movement. There was still no political education or understanding then, and the people relied on Weizmann out of a naive enthusiasm which set no limits on his talent and ability. For his part, Weizmann built all his activity around his contacts, influence and skill, and did not appreciate sufficiently the collective strength of the Zionist movement and the way it could nourish his efforts.

Slowly the rift developed. The movement grew up and developed a sense of criticism. It became aware of its power as a mass organization. Weizmann continued to lean on his own counsel, and did not realize that the blind and naive enthusiasm of the initial period had gone for ever. Personal and party ambitions entered the picture, and at the 17th Congress the leader was pushed aside. Both the leader and the movement faced a severe test. Would the movement be able to exist and operate without this gifted leader? And would Weizmann have the moral strength to fulfil his duty to the movement without the crown of leadership?

During the last four years we have seen both the movement and the leader pass these tests. As Berl Locker pointed out at this midnight 'coronation' party, for four years Weizmann did the job of an ordinary soldier. He went to South Africa on a fund-raising campaign, he helped in political work and so on. Further, he recognized the younger leaders who appeared after his dismissal, was not jealous of them but actually helped them to strengthen their position.

After Weizmann left the Presidency the political task in Jerusalem was placed in the hands of a young leader of the Labour movement — Chaim Arlosoroff. Weizmann was one of the first to recognize Arlosoroff's great abilities. The new political chief followed Weizmann's general path, but knew how to take a different direction when he thought it necessary. Weizmann stood beside him with love and friendship, argued with him as one equal to another, and sometimes accepted his opinion even though he did not agree with it.

Now both the movement and Weizmann have realized that they need one another. The Zionist movement demanded Weizmann's return not out of the naive, all-embracing faith of seventeen years ago, but from a self-awareness and a belief in its own ability, because at this difficult and crucial moment it would be wrong to surrender Weizmann's great talents when he could quite possibly add new conquests to his already remarkable record. And Weizmann himself has returned to the party purified by the pain he has suffered during the four years he was out of the highest office. He knows now that the movement has a desire, a will and a path, and the energy to accomplish what it wants to. The partnership which is being forged now is new and built on a mutual recognition that the times demand we work together.

We separated at a late hour, and naturally immediately afterwards cables flew to all the countries of the Diaspora saying that Weizmann was returning to the Presidency.

The entire Congress breathed more freely. One of the most complex problems had been solved, to the satisfaction of many people outside the two parties who had initiated Weizmann's return. These people conceded that Sokolow's Presidency was nothing more than a fiction and did not reflect any credit on the movement or indeed on Sokolow himself. So ended the episode of the Presidency, and Weizmann was duly elected at the final session of the Congress.

I am writing this letter on a ship travelling from Lucerne to Flüelen and back, on the beautiful lake called the Vierwaldstattersee — in other words, 'the lake of the four forest states,' because it runs along a ridge of green and wooded mountains which crosses four Swiss cantons.

This is the first time I have moved from Lucerne since the Congress began. The journey takes six hours — three hours each way. I am travelling with your mother, and we are now on our way back to Lucerne. The air of the mountains, the charm of the lake, the rest are all marvellous after the weeks of tense conflict at the Congress.

Tomorrow mother and I are going to a small village near Lucerne. She will remain there three or four days, and on Saturday she will sail from Trieste on the same ship that brought us there. I will stay on in the village for another ten days or so, until I feel rested, and then will travel to London. You can write to me there.

Burgenstock
September 9, 1935.

Dear Geula and Amos,

After lunch mother and I left Lucerne and rented a flat in the house of a farmer in the village of Burgenstock. From Lucerne we went by boat for about forty minutes, and then by funicular, a kind of railway climbing up a steep mountain, almost like a wall, for six or seven minutes. From the railway station we walked, carrying all our parcels (most of our luggage remained in Lucerne), because there are no cars here.

The two rooms we have rented are low, rather damp and covered with faded wallpaper. But the house stands on a high mountain, surrounded by woods and green fields. There is a smell of manure from the stable, and the bells hung around the cows' necks never stop tinkling. The food is good and satisfying, so we are told. We can't say yet, because we haven't eaten a meal in the house. The main thing is the rest — the peace and quiet. There is no one here apart from the two of us. Only trees and grass and hay and the mountain air.

Mother will stay here three days and then she'll go to Venice. On Saturday she'll take a boat from there. I'll stay on for a week or ten days, walking and writing. Time will show whether my pen or my legs will be busier.

Dear Geula and Amos,

A thick mist, like grey milk, hangs over the mountain and the forest this morning. A whole choir of cow bells is coming from the valley. The air is cool and moist. The short walk we had in the wood this morning invigorated us but also tired us. We remembered, Geula, that according to the European calendar you are seventeen, and sent you a telegram of congratulations.

And now, after the walk, I am in the low-ceilinged room continuing my tale of the recent Congress.

You know that the new Executive chosen at the end of the Congress is drawn from four parties. But few people at the Congress, even those closest to affairs, know how much work went into forming this coalition and how difficult it was to achieve it. I conducted most of the negotiations, and in addition to delivering a speech and serving on the Political Committee I had to devote a great deal of my time to bringing the four parties together.

Our party, the Labour faction, has reached the point towards which it was moving, consciously or unconsciously, for years: we have become the decisive force in Zionism. It depends on our leadership whether the Zionist Organization will become the dynamic and effective representative body of the Jewish people, or whether it will become a miserable fiction, impotent and sterile.

But our Labour movement is different from other workers' parties. The working class in other countries already has a state and a country and an economy and a civilization — and a class. Zionism, on the other hand, is not a state and it is not a government. We of the Labour wing cannot fight, as other workers do, for a working class economy. We are still fighting *to create something out of nothing.* Our historical aim in the Zionist movement is the building of the state, the creation of an economy and a society, the foundation of a culture. None of these can come about without a general, joint effort by all the constructive forces within the Jewish people.

It is a mistake to see the Zionists of other parties as

enemies. There are indeed some people who hate us. But in every party there are young people who want to work in Palestine, who passionately want Zionism to succeed. The people who are workers in the Land of Israel were not workers in the Diaspora. Their parents were landlords, shop-keepers, traders, members of the middle class. Only a few of them worked with their hands. And thousands of people in the Diaspora, who are not workers now, will become labourers when they settle in Palestine. These people are our potential allies. We must explain this to them, not by waging a class war, but in a peaceful way, with love, patience, faith. It follows that we should seek a coalition, for the sake of the whole of Jewry.

Trogen
September 11, 1935.

Dear Geula and Amos,

How good it is to sit in the afternoon sun on a Swiss mountain and not to think about the Zionist Congress.

When I came to the end of Page 50 in my notebook, which is the last page, I took your mother for a walk along one of the paths I discovered this morning, and we sat down to rest on a sloping field of hay, facing the sun. Beautiful, relaxing Switzerland . . .

In the afternoon Hadassah Granovsky (Samuel) came to visit us and brought along some wine. What was the occasion? Today is the birthday of her husband Edwin.* He is 38. So we drank to his health. Then we remembered that you too, dear Geula, have just turned seventeen (according to the European calendar), so we drank another glass to you. And then we said to one another: Other people, both famous and unknown, must have been born on this day. And why should we not drink to them as well? So we did. And then Hadassah remarked, quite rightly: What about all the people who are going to be born on this day in the future? So we drank another toast. That made up the four glasses which we drink traditionally at Passover.

*Now 2nd Viscount Samuel (son of Herbert Louis, 1st Viscount Samuel).

90

Afterwards we had a rest, and now I am sitting down to continue my description of the Zionist Congress. I am beginning to fear that my long letters about the Congress have been a burden to you. And I'm not even sure that you read them right through, and that you understand them all even if you do read them. However, I will continue, as I want to write about some important things that happened at Lucerne.

Trogen
September 14, 1935.

Dear Geula and Amos,

Now I come to the last part of my description of Congress: my election to the Executive.

You will remember that at the last Congress I never thought of becoming a member of the Executive, for personal reasons and because of my work in the Histadrut. So when at the end of the Congress I found myself on the Executive it was a surprise for me and, I am certain, for most of my comrades and particularly the members of the Histadrut.

I entered the Executive on condition that I was not given a specific department to handle, that I would not have to move to Jerusalem, and that I would still be able to work in the Histadrut. These conditions were met: but they did not reduce my responsibility within the Executive. I was forced to play an increasingly committed role in political affairs, and later in the internal conflicts within the Labour faction. Because I soon realized that we faced total destruction if we continued the internecine strife which raged in Palestine and the movement during the trial which followed Arlosoroff's murder.

I began discussions with all the Zionist parties about how the situation could be improved. And to my astonishment and fear I saw that I was perhaps the only man in the Zionist movement whom all the parties trusted. Even the Revisionist leaders were ready to meet me. This alarmed me. To carry such a heavy responsibility in the Zionist movement is

91

beyond the power of any man — in any event beyond my power. I agreed to serve on the Executive on a temporary basis, as I felt it was a crucial period which required unity. But I could not remain there permanently, because that meant cutting myself off from the Histadrut. For me personally this was completely unthinkable. To leave the Histadrut was for me like leaving the country. Naturally the Zionist movement is not foreign to me. But my deepest links and aspirations, my spiritual and human contacts, my private and public life, my real world as a man, a Jew, a worker, a man of our times — all these are bound up with the Histadrut, or more precisely with the Jewish workers' movement in Palestine. And I was afraid that if I remained on the Executive I would have more responsibility for Zionist affairs, would be swallowed into the Executive sphere, and would in effect be torn away from the Histadrut.

This was my personal reason. And there was also a public reason. I perceived that my views were not the same as those of some of my dearest and closest comrades, particularly those from the Kibbutz HaMeuchad*. I saw before me not only the internal battle between the parties. I saw other fronts as well — the struggle in which the Jewish people are engaged; the Arab front, confronting our efforts in Palestine; the British and international front which our political activities have to tackle. I saw great possibilities — and I saw great dangers. And I saw very clearly the need to close our ranks, and thought I knew how this could be done.

The main thing, I said to myself, is not the parties and the politicians. The real force in Zionism today is the *youth*. The Jewish youth which has no hope, no future, no chance at all in the Diaspora, and whose only salvation is in Palestine. Not in black-marketeering, or shop-keeping, or the civil service. The real future of this youth lies in *work*. And because of this I am not afraid of the young people, and I believe in them. I am confident that they can be unified and brought together in one pioneering camp, despite their ideological differences.

We are now living in an era of implementation, and

*The nucleus of the left-wing Achdut Avodah faction in today's Israel Labour Party.

ideology is not decisive. It's not so important to me what a man thinks: what counts is what he does, what he has to and wants to do. I am familiar with all the dogmas and ideological systems in our party and other parties. But I discern in them one common factor which unites them all, whether they know it or not: and this is the life of work. Jewish Labour in Palestine: this is our Bible and our creed, the meaning of our Zionism and our socialism. That is what I tried to do in the Histadrut: to show that every working man is a brother and a comrade, and that the union of all the workers in a single Labour Federation must come before anything else.

The Zionist movement is of course not the Labour Federation. But it also has a certain objective content and aim, around which a united movement could be built. But I saw that many of my comrades did not agree with me. These disagreements were not about the the aim, but about the way it should be attained. However, during an era of implementation *the way, the path,* is all-important. And so I could not consider myself the emissary of the public, because I found opinions divided between my comrades.

These were the two reasons which prompted me to withdraw from all public service for a time, and first and foremost from service on the Zionist Executive.

During one of the days that congress was sitting (I think it was on August 30), several comrades met in my room: Berl Katzenelson, Tabenkin, David Remez, Zalman Aranne+, Moshe Shertok and others.

I explained to them why I could no longer remain on the Executive. Berl agreed with half of what I said — about the internal dangers in the Zionist movement and the need for unity. And he recognized the difficulty I found in staying in the Executive. But, in his opinion, I could not be replaced by anyone suitable who could handle external politics and also internal politics. He said that no Zionist Executive is conceivable at present without me. The Zionist education of the working public also makes my membership of the Executive imperative. Having me on the Executive made the workers more aware of their responsibility for Zionist matters. But, on the other hand, if the party wanted me to remain then it had to show confidence in me.

Tabenkin said that there was complete confidence in me. It was true that there were differences of opinion, and that we did not always see eye to eye about the path we should follow. But this had never harmed the confidence placed in me.

Moshe announced that he would not serve on the Executive unless I was included.

From the discussions we had held in the past, I told my friends, I saw that I was right and that there were differences of opinion about the way Zionism should be implemented. I could go only in the direction I believed in. As a soldier I could follow others along a path I thought was the wrong one. And I would always accept the opinion of the majority. But I could lead the party only in a direction I thought was right.

My words were in vain. I knew that this time it would be a decisive step. Although formally speaking I might remain in Tel Aviv after the Congress and continue to work at the Histadrut, if I was on the Executive this would swallow up all my time and energy. But my comrades were merciless. The party insisted. And I didn't have the strength to withstand such cruel pressure. This pressure did not come only from the Labour faction. It was applied by virtually the entire Congress. I had no choice but to give in.

The days will show whether I was right or whether my comrades were.

This is the last matter to do with the Congress that I shall write to you about. If you have the patience to read these long epistles, write and tell me what you think about it all.

London
October 6, 1935.

You are surprised that I don't write. I've really had nothing special to write about. After you left Trogen and I finished the letters to the children I felt lonely and sad, and it was difficult for me to stay in Burgenstock. I went to Lucerne for two days. But there too I felt sad. I wanted to write something for our comrades, but I couldn't. I didn't feel any better when I arrived in Paris. And in that city I soon realized that I still needed rest. After a few meetings I became tense again.

The British workers naturally wanted to see Mussolini fall because he is a fascist. But few people in Britain are ready to oppose Italy by force, because a war with Italy could become a world war, and they don't want that. Apart from this, they know that France wants to maintain its friendship with Italy, because it is afraid of Germany. And Britain will not fight unless France does.

For these reasons I think there is no fear of a war between Britain and Italy.

On October 15 there will be a meeting between Malcolm MacDonald, the Colonial Secretary, the High Commissioner for Palestine and a delegation consisting of Weizmann, Brodetsky and me. After that I shall return home.

London
October 22, 1935.

Yesterday I was sorry you weren't here. There was a reception at the Anglo-Palestine Club in honour of Malcolm MacDonald. James de Rothschild+ was the chairman. There were about 500 guests (including representatives of all the British and Jewish press). Speeches were made by Rothschild, Weizmann, MacDonald, the High Commissioner, an English Archbishop*, the Chief Rabbi of Britain**, Professor Haldane*** and others. The most important speeches were naturally those by Malcolm and the High Commissioner. Malcolm said some nice things about Weizmann as a great leader. The High Commissioner paid me a compliment. I sent Moshe the text of all the speeches. Lady Erleigh, the daughter of Lord Melchett and wife of the Marquis of Reading, made a fine, proud and strong speech. There was only one drawback — too many speeches.

*The Most Rev. Richard Downey D.D. (1881-1953), Roman Catholic Archbishop of Liverpool: at the reception he proposed the toast to 'Racial and Religious Tolerance'.
**The Very Rev. Dr. J.H. Hertz (1872-1946).
***Prof. J.B.S. Haldane F.R.S. (1892-1964): he seconded Downey's toast.

I have almost finished my work here, and was all ready to leave the day after tomorrow. But today I spoke with Hexter+ in Alexandria, and I'll have to wait until he comes to London. He'll be here on Friday.

Weizmann is due to leave here next week, and London is starting to empty out. There are only about eight million people left . . .

London
June 14, 1936.

Of all the visits and talks I've had here, today's with Lloyd George+ was the most interesting. I had lunch at the Weizmanns', and at 3 p.m. the three of us, Chaim, Vera and I, set out for Churt, Lloyd George's country home. The drive took an hour and a half, and I soon saw that there are beautiful landscapes not only in Switzerland but also in this misty island. All the fields were green and thick with trees. The roads were perfect, with very heavy traffic — as if the whole of London goes off to the country on Sunday.

When we arrived at Churt we found Lloyd George sitting on a bench in front of his house. This is the first time I've seen him — and he looks exactly like the photographs one sees on all the buses in London, in the *Daily Telegraph's* advertisements featuring Lloyd George's memoirs. His hair is completely white, but his face is full of vitality and his eyes are young and sparkling. With him was his wife, his private secretary Jones* and his daughter.

Lloyd George received us warmly and immediately led us inside for tea. He asked about the attitude of the new Colonial Secretary, Ormsby-Gore+. Weizmann said he had not seen Ormsby-Gore after his appointment had been announced, but he had always been sympathetic. Lloyd George replied at once:

'You don't need sympathy — you need courage, action and driving power.'

He asked about Wauchope, the High Commissioner, and the Mandatory officials. Weizmann said that the officials, as

*Thomas Jones, C.H. (1870-1955): Author of *A Diary with Letters* (1954).

96

usual, displayed emmity or unwillingness to help us, and singled out in particular the Chief Justice, McDonnell*. 'He is a Catholic,' L.G. said, 'and the Catholics are anti-Semites. Can't they realise that it would be far worse if Palestine were in the hands of the Moslems?'

Lloyd George enquired about the situation in Palestine, and we told him. He said: 'The Arabs are afraid Palestine will become a Hebrew State. Well, it will be a Hebrew State,' he added vigorously, emphasizing the phrase 'it will.'

He wanted to know the number of Jews in Palestine today and immediately after the World War. Weizmann told him there were 400,000-500,000 today. 'What is seventeen years of history?' L.G. said. 'It is like a single day; 400,000 is an important step forward.' We told him that the Arabs have also increased in numbers during these years, more than in any other Arab country, from about 550,000-600,000 to 900,000. He asked about the natural increase of the Arabs and the Jews. I gave him the figures: 30,000 Arabs, 7,000-8,000 Jews. 'And so a larger immigration is needed,' he said, 'if the Arabs are not to increase more than you do.'

Then he went on to talk about the debate in the House of Commons, which will take place next Friday. 'You need an important man among the supporters of the Government, someone like Winston Churchill+ or even better Austen Chamberlain, to present your case.'

Mrs Weizmann remarked that we should be a little wary of Austen Chamberlain, as in a meeting with us he had expressed the opinion that Jewish immigration should not lead to a Jewish majority. L.G. answered with emphasis and energy: 'This is nonsense!' Then Weizmann asked him whether he, Lloyd George, would take part in the debate. L.G. said at first that he didn't know the present situation. Weizmann replied that he would find some material for him. L.G. said: 'Good, I'll come to town and we'll talk about it.'

He spoke a lot about the need to arm the Jews in Tel Aviv and the settlements so that they are able to defend

*Sir Michael McDonnell (1882-1956): Chief Justice of Supreme Court of Palestine 1927-37. Not long after retiring from his official post, he acted as adviser to the Arab Delegation on the Joint Anglo-Arab Committee set up in 1939 to examine British commitments to Sherif Hussein in 1915-16. The Lord Chancellor, Lord Maughan, led the British Delegation.

themselves, and he also said that more British troops should be brought to Palestine.

I spoke about the situation in Syria, Egypt and the other Arab countries, and Weizmann told him what one French scholar had said to him in Paris: that if the British Government gave in to the Arabs in Palestine, there would be a revolt in all the French colonies.

We also spoke about farming, the land question and the Bible. Lloyd George asked about the position of Hebrew, and was pleased when I told him we speak Hebrew. 'The revival of the Hebrew language is one of the greatest things,' he said in admiration. The Jews in Palestine should not speak the languages they had brought from the Diaspora, but in Hebrew, he urged.

The conversation lasted an hour and a half, until 6 p.m. Before we left he asked us to sign his visitors' book.

When I told L.G. I had worked on the land, he said: 'Both of us were once farmers.' He is very proud of his farm at Churt, and grows potatoes and strawberries, which are sold as 'Lloyd George strawberries'.

In the evening I was invited to dinner at James de Rothschild's. He also plans to speak in the House of Commons debate on Friday, and asked me to prepare a speech for him. He is extremely pleased with our political activities in Jerusalem, but is angry with Weizmann because he doesn't involve him in what's going on.

London
June 16, 1936.

Today Weizmann saw the new Colonial Secretary, Ormsby-Gore, and had a good talk with him. Ormsby-Gore was in Palestine immediately after the World War, when Weizmann came with the Zionist Commission. O-G served as Liaison Officer between the Zionist Commission and the Government.

He has always been a Zionist. But we were afraid that when he took up his new post he would change. I am sending you a copy of his talk with Weizmann, the contents of which
98

I sent to Moshe today.

Today Weizmann saw Lloyd George and gave him material from his Commons speech on Friday.

Lloyd George told Weizmann that if the Jews have people like me, their future is assured.

I don't know what L.G. could have found out about me from the short visit to him on Sunday. From what Weizmann says, he was particularly impressed by my courage.

We are busy with the forthcoming Commons debate. Meanwhile the news from Palestine is not very good.

It's possible that on Saturday I might go to Warsaw for a day or two. Next week I shall decide whether to return home immediately or to stay on here.

London
June 18, 1936.

I've been busy all week, as has the entire office, with the preparations for tomorrow's debate in Parliament on Palestine, which was demanded by the Labour Party. I've already written to you about my talks with Lloyd George and James de Rothschild. Today I prepared a speech for Herbert Morrison, one of the Labour leaders, who visited Palestine a year ago.

I'm enclosing an editorial which appeared in *The Times* this morning. If tomorrow's debate is in the same spirit, then our position will not be bad at all. True, there will still be riots in Palestine, but these will peter out. Here in London people want the Government to take firmer measures. But our old man is apparently afraid that stronger action will make things worse.

The day after tomorrow I am going to Warsaw for a few days, and will return to London in the middle of next week. I don't know yet how long I shall have to be here. It depends on the way the situation develops.

Tomorrow I'll write to you and give you my impressions of the debate. It will begin at 11 a.m. and end at four in the afternoon. This time many people will probably speak against us, because in recent weeks the Arabs and their friends have been very active. But at the moment not a single man has joined the ranks of our enemies. The Government is on our side at present, and the Colonial Secretary, Ormsby-Gore, is a friend of ours. The few replies he has made in Parliament to our opponents were good. Now we must see what he will say tomorrow. He told Weizmann that he would not make a long speech, but will emphasize the right of the Jews to come to Palestine. He will no doubt also say a few things in favour of the Arabs. I've already sent you the text of his talk with Chaim. It's not bad at all.

I want to know what Amos is thinking of doing when he finishes high school. I would like him to become a sailor. There is a school in England where he could learn how to become a seaman. Then he would have to do practical work on a ship for three years.

P.S. The moment you receive this letter and have finished reading *The Times* editorial, phone Berl and give it to him, and tell him to publish it in *Davar!!!*

Warsaw
June 21, 1936.

Yesterday I sent you by airmail from Amsterdam *The Times* with the report of Friday's debate. I sat in the House of Commons from eleven to four, from the beginning of the debate to the very end, and this gave me some compensation for all the torments we have gone through during the last few months, and which will probably continue.

The actual decision to hold a debate was not inspired by us. The Labour Party demanded it of its own accord. But the debate which took place last Friday was almost entirely the fruit of our work, apart of course from the speeches of our opponents. The speeches by Lloyd George, Leopold Amery+, Tom Williams, Creech Jones, Herbert Morrison, James de Rothschild and Victor Cazalet were wholly or partly prepared by us. Ormsby-Gore's speech was naturally not drafted by us, but by Wauchope, and although it also contained some rather unpalatable things, it was in general full of friendship and respect for the Zionist enterprise in Palestine.

I watched Ormsby-Gore's gestures and his reactions to what other speakers said, more than I listened to his words. And I had no doubt that he is a veteran and well-tried friend of Zionism. I don't know whether this friendship will reveal itself in positive acts. Wauchope will undoubtedly have a great influence on him. The officials at the Colonial Ministry will also exert considerable influence, and the Middle East situation in itself is confusing and difficult. But I hope that at the very least Ormsby-Gore will not handicap us unnecessarily. He is certainly the most friendly Colonial Secretary I have ever had to deal with.

Lloyd George's speech was marvellous. But the best speech was by Herbert Morrison. His remarks on the workers' settlements and the human material which is building these settlements, and the spirit prevailing among them made a tremendous impression on his hearers. It is a pity that there was a comparatively small audience, as on Fridays many MPs go away for the weekend. But after all the speeches are made mainly for the newspapers, and the leading paper, *The Times*, gave the debate prominent, although not major, coverage.

I left London at six yesterday morning. At seven I took a plane from Croydon, and at nine I was in Amsterdam From there I went by plane to Vienna. At 3.20 p.m I took a train from Vienna, and arrived in Warsaw this morning at eight o'clock.

I didn't want to travel through Germany, and I didn't want to arrive in Warsaw on Saturday. That's why I went by such a roundabout route.

I'll be here for two days, and then I'll return to London.

Here in Warsaw I found a full programme of rallies, meetings, parties and talks waiting for me: so I won't exactly be idle during the two days here.

London
June 23, 1936.

I left Warsaw at eight this morning and arrived here at five.

I changed planes twice: from Warsaw to Berlin in a Polish plane, from Berlin to Amsterdam in a German plane, and from Amsterdam to London in a Dutch plane. Altogether I was in the air for six and three-quarter hours. The air was calm, the skies were clear, and the flight was excellent, so I was able to relax on the plane and rest from the hectic two days in Warsaw.

Immediately after my arrival, the day before yesterday at eight o'clock in the morning, I had a talk with the leading Zionists, who met me at the airport. At ten there was a session of the Zionist Council, embracing all the parties, and I addressed the delegates on the situation in Palestine and the economic difficulties facing the Jews there. The Council decided to hold a special fund-raising campaign for our urgent and pressing objectives.

In the afternoon I addressed a public meeting in the Novotsky Hall on the political situation. I've never seen a large crowd at a meeting in Warsaw. And the people here also say they've never seen a Jewish gathering like it. The entire hall and all the balconies were jammed with people. The organizers of the meeting decided to publish my speech in a special booklet. In the evening there was the party's Council, at which I spoke twice, and afterwards they took me to a farewell reception for *halutzim* who left for Palestine the next day (in other words, yesterday), and there of course I had to speak again.

Yesterday morning they arranged a press conference. All the editors and prominent journalists from the main Yiddish papers were there, and after my talk I answered the many questions they put to me.

Immediately afterwards came a press conference for Polish, French and English journalists. All the large Polish papers were represented, and so were the foreign news agencies. I spoke in English on the Jewish-Arab problem, our achievements in Palestine and the basic principles of Zionism. Dr Hindes translated my remarks into Polish, and they were due to appear in the Polish press this morning.

In the afternoon I had a meeting with non-Zionists from the Jewish Agency and the heads of the Zionist movement in Poland, at which I gave them more confidential information

102

about the situation, and I asked them to arrange an immediate fund-raising campaign in order to help the Jewish community in Palestine to survive. And in the evening I sat with the organizers of the Zionist parties until one in the morning. I told them about our relations with the Arabs and particularly with the British Government, in Jerusalem and in London.

I was amazed by my own stamina during all these meetings, after the strain of preparing the House of Commons debate last week, which left me utterly exhausted. But after two intensive days in Warsaw I was too tired to sleep last night. So the 'plane trip relaxed me a little.

London
June 30, 1936.

Thank you so much for your letter of the 24th, which made me very happy. Nothing could please me more than to know that you are content and happy with life. Today I'm sending you two letters. One is from Zalman Rubashov in America, written after he'd seen Brandeis. What Brandeis said to Zalman is similar to what Felix Frankfurter told me when he paid a visit to London a week ago. I hope you will be pleased by what he says. You can show this letter to the children as well, The second letter is from Wauchope to Chaim. A fine and human letter.

I've just come back from the Colonial Office, together with Weizmann. We had a talk with Ormsby-Gore which lasted one and a half hours, from 5 to 6.30. We spoke about land, immigration and the Arabs. He thinks that the Royal Commission* will come to Palestine in September and will stay there about two months. He would like to have its report before Christmas.

The impression O-G made on me was that of a friend. But I'm afraid that this friendship is personal, and what is really important is not what O-G *the man* thinks and feels, but

*The Peel Commission in fact began its sessions in Palestine in November, 1936 and continued them in London in 1937. For terms of reference see p235.

103

what O-G *the Minister* will do. And I'm afraid there may be a difference between the man and the Minister. There must be some discrepancy between these two sides of the man. A Minister cannot do what he himself might like. He is nothing more than an emissary of the state, and he must take into account its political interests, public opinion and the views of his colleagues in the Cabinet. But I fear that in this case the natural difference between the man and the Minister might be too great to bridge.

This is the first time I've met Ormsby-Gore. But this is how I've always imagined him.

On Saturday I'm going to Prague for one day. There members of the Zionist Actions Committee living in Europe (apart from Britain and Poland) will meet me, and I'll give them some information about the situation in Palestine and the overall political picture. I'll be in Prague until Monday morning and will then return to London.

I still don't know how long I'll have to be here. In any event, I don't think I can leave London before the Royal Commission is appointed. This might take another two or three weeks — possibly less.

London
July 17, 1936.

I've been in London for three days. After the four days I spent at home I feel like a new man. When I arrived in Palestine I was tired and depressed. The talk we had with Ormsby-Gore three days before I came home disturbed me very much. He spoke of stopping immigration while the Royal Commission is in the country, and I was afraid he might announce this in Parliament, and then it would be a final decision. The talk I had with the High Commissioner helped to prevent this announcement, and the H.C. also made some favourable remarks about Transjordan and the Tel Aviv port. And speaking about the port — if I'd made the trip to Palestine just in order to see the new jetty, it would have been worth it.

On the way back to London I rested a little. The two days
104

on board ship from Alexandria to Brindisi were a marvellous relaxation, and the plane trip from Rome to London was first-rate. I'll never forget flying high over the Swiss mountains, the lakes, the unparalleled scenery of this country. I reached London at night. And the view of the lights of London from the plane is also magnificent. Here too I found an improvement in the political situation. It seems that there won't be an announcement on the cessation of immigration. So now we have some time to fight the whole idea of banning immigrants.

The press is no longer so interested in the Palestine problem — and this is also in our favour. There's a feeling that the whole thing is cut and dried. The English have other headaches at present: the agreement between Germany and Austria, the tension between France and Germany, the Italian question. And it's good that they'll forget us and the Arabs for a while. But this will be only for six to eight weeks. Then we can expect some trouble. But I think we can overcome it.

The British Parliament closes on July 31, and then I might be able to leave here. But we have decided to summon the Zionist Actions Committee for August 25, and I don't know whether I'll be able to return home before then.

I sent regards to you through someone who will surprise you — Jabotinsky. He phoned me about some financial matter (we didn't talk about politics), and I asked him to give you regards from me.

London
July 23, 1936.

It's becoming increasingly difficult to stay here and to operate effectively. We are suspended in a kind of vacuum, without knowing what the Government is about to decide. And not only don't we know, but the Government itself doesn't know what it is going to do. It's a long time since England had such a confused, hesitant and vacillatory Government. On the one hand, there is pressure on it to stop immigration 'temporarily,' while on the other hand it is afraid to do this, because it knows this would be strongly opposed not only by the Jewish public, but also by important English circles, and particularly in Parliament.

Yesterday several MPs held a meeting, and Weizmann spoke to them. Some time ago the Arabs addressed the same gathering; and the MPs put several questions to Weizmann in order to examine the Arab claims. Apart from two or three friends of the Arabs, the meeting was on our side, and it adopted a resolution to oppose the cessation of immigration. But in another week Parliament will close for the summer, and then until October the Government will be free to do as it pleases, because Parliament only reopens at the end of October. And meanwhile the Royal Commission might start its work in Palestine. Without Parliament in session, it is harder to combat the Government, and then the civil servants can exert greater influence.

The weather also makes it hard to stay in London. I can't understand how the English can exist at all in this climate: cold, rain, leaden clouds, no blue skies, no sun, not a ray of light. A depressing, grey, wet sadness hangs over the dark sky and all one wants to do is to run away. But I have to be here until August 10, when Brodetsky returns from Africa.

London
August 18, 1936.

Read the long letter I've enclosed — and then give it to Eliahu (Golomb)+. You'll see from the letter that I was about to come home, as I was filled with anxiety about what was happening there. But our comrades at home insisted that I remain here for the present and attend the meeting of the Actions Committee later on. I haven't yet decided what to do, and will have to see what the situation in Palestine looks like in a few days' time. In any event, I'll come back as soon as I possibly can.

My dearest Paula, believe me that I too would like to be together with you now, as you want to be with me. But what can I do? I must do my duty. I am a soldier.

London
August 19, 1936.

This is the first day I've breathed more freely, after several days of torment and depression. After all the terrible things the Arabs have done in Palestine, it seemed as if we were to be left to our fate, abandoned. But at last a voice has been heard: this morning *The Times* carried a strong article against the atrocities in Safed and Jaffa*, and for the first time the paper criticized the idea of stopping Jewish immigration. I haven't yet had a chance to read the other papers, as I want to get this letter and the enclosed cutting from *The Times* off to you before the 10.30 a.m. post.

London
August 22, 1936

I'm still here, and I'll apparently be here for at least another two days. I've been very busy lately with two things:

1. Action to prevent immigration being stopped. We've been able to achieve one important thing — *The Times* article which I sent you in my last letter. But we wanted to get the greatest statesmen to sign a letter to *The Times* against the cessation of immigration — and we couldn't arrange this. Most of the people we wanted were not in London. One is in Canada, another in Moscow, a third in the South of France, the fourth in Switzerland and the fifth in an isolated village in Wales which has no telephone. Yesterday I sent a cable to Lloyd George about this proposed letter. But I haven't had a reply yet. I've also written to Lord Melchett, who is in Austria.

2. The second thing was *obtaining funds for the extra policemen who are being recruited.* Until now we've had 1,850 additional policemen. Now they've given us another 1,000, and this will cost us £9,000 a month (apart from what the Mandatory Government contributes).

We approached Warburg, and he refused to help. I asked

*On August 13 an armed group of Arabs attacked the Jewish quarter of Safed and killed a man and his three children.

Simon Marks, and he immediately gave us £10,000. I informed Jimmy Rothschild about the policemen, without asking him for money. He phoned me six or seven times about this development, and I could see he was waiting for me to ask him. But I didn't. In general, I don't like asking wealthy Jews for money, and in particular I didn't want to ask Rothschild. And although I felt he wanted me to ask him, I decided in my heart that I wouldn't. I wanted to see whether he would offer to contribute of his own accord. Last night, at about 10.30, he rang me again and asked, for the seventh or eighth time: What's happening about the policemen? I gave him the latest information I had received the same morning, in a telegram from Moshe. I also told him that after Warburg had received a second cable, he announced that he would reconsider the matter. He asked me several other questions on the phone, and I had the feeling he was pleading with me to ask him for money as well. But I didn't. And then he said: I'll give £1,000 a month if Warburg's Assistance Fund will give what we've asked it for (£6,000 a month). I said to Rothschild — Good.

Now I'm hoping that Warburg will also be forced to contribute. And so we'll be able to maintain a Jewish army in Palestine consisting of nearly 3,000 men.

The reports from Palestine are worrying me tremendously, and I regret the actions that came from our side*. They will cause us great damage. And we must stop them.

Zurich
August 29, 1936.

The meeting of the Actions Committee is virtually over, even though formally speaking it will only close tomorrow or the day afterwards. The focal point of this session was naturally the discussion on the political situation. This debate finished yesterday, and this was more or less the end of the important part. Weizmann left last night. This morning he will be in Paris, and in the evening he will return to London. I

*Reprisals against Arabs in Tel Aviv and Haifa, which departed from the Jewish policy of self-restraint.

am leaving for London tonight. On Monday afternoon at 3 p.m. Weizmann and I will meet Ormsby-Gore.

I arrived in Zurich on Tuesday morning, and that same afternoon Ussishkin+ opened the Actions Committee session. Weizmann made a short speech on the political situation in the world and our particular position. He said some good and true things, but they didn't answer the problems we are facing today.

I followed him and spoke on the way things have developed recently, from the Zionist Congress in Lucerne until now. My speech had even less of an impact than Weizmann's. I was very tired and found it a great effort. And because I spoke in Yiddish, it was even more of a strain.

The general debate, which began that night, was not really important. The opposition praised the devoted work done during the riots. Meir Grossman+ and his friend Robert Stricker+ made an attempt to criticize us. But it was empty and pathetic, and failed completely.

On Wednesday night I summed up the debate and replied to points raised. I spoke from ten until twelve, and explained the political situation and the difficulties we are having with the Arabs and the British. I dealt with the main questions facing us at present: the Royal Commission, immigration, land, government, the civil service, relations with the Arabs. I had originally intended to open the debate with these remarks, but was too tired.

On Thursday morning Eliezer Kaplan lectured on the economic situation. This was the best speech delivered during the entire Actions Committee session. He spoke for about two hours, and the entire audience listened to him eagerly and with bated breath. He described very successfully the Yishuv's great efforts, and in particular the activities directed towards self-defence. Dr Schwarzbart+, who was chairman during Kaplan's speech, proposed that it should be published in full.

Then the Political Committee began sitting. The main question here was whether to co-operate with the Royal Commission if immigration is stopped. I insisted that no decision on this point should be adopted, but that we should elect a small committee which would reside in Palestine and would decide on this question (and also other questions) when the time comes. After a lengthy debate my proposal was accepted by a large majority.

My opinion was that in certain conditions we should take part in the Royal Commission's work, even if immigration is stopped temporarily. But we should not decide this now, in order to be able to threaten the British Government with a refusal to co-operate. But I noted that a situation could arise in Palestine in which we would not be able to participate in the Royal Commission's meetings, or that the whole question might be abandoned.

Meanwhile we received from Moshe disquieting news about the negotiations between the High Commissioner and the Arabs on halting Jewish immigration, and also on even more important matters. We contacted London. Weizmann phoned Ormsby-Gore, and arranged to meet him next Monday. So the danger that immigration might be halted at once, this week, has been postponed for at least another week. And yesterday we informed the Political Committee that the situation is extremely grave, and that it should stop its deliberations and choose a small committee which should stay in Palestine all the time and should be authorized by the Actions Committee to decide all these questions. The Actions Committee itself will only publish a political manifesto and not take any other steps at the moment.

We also decided to transfer the meeting of the Administrative Committee on September 2 to London.

This means I'll be in London until Friday (September 4). That afternoon I'll leave for Alexandria. I arrive there on Sunday afternoon (September 6). The next morning I'll take the train to Ramleh, and that evening I'll be at home.

London
September 1, 1936.

I left Zurich by train on Saturday night. Then I flew from Paris the following day and arrived in London on Sunday afternoon. The Actions Committee is still meeting in Zurich, but the political part is already over. Once again London has become the centre of attention.

Yesterday afternoon at three we — Chaim and I — had an interview with Ormsby-Gore. Also present was Sir John Shuckburgh*, who is taking the place of Parkinson** in the Middle East Department of the Colonial Office.

At first Ormsby-Gore did not realize with how much bitterness and mistrust we were coming to see him this time. He opened the conversation in a friendly and intimate manner, as good-humoured as if we were old friends having tea together. But he soon saw that things were far more serious than he had imagined. He read us a secret telegram he had received from the High Commissioner the night before, in which he describes the gravity of the situation and the Arab demands and asks whether he should accept the intervention of Nuri As-Said+. When Ormsby-Gore had finished reading the telegram he asked us what we advised him to do.

Chaim shrugged his shoulders, as if to say: I can't give you any advice. O-G became confused, went red and then pale, and asked: Is this non-co-operation? Chaim replied: Yes. We have not caused this situation. And we can't advise you how to get out of it. First Chaim and then I explained the situation in Palestine from our point of view: the virtual absence of a British Government and consequently the handing over of authority to the Mufti*** and his terrorist helpers. We said that with all the respect we had always felt for Wauchope, we had no confidence in him at present, and saw no point in continuing the negotiations with him. He was effective when things were peaceful and quiet. But when war broke out he was unable to cope. A large part of the civil service carried on sabotage all the time and assisted the leaders of the murder groups.

Ormsby-Gore was bewildered and did not know what to say. He cut a sorry figure. I saw him as the symbol of the present Government in England and the Mandatory Administration in Palestine. This time as well I had no doubt

*Assistant Under-Secretary of State (1921-23); Deputy Under-Secretary of State (1931-42).
**Assistant Secretary of State for the Colonies (1931-37). Permanent Under-Secretary of State for the Colonies (1937-40).
***Amin El-Husseini, see glossary.

that he is a true friend of ours. But he is powerless and indecisive, and tries to keep his ties with both the Arabs and ourselves, because he is afraid of them and us.

Tomorrow the Cabinet will meet. But I don't think they will take any final decision. From what we hear, not all the members of the Cabinet will be present tomorrow, and Baldwin will not be there. The meeting will be chaired by Eden, the Foreign Secretary, who is not one of our friends.

Today there was an editorial in *The Times* — not altogether favourable, but not bad. In any event, it will frighten the Government off from taking a decision along the lines that Wauchope would like. There was an excellent article in the *Manchester Guardian* yesterday. We are in contact with all the leading papers, and most of them are inclined towards us. Many of the political leaders are not in London now, and this makes our work more difficult. But Chaim might meet Lloyd George today.

I'm leaving here on Friday. Moshe phoned me and said I have to be in Rome on September 7 or 8. But it's still not clear why. I'm waiting for a cable from him.

Heliopolis, Egypt
January 26, 1937.

After spending a day in Cairo I moved over today to Heliopolis — which reminds me of Tel Aviv in its early years. The noise in Cairo drove me away. Here it is quiet and boring. And there is no danger that unwelcome visitors will come along to bother me, as happened this morning in Cairo. A young fellow from an Egyptian paper came to interview me. The devil alone knows how he found out I was there. I sent him packing and fled from the hotel. Here I hope no one will discover me.

Contrary to expectations, the plane journey was easy and uneventful. This time I didn't pass through Port Said at all, and flew straight from Lod to Cairo. This took two and a quarter hours, from 2.30 p.m. to 4.45. Vilensky, who represents the Jewish Agency in Cairo, was waiting for me at the airport.

112

The last time I was in Cairo was fourteeen years ago, I think. But the city doesn't seem to have changed at all.

Is it still raining in Tel Aviv? Here, of course, there's not a drop of rain, and the local people say it's the coldest winter for many years. But I don't feel the cold. The weather is like the autumn or spring in Palestine. But it's a good thing I took my warm coat, because at night it is a little cool.

Alexandria
April 30, 1937.

It's 8.45 in the morning, and we're just entering the harbour of Alexandria. It's cloudy and misty and cold. I don't intend to go into town. I'm pleased I decided to travel yesterday. I had a day of rest. After we sailed from Haifa I slept for about two hours, and felt refreshed. In the evening I ate chicken, and next morning I was able to go back to normal food. The headaches and stomach pains went away.

The sea is calm, and I hope the whole voyage will be like this. During the remaining four days on board ship I shall enjoy what I have missed for such a long time — rest.

Please phone Even-Zohar and say that I request him:

1. To send *Davar* to me *every day* — by *airmail;*
2. To send the other papers every day by *surface mail.*

May 4, 1937.

In another half an hour or so we shall dock. Since yesterday the sky has been overcast. But the sea has been calm all the way, and no one could want an easier voyage.

At Alexandria they changed my cabin, as they had promised. They gave me a larger room with a bath, on a higher deck. And I enjoyed the rest thoroughly. An ideal journey, and it's a pity it passed so quickly.

The day before yesterday I received a cable from Weizmann saying that he was leaving London and going to Switzerland in order to convalesce. He will be in Paris for two

113

days — today and tomorrow — and wants to meet me. I replied that I would come to Paris tomorrow. There is an express train today, which goes through the Simplon Pass. It leaves Venice at 3 p.m. and arrives in Paris tomorrow morning. But it only has sleeping cars, and I'm not certain I'll be able to get a place, although I cabled Venice yesterday and asked them to reserve one for me. If I can't get on that train, I'll take one at 7 p.m. which reaches Paris tomorrow afternoon at one.

For the last few days I've had no idea at all of what's happening in the big wide world. But I don't regret this in the slightest. I'm sure I did not miss the salvation of the human race while on board ship . . .

Most of the passengers on the ship are going to London for the King's coronation, and they say it's impossible to find a hotel room in London at present. All the same, I hope there will be a room for me somewhere. I'll be in London the day after tomorrow, on Thursday.

London
May 29, 1937.

Dear Renana,

Thank you so much for your lovely letter. You want me to describe the coronation* to you, but although I was in London that day, I did not go to see the procession. I saw it only afterwards in the cinema. I'm sure you'll see the same film in Tel Aviv. Today I saw a small part of the procession, by chance. I went to see Pinchas Rutenberg+, and I had to pass not far from the King's palace. And they happened to be having a procession of the King's family. So I saw the golden coaches in which the members of the royal family were riding. Not cars, but golden carriages drawn by horses. And rows and rows of the guards with their special hats and uniforms and swords. Of our friends only Yitzhak and Rachel Ben-Zvi saw the whole ceremony in Westminster Abbey — the most important and oldest church in London.

Rachel told us that she imagined she was in our temple

*The Coronation of King George VI.

114

3,000 years ago, because the ceremony is taken from Jewish customs of that time and most of the prayers come from our Bible. If I'd known you were so interested I would have gone to see it. When you see that the cinema in Tel Aviv is showing the film of the coronation, ask Mother to let you see it, and ask her to go with you, because it's worth seeing.

When Eretz Yisrael is ours we won't have a king. What do you think about this?

I'm sending you the picture of the King and Queen, on the stamps issued for the coronation.

London
May 29, 1937.

I still don't know when I'll be able to leave here. I thought of going to Poland for a week at the end of next week. But I can't leave London now. The Royal Commission has not finished its work, and during the next fortnight it will take some crucial decisions. So I have to be here. Weizmann, who has been in Switzerland, thought of coming here next week. But he has also been forced to leave Merano and come to London. He was in Paris yesterday and saw Leon Blum+, and tomorrow he'll be in London.

We don't know yet what the Commission is thinking of doing. But we've learned that they have changed their plans — and I fear a change for the worse. We might know the day after tomorrow.

Parliament opens this week, and the Ministry changed hands yesterday. The next few days will be decisive for us. I assume that you see the daily report I send to Moshe, and that you know everything that's going on. If the Commission's report is published in the middle of July, I'm afraid I won't be able to be home before the Zionist Congress. But at the moment we don't know anything. Ormsby-Gore has virtually promised to publish the Government's decisions as soon as the Commission completes its report. This will be in approximately another three weeks. But everything can change overnight at this delicate time.

On Tuesday I am meeting the Prime Minister of New

Zealand, who belongs to the Labour Party. On the same day I shall see the Egyptian Minister in London. In my next letter I might be able to write more fully about the political situation, although I'm not sure I'll be able to.

The commotion of the coronation has not yet died down, and it is still difficult to get down to any systematic work. The banquets and journeys and processions of the Royal family and the many guests still continue. But at present we are busy not so much with Englishmen, but with Arabs, who have come to London in large numbers. All the Arab Kings and the Emirs and the Sheikhs have emissaries in London, and we are trying to meet them and to clarify their attitude to the Palestine question.

Yesterday I had two important meetings with two Englishmen who have close ties with the Arab world. The one is Philby*, who is a confidant of King Ibn Saud of Saudi Arabia. Eighteen years ago he was the representative of the Palestine Government in Transjordan. Then he became friendly with Ibn Saud. He has written many books about the Arabs — and became a Moslem himself. He calls himself Abdullah Philby.

The second is Captain Armstrong**, who wrote the biography of King Ibn Saud. The first, although he is English himself, hates the English and the Jews and talks as if he himself were an Arab. The second is a British imperialist and treats us without too much friendliness but at least with some sympathy. The first proposed to me a plan for an agreement with Ibn Saud so that the British leave Palestine . . . I said to him that not only the Jews but also the Arabs would not agree that Ibn Saud, who is nothing but a Bedouin, should rule over Palestine. Philby promised that we would receive more from Ibn Saud than we would from the

*Philby, Harry St. John Bridger.

**Captain H.C. Armstrong, author of *Lord of Arabia, Ibn Saud* (1934).

116

British. Ibn Saud's son, Crown Prince Saud, is here now. He came for the coronation, and Philby and Armstrong want to talk to him and his party.

No news yet from the Royal Commission. Yesterday one English newspaper declared that the report will be published in another two days. But there is no basis for this forecast.

Yesterday the Anglo-Palestine Club gave a reception for Ben-Zvi and Rachel. Blanche Dugdale+, Balfour's niece, was in the chair and Ben-Zvi spoke in English. Rachel also spoke, in Hebrew, and Dov Hos+ translated her words into English.

London
June 1, 1937.

Weizmann returned to London the day before yesterday, and the things that matter to us are starting to move in earnest. The Royal Commission has now reached the stage of taking decisions. It seems it will recommend the partition of Palestine (all this must be kept secret!). According to the reports we have heard, we shall be given the whole of Galilee and the Emek* and the entire coast from the Lebanese border (Ras el-Nakura — you remember the place where they examined our passports when we went to Beirut) until somewhere not far from Gaza in the south. Chaim thinks that Haifa and Jaffa will also become part of the Jewish State. But I have my doubts about this. The Commission has been discussing this proposal now, and that is why I've been forced to cancel my visit to Poland. I won't leave London until the report is finished. Dov was thinking of going to Lithuania, and he too has changed his plans and will stay here.

I've already written to you that I don't know whether I shall be able to return home before the Zionist Congress. And I think you should get ready to talk with Geula about your plans. Geula can stay in Paris, and you can be with me in London.

I hope that in another fortnight we'll have some definite news of the Commission's recommendations. If I find out then that I cannot come home, I'll cable you and you'll be

*The Valley of Jezreel.

117

able to come here.

This coming weekend I might go to Paris for two days. Poalei Zion is holding its annual conference, and they want me to speak.

Ben-Zvi and Rachel are leaving here tomorrow, and will be in Palestine next week. Eliahu Epstein (Elath)+ is also going home soon.

London
June 4, 1937.

I see from your letter that Geula will still be busy with her studies for another month, and so you won't be able to travel before the beginning of July. By this time I should know whether I'll be able to come home or not.

In the political field there is nothing new, except that it is becoming clearer that the Peel Commission will recommend the partition of the country. If we receive the minimum of territory that we need now, I think that would be the most desirable solution at this time. If we get the whole of Galilee — and there is some hope of this — we will be able to settle also in the area belonging to Lebanon, over the border at Ras el-Nakura, the area we drove through along the coast on the way to Beirut. But there are three big questions:

1. What will be the fate of Haifa — will we get the town, or will it be English?

2. What about Jerusalem?

3. What will happen to the Negev — the whole area as far as Akaba, which we visited two years ago?

There's no chance that we shall get Akaba and the Negev at present. But it is possible that this part of the country might be controlled by the British and that we'll be able to settle there. There is also a slight hope that we'll be able to settle in Transjordan.

London
June 12, 1937.

The Commission finished its work the day before yesterday. But we don't yet know the contents of its report. This is the last stage of anticipation and decision, because now the British Cabinet will discuss the report and act on it. I am extremely concerned. We've been told that the Commission's conclusions were adopted unanimously — and I can't believe that all the members of the Commission would agree on something which is good for us. You haven't said whether you receive the daily report that I send to Moshe. Today I sent him the summary of my talk with Mrs Dugdale. It will give you some idea of what I'm worried about.

I think it would be best for you to travel via Marseilles, as it is closer to Paris. You should go through Trieste only if you receive free tickets on an Italian ship.

London
June 16, 1937.

You say you are surprised I suggested you should come here, when I'm thinking of coming home myself. But I can't tell what is going to happen in another three or four weeks' time. And I don't travel to London or Jerusalem out of some kind of caprice, but because I have to.

This is the position: next week the Commission will complete its report and submit it to the Government, unless this is postponed because of the High Commissioner's arrival. After the Government receives the report it will have to decide whether to publish it at once, to hold a debate in Parliament and only then to decide its own stand — or to take a decision based on its own reaction, to make this decision public together with the Royal Commission's report, and only afterwards to arrange a parliamentary debate.

I'm afraid that the High Commissioner's visit to London will spoil several things. If the report is made public, there might be riots in Palestine, and then I'm not sure the

119

Congress will be well-timed. A lot also depends on the contents of the report. For all these reasons I can't be absolutely sure where I'll be in a month's time. It's quite possible I might have to go to America.

In any event, you and Geula should leave Palestine at the end of June. I will meet you in Paris and bring you to London. What will happen afterwards we don't know. It doesn't depend on me. Perhaps everything will be all right, and the Zionist Congress will meet as planned on August 3. Then we would travel together to Zurich. But something might happen to upset this schedule. And I shan't be able to do anything about it.

Next week might be a crucial week in our history. At the moment all we can do is *to wait and see.*

London
June 22, 1937.

Today the members of the Royal Commission signed their report. Apparently it will be published in another week or two. We still don't know what's in it. But it's clear that they are proposing partition and the establishment of two states: Jewish and Arab. We shall be given Galilee, the Sharon Valley and the area around Tel Aviv. It's not known what will happen to Haifa or Jerusalem, nor what will be the fate of the entire southern part of the country, the Negev: whether it will be given to the Arabs, the Jews or the British. Weizmann is optimistic: but to my great regret I cannot share his optimism. In any case, we are facing a fateful decision, and during the next few days history will be made.

Weizmann went to Paris today and will not return until after the weekend. If I could escape for a few days to somewhere quiet I would gladly do so. My nerves are tense and almost at breaking-point, and I can't sleep at night. Before us lies perhaps an unprecedented battle. And in six weeks' time there is the Zionist Congress. I am now trying in various ways to find out more about the Peel Commission's report, and perhaps I shall have some more news in a few days' time.

I was happy to receive your telegram telling me that you have fixed the date of your departure. But why did you postpone this to July 8?

London
June 29, 1937.

It's difficult for me to describe to you the spiritual tension and turmoil in which I've been living these last few weeks. We are facing a complete revolution in our life in Palestine, and perhaps in Jewish history. But we don't know whether it will turn out to be a grave disaster or a great triumph. Either of these is possible. The report has been completed and several people have read it already. But *we* still don't know exactly what it contains, although we have had some incomplete news of its proposals. But the matters it deals with are so serious and important, and the nuances in formulation so crucial, that without a detailed reading of the entire report it is impossible to judge whether it is a death drug or a healing potion. In a few days' time the Government might hand us the report, and then we will know.

Yesterday Chaim and I saw Ormsby-Gore. I am sending you 'the contents of our talk, in English. *This is secret!* We weren't much the wiser for the talk, and we weren't even promised that we'd be shown the report before it is published.

As you probably know, our comrades demanded that I come home to attend our party's Council session. This time I could not comply with their demand. I don't know whether I'm doing the right thing or not. But I feel I have to be here in London during these crucial days, and although I know how important the debate within the party is and how vital it is that I take part in it, I don't consider myself entitled to leave this place at present.

I cabled you saying that you should leave this week, so that you will be here when we receive the Commission's report. But I see from your reply that you can't travel this week. A great pity!

Apparently the report will not be published on July 7, as

121

we thought, but on July 14, and even this is not definite. The international political situation is grave. There is great tension between Italy and Germany, on the one hand, and France and Britain on the other. The fall of Blum in France and the shooting of the generals in Russia have increased the impudence of the two Fascist dictators, and the position is extremely serious. True, there won't be a war now, because Britain isn't ready for it, and London will try to appease Germany. But things are tense, and some people think that in the prevailing atmosphere the British Government will not want to publish the Peel Commission's report, as it might lead to riots in Palestine.

I've just heard (it's 5.30 p.m.) that Moshe will phone me from Jerusalem tonight at nine.

Paris
July 27, 1937.

Dear Amos,

It wasn't right of you not to write to me even once during all this time. The fact that I didn't write to you doesn't excuse you. I wrote home regularly, and you could have known what I wrote about. And I think I had more to worry about than you did. Don't do this again. True enough, Mother told me all the time how you were. But I don't want to know only whether you are healthy and studying and working. It's very important for me also to know what you are thinking and what your attitude is to some of the great questions facing us today.

I'm going to try to give you a comprehensive survey of the way things stand at present.

I left London yesterday at the end of a very important episode, concerned with the Royal Commission and the British people's initial reaction to its proposals for Palestine. Now we are about to see the Jewish people's reaction, as expressed through the Zionist Congress. Tomorrow morning I'll leave for Zurich together with Mother (Geula is going to Antwerp tomorrow to the Workers' Olympic Games, and will

122

be in Zurich the day the Congress opens). So this is a good moment, after the Commission's report has appeared but before the Congress meets, for summing up the past and discussing the future.

In particular I want to note down the developments which led up to the present proposal for partitioning Palestine and setting up a Jewish State.

The nature of the 1936 riots.

The riots which broke out in Palestine in April, 1936 had several things in common with other riots in 1920, 1921, 1929 and 1933. But they were wider in scope and had greater political influence. This time it was clear that we were facing an Arab rebellion against Britain and also against the Jewish national home. If there had been a decent, fair and strong Government in Palestine the massacre in Jaffa would never have been allowed to become a general uprising. I doubt whether the Arabs and their leaders believed it possible to arrange a strike lasting six months, and to hold it against the police and the army. The civil service, and the High Commissioner above all, must bear a large part of the blame for the way the rebellion spread.

But facts are facts, whatever their causes. For six months the country was in a state of chaos, the Arab economy was strike-bound, there was no security of life and property, and the Government forces were impotent. And not only our small country, but the entire world was shocked by the disturbances.

The Arabs of the neighbouring countries also played an active part in the riots, through military intervention (armed bands from Syria and Iraq) and diplomatic intervention (by the Arab Kings and Iraqi Ministers). The question of Palestine, which had apparently been solved by the Balfour Declaration and the British Mandate, was reopened.

From the day the British Army conquered Palestine the British Empire has become the decisive factor in the political fate of Palestine. Only relatively few Englishmen have ever been interested in the Land or Israel and know about the Balfour Declaration and the Mandate. The British Empire is so large and widespread, the problems it faces so complex and involved, that Palestine is only one of the things that

123

concern the British people. Most of the British who followed the developments in Palestine closely were officials, in the Colonial Ministry and elsewhere, whose duty it was to be interested in Palestine and what happened there. Some statesmen and writers also knew more or less what was taking place in Palestine.

But the riots forced every British citizen to rethink the question of Palestine. Each Day he read in his paper about bombs, shooting attacks and murders. And he could not help thinking: What does it mean? What is all this fighting about? And which of the two sides is right?

And the British were confused. On the one hand, they knew that Britain had promised the Jewish people to help set up its National Home in Palestine. But what is a 'National Home'? No one knew exactly what it meant and what its purpose was. Was it a Jewish State? If so — why did they say 'National Home' and not 'Jewish State'?

The British people knew that the situation of the Jews in Germany, Poland and the other Eastern European countries was terrible. Now the British, more than any other people in the world, sympathize with the suffering of another people, and they are less infected by anti-Semitism than others. They also know, more or less (rather less than more, I am afraid) that the Jewish achievements in Palestine have not harmed the Arabs — quite the contrary.

But, on the other hand, the Englishman sees that the Arabs, who have been living in Palestine not since yesterday but for about a thousand years — which is longer than Britain itself has existed — are rising up against the 'National Home' and the British Mandate, and are demanding independent rule and a national government. And he is sympathetic to these demands, because he has been brought up on democracy and self-government. And so the Arab claim seems logical and just to him. This is their country, they have been living in it for hundreds of years, and they don't want foreigners to settle in it and to dominate them.

And the British became perplexed, confused, without knowing in their heart of hearts which of the two sides was right, and thinking eventually that both were right, the Jews and the Arabs.

124

The British are not concerned only with the justice of this problem. They know that they have an empire which spreads over the entire globe, and that there are many people who hate this empire and are jealous of it. Now England wants to increase the number of its friends and supporters. This is why it gave the Balfour Declaration during the first World War — in order to acquire the sympathy and friendship of the Jewish people, who are scattered all over the world. But at the same time Britain also gave assurances to the Arabs, because it also wanted the assistance of the Arab people in the difficult war against Germany and its ally Turkey.

After the war as well, Britain sought the friendship of both the Jewish people and the Arab people. But here in Palestine it faced a bitter dispute between the Jews and the Arabs. The British could not help one without antagonizing the other. So they became confused and could not decide what to do, both from the standpoint of justice and moral sympathy and for the sake of their own interests. Only few Englishmen were wholeheartedly in favour of one side or the other — the Jews or the Arabs. But the great majority of the people, although inclined towards the Jewish side, was not entirely convinced, and so they tried to sit on the fence. This is the reason for setting up the Royal Commission.

The role of the Royal Commission.

This Commission was established by the British Government. Its function was to examine the cause of the riots, to study the claims of the Jews and the Arabs, and to decide whether the Mandate has been carried out properly or not. But in reality the Commission had a greater task to perform. It was not only a committee of the Government, but of the British people, of British public opinion. The man in the street wanted a committee of experts who could visit Palestine, check all the arguments, and offer a solution to this complex problem about which he was reading in his newspaper, without being able to decide who was right.

True, when the Committee was nominated its duties were clearly defined and limited. The Colonial Secretary stated expressly in Parliament that the Royal Commission was not authorized to change the terms of the Mandate or to go beyond it. But from the very first moment it was appointed it was clear to me — as it must have been clear to anyone who understands something about politics — that this formal limitation was valueless. The question of Palestine was in effect being thrown wide open once more, and this meant that the Commission could make far-reaching proposals.

Naturally it was impossible to forecast what the Commission would recommend. The members of the Commission are not robots, but individuals with various political philosophies and sympathies. But one thing was clear to me all the time: this Commission would not content itself with temporary, stop-gap proposals, but would try to find a final, decisive solution to the problem.

In effect the riots last April asked this question: would Palestine become a Jewish State — or would it remain an Arab country? This time the conflict between us and the Arabs was not about the Wailing Wall, as it was in 1929. The central question was immigration, or more accurately the extent of immigration. Before the 1936 riots Jewish immigration reached 62,000 a year. If immigration continued at this rate, Palestine would become a Jewish country in another few years, because then the Jews would be a majority. In 1929 the Arabs told the Shaw Commission that the Jews were forcing the *fellaheen* off their lands. This time too they argued that we were taking their land away — not the lands and the soil (that claim has been shown to be false), but their actual homeland. So the question is: to whom will this homeland belong — the Jews or the Arabs?

And although this question does not appear in the directives given to the Royal Commission, it has been asked by history, which has insisted that the British people and the British Government give an answer to it. Any resolution or decision which allows Jewish immigration to continue at its present level means in effect handing Palestine over to the Jewish people. Will Britain allow this, or will it limit Jewish immigration artificially in order to avert a Jewish majority — in other words, to condemn the Jews to remain an eternal minority in Palestine? This was the actual concrete, factual question which the Commission had to decide.

In our statements before the Commission we did not demand a Jewish State, but concentrated on fighting for a

126

level of immigration 'in accordance with the country's economic absorptive capacity', which would of its own accord bring about the creation of a Jewish State.

The possible solution.

During most of the period of the riots I was in London and followed the trend in British public opinion. At that time I had one central objective: to prevent immigration being banned. As you know, this was the main demand by the Arabs. The British officials in Palestine also wanted to halt immigration, because they thought this was the only way of stopping the riots and averting bloodshed. Public opinion in Britain was also inclined towards stopping Jewish immigration.

When the riots broke out in 1921 the Jewish High Commissioner at the time (Herbert Samuel+) banned immigration. After the 1929 disturbances the British Government in London did the same thing. And this time as well, the Government wanted to stop immigration on a temporary basis. But it was clear that the question in 1936 was not of a temporary stoppage, but of the fate of all immigration in the future. Many Jews also thought immigration should be halted for the moment 'for the sake of peace'. But it was obvious to me that this time any cessation of immigration, even a temporary cessation, would be a sentence of death. Because the struggle this time is against our right to immigrate, against our immigration 'by right and not as a favour'. And halting immigration undermines our right to settle in the country, and could perhaps destroy it altogether.

As you know, we won this battle. Immigration was not stopped. But the Arab onslaught did not stop either. And the Royal Commission had in effect to be the final arbiter.

The mood in England during the riots gave me the key to understanding the mood of the Commission. Most of the British public, in the press and in Parliament, was sympathetic towards the Jewish people and towards Zionism. But this sympathy had a certain limit. It opposed the cessation of immigration. But public opinion in Britain did not support us when we demanded increased immigration, as the most effective way of preventing the riots being resumed.

127

We argued: Increase Jewish immigration, create a large Jewish population in a short time, and this will take away from the Arabs their desire to attack us. If they see the Mandatory Government is determined to implement the policy of the National Home, the Arabs will no longer dare to use violence, and things will become quiet again.

But we found no response in Britain to this just and logical demand. Apparently the British did not want to provoke the Arabs too much and to arouse the hatred of the Arabs and Moslems outside Palestine. And all the Englishmen who were outwardly our friends told us: After the riots die down, there will have to be some concessions to the Arabs — naturally not far-reaching concessions, like stopping immigration completely or setting up an Arab Government, but partial concessions: for example, reducing the scope of immigration.

I found the same trend inside the Royal Commission. Although its members were careful not to express any opinion, it was not difficult to discern the way they were thinking from the questions they put to us.

Before the Commission we demanded that immigration be speeded up and that the National Home be allowed to grow faster. The Commission did not accept this demand, probably because it would have meant turning the whole of Palestine into a Jewish country. Britain was not ready for this, and for such an open conflict with the entire Arab world.

After the Commission had left Palestine I came to the conclusion that we faced a real and terrible danger of immigration being restricted. And I asked myself: Is there no other way out? Is it essential and desirable that Britain should take a final decision now on whether Palestine should belong to the Jews or to the Arabs? If it is forced to take any such decision, it will not decide in our favour. So is there an alternative?

And at the beginning of February I summoned the Central Committee of the party. I addressed it on the grave fears I had about the Commission's proposals. I told our comrades I was afraid the Commission would propose the reduction of immigration, a ban on the purchase of land in certain areas, the formation of an Arab Agency in which the Arab Kings would be represented, and so on. I said that even if the status

128

quo was allowed to remain, immigration would slacken off, as happened immediately after the riots. So we had to find a positive, radical solution.

This could, I suggested, be in the direction of 'partitioning the country into two parts, so that in one part will arise a Jewish State, which would make a pact with Britain, as Iraq, Egypt and Syria have done', and the other part would become an Arab state. I also worked out a detailed proposal for partition, according to which there would be about 300,000 Arabs in the Jewish State, which would have a Jewish majority. Under the scheme the Jewish State would include the areas of Safed, Nazareth, Tiberias, Haifa, Beit Shean, Tulkarm (as far as the mountains), Jaffa, Ramleh and half the Negev. I proposed that Jaffa, Lod and Ramleh should remain in Arab hands and should be linked to the Arab State by a corridor. Jerusalem, Bethlehem and Nazareth should be allocated to Britain, and the areas around Acre and Gaza, which are inhabited almost solely by Arabs, should be autonomous, like the province of Alexandretta in Syria.

I said on that occasion:

'At first this plan might seem utterly fantastic. And indeed it might have seemed fantastic a year ago, and could appear absurd in another year. But at this particular moment it is not fantastic, because there are factors which favour it. The question of Palestine has been presented anew and thrown wide open. There have been riots in the neighbouring countries, and the question of Syria has also been solved in this way. An independent kingdom has been established in Syria and a second kingdom in Lebanon, and the province of Alexandretta has been declared an autonomous Sanjak.

But I added:

'If this proposal comes from the Jewish side — it is doomed. It must be presented as a British idea. If we can find people in all the British political parties — Churchill, Chamberlain+, Lloyd George, Amery, Greenwood+, Attlee — who can adopt this plan and sponsor it, it could be accepted. And if the League of Nations knows that the Jews will agree to it — they will not interfere. In my opinion, this plan is feasible politically.'

Why did I insist that this programme should not be

presented as a Jewish proposal? Because partition would mean the abolition of the Mandate. If we suggested partition, Britain might accept the first part — the abolition of the Mandate — but there is no guarantee that it would accept the second part — which is the establishment of a Jewish State. And at present our entire political leverage rests on the Mandate, and we cannot abandon it so long as we have not received something worthwhile in its place. A Jewish State in part of Palestine, covering a suitable area and with proper borders, would be better than the Mandate. But we cannot force Britain to set up a Jewish State and to give it the frontiers it needs. We can only agree or not agree that the Mandate be abolished. So at present we should press our demand that the Mandate be carried out faithfully. The partition proposal should come from the British, and if we see it is favourable, we can accept it and give up the Mandate.

The meeting at which I proposed this plan took place in our house, in my study, on February 4. During the discussion several of my comrades said the idea was unrealistic. Both Berl Locker and Yitzhak Tabenkin argued vehemently that there was no chance Britain would propose any such plan or would agree to it, and in putting it forward we would only harm our own cause, because we would weaken the Mandate. The debate continued until I left for Lonon.

To these comrades I replied: I can't be sure that this plan will be accepted by Britain. But it is clear to me that there is *a realistic chance* of its being adopted as a British proposal, not a Jewish one. We should aim for this because it is the only solution which will advance our own interests. Otherwise we will face restricted immigration, an economic crisis in Palestine, a worsening of the Jewish position in the Diaspora and a weakening of the Zionist movement.

The conclusions of the Royal Commission.

I presume you have read the Commission's summing-up. To my great regret, all my worst fears were realized. In the second part of the report all kinds of limitations and restrictions are proposed on immigration, settlement and land purchase.

I'm enclosing a short survey I drew up immediately after reading the full report for the first time. Also attached is a

130

short but detailed analysis (in English) of the Commission's proposal for partition.

This proposal differed in various respects from the one I brought before the party's Central Committee. Some changes were for the better, others for the worse. Here I note the main differences:

1. *Changes for the worse:*

a) According to my plan, *the entire coastal plain* from the southern border of the Acre area to the northern border of the Gaza area was included in the Jewish State. The Commission gives us only part of this coastal plain. Further, I placed our eastern border near to the hills of Judea and Samaria. The Commission makes the border go through the plain itself.

b) According to my plan, we should have received half the Negev, from Beersheba southwards to the Egyptian border and the Gulf of Eilat (Akaba). The Commission, however, hands this over to the Arab state (apart from the north-east corner of the Gulf of Eilat).

c) In my proposal the towns of Tiberias, Safed and Haifa were to have been Jewish. The Commission suggests a provisional mandate over these towns.

d) I wanted the Jews to have *full control* over the whole Jewish State, apart from the privileges Britain would enjoy in Haifa on the basis of an agreement between it and the Jewish State. The Commission limits the authority of the Jewish State to the ports and the shores of the Sea of Galilee.

2. *Changes for the better:*

a) Whereas I removed the province of Acre from the Jewish State, the Commission gives us the entire province, while proposing a temporary mandate on the town of Acre itself.

b) Similarly, I omitted the entire province of Gaza from the State, while the Commission gives us part of it (admittedly the smaller part).

c) I proposed *an Arab corridor* from Jaffa, Lod and Ramleh to the Arab state. The Commission suggests an *English* corridor from Jaffa to Jerusalem, and removes Lod and Ramleh from the Arab state. This is important

131

for two reasons: first, Jews will be able to settle in the corridor, as it will not be Arab or English land; the second, this corridor would enable *New Jerusalem* to become part of the Jewish State.

d) The Commission wants to remove all the Arabs living in the coastal plain, the Valley of Jezreel, and the Western Jordan Valley from the Jewish area and to resettle them in Transjordan or in another Arab area. This would mean that the Jews would receive these valleys completely empty of Arab villages, and could settle more Jews there. This proposal has a tremendous advantage, and is worth as much as having the Negev, in my opinion. But I forgot to mention the two principal *drawbacks* of the Commission's report:

e) It places Degania and its sister kibbutzim, as well as Rutenberg's power station at Naharayim, outside the Jewish State.

f) Another place left out of the Jewish State is the Dead Sea plant, which is important in itself and also for the development of the chemical industry.

When I come to weigh up the advantages and disadvantages of the Commission's proposal compared to my own plan, I find that generally speaking it is better. This is particularly true of two priceless things:

a) The fact that the whole of Galilee is given to the Jews and our northern border is placed along the Lebanese frontier. This proximity has tremendous political value, as both Lebanon and the Jews are interested in being neighbours. The Christians in Lebanon could scarcely exist at all without a Jewish State next door, and we are also interested in an alliance with Christian Lebanon.

b) The proposal to transfer the Arabs from our valleys. We cannot and are not entitled to propose anything like this, because we have never wanted to dislodge the Arabs. But as Britain is giving part of the country which was promised to us to the Arabs for their state, it is only right that the Arabs in our state should be transferred to the Arab part.

Another advantage of the Commission's proposal is that it gives us *three-quarters of the Palestinian coast*. If we wish to

132

bring many Jews to Palestine we must concentrate on three branches of the economy: farming, industry and the sea. All the built-up area containing our industries is allocated to us (apart from the Dead Sea). If the valleys are emptied of Arabs we will be able to irrigate them and to settle a family on 20-50 dunams. And the sea will make it possible to have ships and fishing.

Paris
July 28, 1937.

Dear Amos,

I didn't manage to finish my letter to you yesterday. I was thinking of going to Zurich this morning. But I changed my plans. Dov Hos came here yesterday from London, in Weizmann's car, and I decided to travel to Zurich with him by car this afternoon (Mother will come with us).

I'll use the time before our journey to finish this letter. Even before the Royal Commission published its report* we knew more or less what it contained and we began taking political action to correct it. We discussed it with the British Government, our friends in Parliament and the leading papers. The amendments we wanted were:

a) To include New Jerusalem (i.e. that part of the city outside the walls) in the Jewish State, as part of the British corridor.
b) To extend the corridor to the Dead Sea, so that the potash plant would belong to the Jewish State and there would be a link with our State through the corridor.
c) To include Transjordan, between the Yarmuk. the Jordan and the Sea of Galilee, in the Jewish State.
d) To broaden the coastal plain as far as tne hills of Judea and Samaria.
e) To place the Negev under a British mandate, so that the Jews can settle there.
f) To annul the 'provisional' mandates over Haifa, Acre,

*On July 7, 1937.

133

Tiberias and Safed, or to decide in advance that they would end after a fixed period, which should not be longer than three years.

g) To lift the restriction on the construction of the Tel Aviv port, and in general to remove all limitations on the sovereignty of the Jewish State.

h) To include the entire province of Beit Shean in our state, so that we can incorporate the new kibbutz of Tirat Zvi.

i) To annul the proposal for the payment of an annual tax to the Arab state. We are ready to pay some compensation to the Arab state, and to reach a mutual agreement about this, but not to pay this sum by decree.

The debate in the British Parliament.

You've probably read a summary of the speeches during the recent debate in both Houses of the British Parliament. The most important speakers supported most of our demands. We were able to persuade the Archbishop of Canterbury (a sort of English High Priest) to demand that New Jerusalem be given to the Jews. But this debate revealed strong opposition to partition on the part of our friends, while the supporters of the Arabs agreed to partition. Our friends among all the parties thought the Jews were really against partition (because this has been our official and public stand all the time), and they believed that by opposing partition they were helping us . . .

And so two of our greatest friends, Lloyd George and Winston Churchill, brought about the rejection of the Government's resolution, and in its place Parliament adopted a resolution authorizing Britain to submit the partition plan to the League of Nations. But the entire question will still have to come before Parliament once more, if the League of Nations does not oppose partition, and the Government could change the entire plan or even drop it altogether.

This debate was mostly in our favour (when I sat in the House of Lords and then the next day in the House of Commons I felt I was at a Zionist Congress!). The speakers praised the Jewish people, Zionism and our achievements in Palestine. The debate strengthened our political and moral
134

position. It enabled the partition proposal to be changed in our favour. But, on the other hand, it cast doubts on the partition plan as a whole and brought in some changes for the worse. I am paticularly worried about the fate of Upper Galilee.

One of the chief opponents of partition was Winston Churchill of the Conservative Party. He is one of the most influential men in England (but is hated by the Government). Churchill's opposition to partition springs not only from friendship for Zionism, but from a completely different reason, and an imperialist one. He is convinced (and rightly!) that the Jewish State will build up a strong army, with the best available weapons, and that the Arabs won't be able to withstand it. And that after the Jews are strong they will not content themselves with their narrow borders but will burst into the undeveloped areas — and then England will have fresh headaches . . .

Another voice was raised against partition — and this was the voice of Herbert Samuel. You probably read his speech in the Hebrew press.

Before I left London I sent a circular to all the Zionist organizations and parties in the world asking them to protest vigorously against Samuel's treacherous conduct and his advice to the Jews to remain a minority in Palestine. He wants in effect to turn the whole of Palestine into an Arab state. This morning I read in *The Times* the first protest against Samuel, by the National Committee for the Jews of Palestine.

Now let me return to the League of Nations in Geneva.

The next move.

As far as we know, the members of the Permanent Mandates Commission, which forms part of the League of Nations, also thinks that the Mandate cannot be implemented as we would like. The alternative, a restricted immigration, condemns the Jews to remain a minority, and this is against justice and the promises given to the Jewish people. So the way out is partition.

Now the Zionist Congress has to decide its stand. And this depends mainly on our party, as we will have about 45 per cent of the delegates.

What I would like Congress to do is:

a) To protest vehemently against Samuel's position.

b) To oppose strongly all the Peel Commission's proposals for restrictions on immigration, land purchases and so on. .

c) To take issue with the Commission's basic premise that the Mandate cannot be implemented.

d) As far as partition is concerned, the Congress does not yet have to say 'yea' or 'nay'. But it must empower the new Executive to discuss the proposed amendments to the Commission's plan with the British Government. And if the Executive can obtain a satisfactory proposal, then a *special session* of the Congress will be held, probably in the winter, to take a final decision.

I am very tired and worn out by the terrible strain of the last two months. I can hardly do any work, and I find it particularly hard to take part in discussions. But the Congress will open in a few days' time, and a new effort must be made.

September 2, 1937.

We'll be in New York tomorrow. The journey was excellent, although I had an inside cabin. But it wasn't bad at all. The main thing is that I hardly spoke to anyone and had a complete rest. The pains have almost disappeared, and I slept almost normally. Warburg was also on the ship, and he is the only person I spoke to on the journey. The day before yesterday I received a cable from Moshe about the people killed in Jerusalem and the villages in the new riots. I contacted London and New York, and the reports are reassuring. I hope the attacks have stopped by now.

I trust you also had a good and comfortable sea voyage home.

New York
September 3, 1937.

The moment I arrived here I sent a cable to Genoa, to

reach you on your ship. I hope you received it safely.

Tonight I'm going to Chatham — a small town in Massachusetts where Brandeis now lives. I wanted to rest tonight. But I received a cable from Brandeis asking me to be at his house tomorrow morning. It will take me most of the night to get there. I don't know when I'll return to New York.

This morning a lot of journalists, Jewish and non-Jewish, came to the ship to meet me. So after six days of silence I was forced to open my mouth.

It's dreadfully hot here. Worse than the Jordan Valley.

Ile de France
September 13, 1937.

This is my third day on board ship, on the way back. This time I'm not travelling first class, but tourist. I have a better and more comfortable room than on the *Berengaria*. There I had an inside cabin, without any air, and with someone else in with me. This time I have a large outside cabin and am alone. There is a special bathroom, with hot and cold water and iced water.

The first day at sea was stormy. The waves spat against my window, and the ship was buffeted about. But it didn't bother me particularly, and I ate my meals as usual. Yesterday the storm died down a little, and today the sea is smooth and calm.

This is the first time I've crossed the Atlantic on a French ship. It all happened by chance. I had booked on the *Berengaria*, which was due to sail the day before yesterday at midday, as was written on my ticket. When the day came I left the hotel at eleven and went to the quay. When I arrived there, I couldn't see the *Berengaria*. The ship's agent was waiting, and informed me that it left at ten instead of twelve . . . When I expressed my annoyance, he said he would give me a cabin on the *Ile de France*, which was sailing a little later the same day. I had no choice, so I transferred my luggage to the French ship, which sailed at 12.15.

137

Ile de France
On the Atlantic Ocean
September 14, 1937.

I'm enclosing the letter I've written to Eliezer Kaplan about my talks in the United States.

I might spend a few days in Europe before returning home. Meanwhile I'll give you a general account of my brief visit to America.

I had two objectives during this rather hurried journey: à) To maintain the connections with Brandeis and his circle, which have been somewhat upset because of the partition plan; b) to examine the chances of success at the next Zionist Congress, if it is summoned during the coming year.

Things didn't work out exactly as I would have liked. But in general I am very satisfied with the results of my visit.

The night before I sailed from Europe I had a severe attack of the pains that bothered me after Zurich, and I wasn't sure I would go. But on the day of my departure I felt better and decided to travel, and on the way the pains died down.

On the *Berengaria* were Louis Lipsky+, Warburg and his group. At the first opportunity I told Karp, one of Warburg's friends, that these few days at sea were my time for resting. He took the hint and let me travel undisturbed all the way to New York.

Warburg came to see me a few times. The first time he was sarcastic and prickly and full of complaints: about the contempt shown for his 12-point non-Zionist platform, the lack of contact, attempts at dictatorship and so on. But after I had given him a fair yet firm answer he became friendlier and assured me he had been extremely satisfied with the Zurich meeting. For some reason he seems to feel that he rescued Weizmann, after the latter's 'failure' at the Congress.

From what Warburg said it is clear that he is not a great friend of Weizmann's and does not believe in him. He also does not particularly care for our party, but respects our honesty and devotion. All in all, he is far too dependent upon his informants and takes all his opinions from them.

I saw before me a man who undoubtedly loves the Land of Israel and has a Jewish heart. But he is shortsighted . . . and

138

finds it difficult to accept a broad-based, democratic movement like Zionism, much less to understand it.

I spent seven and a half days in America, from Friday, September 3, to Saturday, September 11. The Jewish Telegraphic Agency announced that I was en route to America, and while on the *Aquitania* I received a telegram from Wertheim complaining that I had not informed the party of my arrival. I replied that my visit was private and short and that I didn't want to address any public meetings. And in fact this time I was able to leave America without having to make any speeches — a great relief.

The first person who came to see me was Stephen Wise. It appears that the proposal he made at Zurich — a joint talk with L.D.B., Felix, Mack, Bob and himself* — won't work out. Frankfurter is ill and cannot leave his house. Wise can't leave New York just before Rosh Hashana. So he suggested I should go straight to Chatham. I wanted to have one day's rest in New York, but Wise was insistent. So we compromised, and cabled Brandeis saying I was ready to come to him on Sunday, September 5, but that if he preferred me to come on Saturday I would do so. In about an hour we had a reply cable asking me to come at once if I could. So I left by train the same evening for Hyannis, from where I would continue to Chatham, as there is no train to Chatham.

The overnight journey brought me to Hyannis at 7 a.m., and there I found Gilbert, Brandeis's son-in-law, waiting for me. He took me by car to Chatham. I had breakfast in Gilbert's home, and from his wife, B.'s eldest daughter, I learned the background to this group's opposition to partition. The source of this opposition, or one of the sources, is a lack of confidence in Weizmann ... It goes without saying that Brandeis did not hint at this in my talk with him, and backed up his opposition with other reasons.

Brandeis received me with great friendship, and I was glad to see this old man (he is over 80) while he still has his spiritual power. His physical vitality has also not yet left him. He stands as straight as a man of forty and walks with a steady, confident tread. I think he looks better now than

*Brandeis, Frankfurter, Julian Mack and Robert Szold.

when I saw him in Washington two and a half years ago. I told Brandeis that my father is eighty-two and still vigorous, and he asked about my father's health and what he does.

My talk with Brandeis, which was arranged for a quarter past nine, went on for two and a quarter hours, with a break for a quarter of an hour at the end of the first hour. For an hour, less a few minutes, I spoke, and he listened without a break and without asking any questions or making any comment; and then he spoke for a little over an hour, without any interruption on my part. But immediately after he had begun speaking, when an hour of our meeting had gone by, he stopped, asked me to talk to his wife and went out to walk by himself for a quarter of an hour. His wife told me that this is how he arranges his life. He works according to a timetable and a fixed programme. His features are excellent, he stands up straight, his brain is alert, his conversation is alive and energetic, and you don't feel for a moment that you are talking to an old man of eighty. From what he says it is clear that he knows everything it is possible to know about Palestine from reading, and he knows that he knows.

I told him about the reaction of public opinion in Britain during the riots, how the British public cannot decide between the claims of the Jews and the claims of the Arabs, both of which seem to be justified, and how much of a struggle it is to continue the immigration; the mood among the Royal Commission when it was in Palestine; the reasons why the British are unwilling to decide the historic dispute between the Jews and the Arabs, even when they recognize the justice of the Jewish case, as the Royal Commission has done this time. I told him about the attitude of the British Mandate civil service during the seventeen years they have ruled the country, and why this stand is unlikely to change for the better even if the Mandate continues; why it is difficult for Britain to continue the Mandate with confidence; the increased Arab opposition, and the reasons for it; what we can expect from the Mandatory regime in the near future, if it does continue; and what the chances are that a Jewish State will be formed, even in a part of the country; and whether this part on its own would meet our basic

140

demands.

I told him that I would certainly choose a state in part of the country instead of a Mandate in the whole country, but that until the report appeared I had not believed that Britain would agree to found a Jewish State. And even now the main argument against the report in my eyes is that the Jewish State is still not a fact, and our trust in the British Government's promises has not increased of late. On the other hand, my experience in Palestine has increased my confidence in the ability of the Jewish people, and if we are given freedom of action even in a limited space — but space that we control — this will lead in the course of time to far greater results than dependence on the British civil service over the whole of the territory.

In his reply Brandeis said that he agreed with my appraisal of Britain in the past and the present, but did not agree with my conclusions. Things did not have to develop in future exactly as I thought they would. I was making the mistake Herzl made with regard to Uganda*, he said. After Herzl had seen the suffering of the Jews in Poland and the difficult conditions in Palestine, he came to the idea of Uganda. This was the greatest mistake of his life. An agreement to annul the British Mandate would be a mistake of this order.

It was true, Brandeis said, that Britain was confused, weak and in error at present. The best people in Britain had been slaughtered in the war, and the British did not have good leaders now. Britain's political and moral weakness had been revealed not only in Palestine. Britain had been wrong in Japan, in Ethiopia, in Spain. But this weakness would not continue for ever. Britain would return to its former strength — and would also change its course in the Holy Land. The British were as interested as we were in a Jewish Palestine.

The dreadful situation of the Jews in Germany and Poland must not be taken into account, Brandeis said. Even if 100,000 immigrants a year come to Palestine, as I hope they will, this will not solve the problem of the Jews in Eastern Europe, because the natural increase of the Jews in these

*In 1903 the British Government made the Zionist Organization a tentative and provisional offer of the Guas Ngishu plateau (part of what is now Kenya) for Jewish settlement. The offer was rejected, after Herzl's death in 1904, by the Seventh Zionist Congress, in the following year.

141

countries is over 100,000 a year. During the next few years immigration would be reduced, if the status quo remained in force: but this was not a catastrophe. Because I was living in Palestine and was under the pressure of our immediate needs, I did not see things correctly, Brandeis said. We had to see the matters at hand from the perspective of the generations who would come after us.

We should not be afraid, he added, of the Arabs' large natural increase. This was a transient thing. In America and England there had also been a high rate of natural increase. But this didn't last long. It wouldn't last long with the Arabs either.

The rapid progress which I thought a Jewish State would bring about was by no means certain. Brandeis said. We could not ignore the presence of the Arabs in a Jewish State. They would interfere with the building of the country. A Jewish State would not block Arab irredentism.

Precisely because he was far from Palestine geographically, he said, he could discuss things from a historic viewpoint. His faith in Britain has not been shaken. We should not surrender the Mandate, because there is nothing better than it.

The Royal Commission had exceeded its brief. It had no authority to stop the Mandate. Further, it had proposed something which had not been clarified during its investigations. No one in Palestine had been asked about partition, and the Commission's conclusions about the plan were therefore unsound.

Brandeis expressed his appreciation of our work in Palestine and praised Moshe's activities. We parted with great friendliness. The second part of the talk lasted over an hour, and from the gestures of his wife, who appeared at the door, I could see she was anxious in case the timetable should be upset. I couldn't continue the conversation myself. But I said to Brandeis as we parted that in the same way that he regretted his inability to agree with my views, I regretted my own inability to agree with his.

The debate was continued with Mack, after I returned to New York.

I first met Mack the day after Rosh Hashana (September 7), together with Bob Szold, for a short talk, and then a

142

second time on September 8 for two and a half hours. The second time Mrs (Rose) Jacobs of Hadassah was also present.

Mack changed his position a little. At the end of the second talk he turned to Bob and Mrs Jacobs and said:

'He made out a very strong case.'

I also spoke to Szold about security matters, and from what he said I understood that there is no chance of large sums from the special committee formed for this purpose.

Incidentally, Mack insisted that the agreement we made a year ago about L.D.B.'s 4,000 Palestine Pounds* must be kept to the letter. *All* this money will be devoted to maritime activities and work connected with the sea.

Wise did not take part in these talks, because he was not in New York. When he returned from Zurich he did not feel too well, and immediately after Rosh Hashana he went for a rest. Mack wrote to him that I was returning to Europe on September 11, and he came back to New York the day before. He phoned me immediately and said he would like to see me next morning before I sailed. I said to him that at 8.30 a.m. I was meeting a delegation of Jewish workers. Wise offered to meet me at 7.30, and I agreed. And at precisely 7.30 he arrived at my hotel.

I told him about my talks with Brandeis and Mack, and I saw that Wise has also moved his position somewhat. He said he was sorry Felix's illness had prevented our meeting, because 'Felix is less intransigent than the old man.' Wise agreed with my assessment that Brandeis approached the question from a *legal* standpoint, and not from a *political* one. Further, Brandeis underestimates the time factor, plays down the Arab danger and Arab opposition, does not appreciate how important immigration is not only because of the Jewish people's needs, but also because it conquers the land — and relies too much on the chances that Britain will change for the better and come out in our favour.

Wise is ready to come to London in November or December for political work, if necessary. He also discussed with me my virtual disappearance from the Jewish Agency Executive.

While in New York I examined the possibilities of military

*Then equal to £4000 sterling.

143

training in America. It's not worth sending people from Palestine to America for this training. But young American citizens should be given military, aeronautic and naval training. A young man between the ages of nineteen and twenty-five with a college degree can get into a military aviation school for a 14-month course, and receives $70 a month salary. Anyone who finishes this course is an expert pilot and instructor. I don't see why we can't find dozens of young Jews to take this course.

Youngsters can also be sent to naval academies. True, it's not easy for Jews to get into them. But with some recommendations from Senators and Congressmen it's not impossible. Why shouldn't we train naval officers for Palestine at the expense of the American Government? We don't need American *halutzim* of the usual kind. But perhaps pioneers like these can only be trained in America.

The other matter I handled in New York was the preparations for the next Zionist Congress.

If the chance of a Jewish State seems realistic, and a special session of Congress is summoned to discuss it, people are going to flock to the Congress. The mood of the Jewish masses in Eastern Europe is known. And I saw now in America that the same applies over there. Only the assimilated minority is against the idea. They told me that one wealthy American Jew said that if a Jewish State is established, he will convert to Christianity. But the masses of Jews, even those who have not been close to Zionism, favour a Jewish State. So does the Yiddish press in New York.

If the British Government does not change its mind, and if no unforeseen international disaster takes place, I am confident the special session of Congress will approve the partition proposal. But we of the Labour faction in Palestine must ensure the widest possible backing by other Labour groups and supporters of partition. So I spent a lot of my time in New York persuading the various Jewish workers' organizations to form a single unified body which will take part in the elections to the forthcoming Congress. This was the theme at the second breakfast I had on the morning of September 11 (the first breakfast was with Stephen Wise at 7.30 a.m.).

The discussion with the workers' representatives went on until 10.30. At eleven I left the hotel and went to the port, to find that the *Berengaria* had left at ten, instead of twelve. As I wrote to you, the agent who had sold me the ticket arranged a cabin on the *Ile de France,* which left shortly after twelve. So it turned out well in the end. I have a large cabin to myself, and am enjoying a complete rest. I know none of the passengers, and none of them knows me. So I haven't been forced to speak a single word until now. Perhaps we should hold a Zionist Congress under these conditions.

From London I will talk to Moshe, who is in Geneva, and then I'll decide my plans. I have no desire to go to Geneva, and would like to come home as soon as possible.

Ile de France
September 15, 1937.

At 12.30 after midnight they brought me a telegram from Moshe in Geneva:

'EDEN ANNOUNCED: HIS MAJESTY'S GOVERNMENT WILL APPOINT A COMMITTEE WHICH WILL VISIT PALESTINE, MEET WITH JEWS AND ARABS, AND PROPOSE A DETAILED PARTITION PLAN WITHIN PROVISIONAL BORDERS, WHICH A SPECIAL COMMITTEE WILL FIX PERMANENTLY.'

The ship's newspaper this morning carried a dispatch from Geneva:

'Au cours de la séance de l'apres-midi, M. Eden a posé la question du partage ethnologique de la Palestine.'

Does Eden's announcement mean that he has submitted to pressure from the Arab Kings and the Mandatory officials? Has the idea of an international committee to fix the borders been dropped? What does the reference to 'provisional borders' mean? And why does the statement refer to 'partition', but say nothing about a Jewish State? I'll have to find these things out in London.

After lunch a storm blew up and soon grew stronger. In the library tables were overturned. It's impossible to sleep. The whole cabin is rocking from side to side.

The sea is a mass of mountains. The sky is black. To walk about you have to be an acrobat. The whole ship is creaking, as if it is about to fall to pieces.

This afternoon at four I received a telegram from London saying that Moshe suggests I go to Paris to see Chaim and that from there I should continue to Geneva. Moshe and Berl Locker will be in Geneva only on the 24th. So I have changed my Plymouth-London ticket for one from Le Havre to Paris.

I arrived here from Le Havre at 11 p.m. The storm delayed the ship by several hours. Marc Yarblum* told me that a decision has already been taken in Geneva. The committee studying the partition plan will visit Palestine in October and will spend about four months there. One or two members of the Peel Commission will serve on this new committee.

According to Yarblum, Chaim is pleased with the new development in Geneva. He asked me to phone him tomorrow morning. Moshe phoned Yarblum today and left a message asking me to proceed to Geneva at once.

On Saturday morning, the day after I arrived, I saw Chaim, who had just returned from Geneva. He asked me to go to Geneva before I went to London. That same afternoon I flew from Paris to Geneva.

In actual fact, the matter was settled here last week. You know already from the newspapers that Anthony Eden announced that a new British committee will visit Palestine and discuss the partition plan with the Jews and the Arabs.

*French Zionist leader.

146

Chaim told me that this delegation will consist of three people. One of them will be Morris Carter, who was a member of the Royal Commission. I personally am worried by this new delegation. I fear it might mean that the entire matter will pass into the hands of the Palestinian civil service, and that the Arabs will organize a new attack against the formation of the Jewish State. Chaim was far more optimistic.

Today the Iraqi Minister addressed the League of Nations, and delivered a vehement attack on both the Balfour Declaration and the partition plan.

Berl is going to London tonight. I'm staying on until tomorrow. Then I'll go to Paris, and after a day or two there will continue to London, where I will ascertain the nature of the new committee, its composition and function. I hope to return home at the end of September.

London
September 24, 1937.

I'm enclosing a copy of a letter I sent to Kaplan this morning, from which you'll see what I think of the present situation, and also what Chaim thinks of it (we don't agree on everything).

Next week the Political Committee which was elected in Zurich will meet. I shall have to be here for another two weeks, and then I hope my work on the Executive will be completed and I shall be able to concentrate on the Histadrut once more.

London
September 24, 1937.

I arrived here last night, and only this morning could I meet our people and look at the post, including your letter of the 19th.

My four days in Geneva were almost unnecessary, as the main action had been taken before I arrived. This was the

147

League of Nations resolution on Palestine. The subsequent debates at the League's Assembly and the Mandates Commission were of purely platonic and moral value.

In my opinion the League of Nations resolution is excellent. It annuls the British decision about a political limit to Jewish immigration, and at the same time demands that the Mandate be continued. A minor defect in the resolution is that in the passage referring to partition there is no explicit statement about the establishment of a Jewish State. But this is only a technical defect. The content of the resolution meets all the wishes of the Zionist Congress and of both those who favour partition and those who oppose it.

You probably read about the debate in the press. The Iraqi speaker was extremely impudent. At the Mandates Commission there were some Zionist speeches, particularly one by the Norwegian delegate. The Egyptian Minister also apparently retracted his hostile stand and praised the Jews. He identified himself with the Norwegian delegate's pro-Zionist remarks and with Eden's position. Only he attributed to Eden the exact opposite of what he said. The Egyptians implied that Eden does not think partition is the only solution, whereas he said expressly that partition *is the only ultimate solution*. Although the word 'ultimate' could be misinterpreted, one can't claim that Eden said the opposite.

The formation of the new committee which is being sent to Palestine, and which is officially being called the new 'body', gives grounds for much concern.

The transfer of the focal point of the debate from London to Palestine means increasing the Arab pressure and the influence of the Mandatory civil service. This does not bolster our already shaky trust in the British Government's decisions and announcements.

I am afraid that the publication of Chaim's talk with Ormsby-Gore played some part in this shift, if the creation of this new 'body' is indeed a shift.

We must demand the maximum punishment for the man who published this talk — a ban on re-election for a considerable period and expulsion from the Zionist Actions Committee. His action undermines the political work of the

Four American Zionists: Rabbi Stephen Wise (top left), Louis Lipsky (top right), Louis D. Brandeis (bottom left) and Felix Frankfurter.

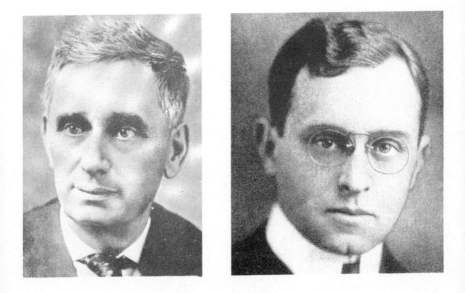

Major-General Orde Wingate, creator of the Special
Night Squads.

Prime Minister Neville Chamberlain presides over the Jewish
representatives at the London Conference of February 1939. Foreground,
left to right: Rev. M. L. Perlzweig, N. Goldmann, S. Brodetzky,
C. Weizmann, D. Ben-Gurion, R. Jacobs, M. Shertok (Sharett), A. Lourie.

Zionist spokesmen, and it cannot be tolerated for a moment.

Moshe and (Nahum) Goldmann+ are due here tomorrow evening.

This morning I had a long talk with Chaim. He does not see things in as dark a light as I do. On the contrary, he is optimistic. The situation in the Arab countries is working in our favour, he says. The confusion, instability and internal differences, and the negative attitude towards Britain, all make the Arab countries a less important factor in British policies. (In my own opinion, this also works in the opposite direction: precisely because the situation is so bad, the Arab politicians can grasp the Palestinian slogan even more intensely, as the only fulcrum which could bring about internal unity).

Chaim is pleased that Shuckburgh will handle Palestinian affairs from now on. Although Shuckburgh never was and is not now a Zionist, he is a sincere and honest man. When he says 'no' he means no, and when he says 'yes' he means yes. Parkinson, on the other hand, criticizes you one minute and compliments you the next, and you never know if he is with you or against you.

As far as the the new body is concerned, Chaim doesn't know definitely yet who its members will be or what its function and authority is. Carter has been proposed as one of its members. But according to the Professor* (with whom Chaim talked a few days ago), Carter can't stand the climate of Palestine, and so it's possible he won't accept the post. In this case the Professor himself might be nominated. Another possibility is Laurie (Hammond). Chaim thinks Laurie would be better than the Professor, because the latter has a very doctrinaire approach and he would not easily agree to any changes in his plan. For example, Chaim spoke to him about Jerusalem and encountered some stiff opposition. Laurie, on the other hand, is more open, and at the same time he is rigid about the Galilee question. Here Laurie's influence probably tipped the balance on the future of Galilee, and Chaim is convinced he would insist on keeping our northern border and would perhaps also help us to obtain other amendments in our favour.

*Professor Reginald Coupland.

At present there is 'no one' in London — in other words, Ormsby-Gore and Shuckburgh are away, and it's impossible to do anything.

As far as the loan from Lloyd's is concerned, Chaim is optimistic. He says Sieff is certain we will receive it very soon, but Hoofien+ is much more pessimistic. Abel is in favour of the loan, and says all he needs now are two letters from Chaim:

1) Promising to do all he can after the State is established to see that the debt will be taken over by the State:

2) Promising also that the Anglo-Palestine Bank will be recognized as the bank of the Jewish State, when this is established.

In arranging this loan now I am doing something big not only from the economic standpoint but also from the political aspect. The loan will not only enable us to improve the economic situation and expand settlement, but will also have a good psychological effect on other branches of the economy and will increase our political strength vis-a-vis the British Government and the Arabs.

Chaim is depressed — not without reason — by Meir Grossman's trick in leaking the document* — Isaac Naiditch+ told him that two of Grossman's friends came to him and assured him that Grossman obtained this document from Hexter. I doubt whether Hexter would do anything stupid, although he is capable of other foolish things. Chaim wants to set up a small committee to conduct an enquiry in the office and other places and to find out how the document came into Grossman's hands.

Chaim himself is leaving for Palestine on October 30.

This morning I sent a telegram to the Actions Committee in Tel Aviv saying that I'll return in another two weeks.

Perhaps I should add a word here about my own position. I am still functioning as a member of the Zionist Executive. If Mrs Jacobs doesn't take a final decision about joining the Executive by the time I arrive in Palestine, I will not serve on the Jewish Agency Executive, and then I will have to decide whether I can continue as a member of the Zionist Executive.

*See page 146 (bottom).

150

While in New York I explained to Mrs Jacobs that my feelings about not being able to serve together with her on the Executive have nothing to do with my personal attitude and her. On the contrary, from a personal viewpoint I favour her nomination, both because she herself deserves to be on the Executive and because it is important to have a woman serving on this body, especially as she will represent American Zionism and Hadassah, the largest and most important Zionist organization in the United States. But I cannot accept that Warburg should nominate anyone for the Executive who was not elected at the Zionist Congress. This would strike a dangerous blow at the sovereignty of the Congress and harm morale within the Zionist Organization, and I will never agree to it under any condition.

This winter I intend concentrating on the fundamental problems connected with the creation of the State: the question of the constitution, arrangements for immigration, the way land will be organized and relations with the Arabs.

There are other basic questions which we should examine at once: the economy, defence and the position of the Zionist Organization after the State has been established.

In my opinion, we should immediately set up several committees to study these questions. We should quickly work out an overall plan of action, along general lines, for organizing the State and its activities.

In Geneva Moshe and I visited the director of the International Labour Office and discussed the affiliation of Palestine. At the moment this is impossible, because the ILO's constitution makes no reference to Mandatory territories and only accepts independent states if they belong to the League of Nations.

London
October 5, 1937.

This morning I received the first letter you've written to me since you returned home. Better late than never. Since my last letter to you there have been great and possibly crucial changes in the situation. There has been a development which

151

is new, and in any event sudden and dramatic, although it comes eighteen months late. The Government has now done what we demanded it should do at the beginning of May, 1936. But here too I say: better late than never. You know more about this than me, because you are on the spot. I see from the cables that things are quiet in Palestine at present, and that the British fear of the Mufti was imaginary.

Naturally it is not absolutely certain that this quiet will continue. But in my opinion this depends not on the Arabs but on the Government. The Mufti will certainly not give in and will not stop his intrigues. But if the Government is not deterred and perseveres with its current policy, nothing will happen. The Arab masses are tired of all the confusion. Those who hate the Mufti are pleased, and the extremist youth will not dare to try anything, once they see the Government is showing a firm hand, because the Arab public at large will not encourage the extremists. So the main question is: will the Government continue its new strong policy?

No one has seen Wauchope, and I don't know whether he is coming back or what he thinks about the riots. For him the new development is a considerable defeat. If the present calm continues even though the Mufti has been outsted, it will become clear to everyone that Wauchope failed and deceived the Government.

The new committee which is supposed to come to Palestine will not arrive in October, as it was originally supposed to, but at the end of November. It will spend several months in the country. The British have told us that if the Arabs don't want to negotiate with the committee, the Government will set up the Jewish State, and the rest of Palestine will remain under British administration.

But after the downfall of the Mufti I don't think the Arabs will boycott the committee. Emir Abdullah+ wants partition, and so does Nashashibi+. And these two will now be the principal forces among the Arabs, as long as Wauchope does not bring the Mufti back.

Chaim saw Shuckburgh a few days ago, and he told Chaim he thinks that in May a decision will be taken on setting up a Jewish State, first by the British Parliament and then by the Council of the League of Nations. At first there will be a provisional Jewish Government, which will handle the three main things: immigration, defence and finance. The final arrangements will take several years. This doesn't bother me. The main thing is that we should control immigration.

But who knows what could still happen this winter?

The world situation is terrible. At the end of Eastern Asia there is one war, and at the end of Western Europe another war. Under these conditions, can peace be maintained?

At present all we can do is *to wait and see.*

I'm very worried about the economic position in Palestine. We are trying to raise a loan of £300,000 here, from Lloyds or Barclays, so that we can avert unemployment and strengthen the settlements and our security. We might know by next week if there is some hope of this loan coming through.

Chaim has asked me to stay here a little longer until the political situation becomes somewhat clearer. I was anxious to leave London this week and I certainly won't remain longer than October 18—20. I might even leave earlier.

London
October 5, 1937.

Dear Amos,

I would like to make some comments on the conflict you say you feel between your logic and your emotions over the question of the State. There is no room in politics for sentimental considerations. The only thing we must weigh up is: what is desirable and good for us, what is the path that leads to the goal, what policy will strengthen us and what policy will weaken us.

I think I too have 'feelings'. Without these feelings I would not have been able to carry on our difficult work during all these years. My feelings are not hurt in the slightest by the idea of establishing a Jewish State, even a small State. Naturally, I don't like the partitioning of the country. But the country which is being partitioned is in effect not in our hands. It is in the hands of the Arabs and the British. We

153

control only a small percentage, less than we are being offered for a Jewish State. If partition is implemented we shall receive more than we hold at present: but less, far less, than what we are entitled to and what we want. True. But the question is: would we receive more if there were no partition? What we want is not that the country should be whole and unified, but that the whole and unified country should be *Jewish*. I would not be happy in a whole Palestine if it were Arab.

For us the present situation is the kiss of death. We want to change it. But how to bring about this change? How to have our own country?

And here the key question is: would the formation of a Jewish State help us turn the country into a Jewish one, or would it hamper this?

I am an enthusiastic advocate of the Jewish State, even if it involves partitioning Palestine now, because I work on the assumption that a partial Jewish State will not be the end, but the beginning. When we acquire 1,000 or 10,000 dunams of land we are happy. Because this acquisition of land is important not only for its own sake, but because through it we are increasing our strength, and every increase in our strength helps us to acquire the whole country. The formation of a State, even if it is only a partial State, will be the greatest increase of strength we could have today, and it will constitute a powerful lever in our historic effort to redeem the country in its entirety.

We will bring into this State all the Jews we can possibly hold; we firmly believe we'll be able to bring in over two million. We will set up a varied Jewish economy, agricultural, industrial and maritime. We will organize a highly effective defence force, a first-class army — I have no doubt that our army will be one of the best in the world — and then I am certain we will be able to settle in all the other parts of the country, whether through agreement and mutual understanding with our Arab neighbours or in another way.

We must always remember the basic facts which bring us to settle in Palestine. These are not the British Mandate or the Balfour Declaration. These are results of our settlement urge, not causes of it. Some of these facts might not have

154

emerged if there had not been a world war, or if it had finished differently. But there are certain fundamental historical facts which will not change as long as Zionism is not implemented in full. These are:

1) The plight of the Jews in the Diaspora, which drives them to Palestine with an iron determination;
2) The comparative emptiness of the country. This gives it a great potential for settlement, which the Arabs do not need and are not capable of exploiting (because they do not have to). There is no problem of Arab immigration, there is no Arab Diaspora, and the Arabs are not being persecuted. They have a homeland, and a large one too.
3) The Jews' creative ability (which is the fruit of Reason 1 above). We have the ability to make the desert bear fruit, to create industry, to build an economy, to develop a culture, to conquer the sea and the air with the aid of science and the pioneering impulse.

We will be able to penetrate deeper into the country if we have a State. We will be stronger vis-a-vis the Arabs. We will be able to build more quickly. And the more the Jewish strength grows in the country, the more the Arabs will realize that it is impossible to oppose us and not worthwhile doing so, and that, on the contrary, they will be able to derive considerable benefits from the Jews, not only material but also political.

I am not dreaming, and I don't like war. And I still believe, more today than before the possibility of the State emerged, that when we are numerous and strong the Arabs will realize that it would be best for them to work together, to enjoy our assistance, and to allow us to settle in all parts of the country, of their own free will. The Arabs have many countries which are under-populated, which are undeveloped and weak, and which cannot stand up to their external enemies. Syria could not survive for a day in the face of Turkey, if it wasn't for France. The same applies to Iraq. And it will be true also of the new State. All of them need the protection of France or Britain. But this protection means enslavement and dependence. The Jews could be equal allies, true friends, and not conquerors and tyrants.

Let's assume that the Negev won't be allocated to the

Jewish State. Then it will simply remain arid. The Arabs are unable to develop it, and they don't need to. They have enough deserts of their own, and they haven't enough people, money and initiative. It's very possible that in return for our financial, military, organizational and scientific help they will agree that we develop and build up the Negev. But they might not agree. A nation does not always act in accordance with logic and commonsense and practical advantage. So it's possible that the Arabs might act from sterile nationalist feelings and will say to us: We don't want your honey or your sting. We would rather the Negev remained a desert than that it should be settled by Jews. And then we shall have to speak to them in another language. And we will have another language then — which we should not have without a State. Because we won't be able to tolerate large empty areas remaining uninhabited when they could take tens of thousands of Jews.

Of course if this happens we shall have to deal not only with the Arabs of Palestine. It's quite possible that the Arabs of the neighbouring countries will come to their aid against us. But we shall be more powerful. Not only because we'll be better organized and equipped, but because behind us is a force which is greater in both quality and quantity. We have a reservoir of millions in the Diaspora. The entire younger generation of Jews in Poland, Rumania, America and other countries will flock to us in the case of a dispute with the Arabs, which I hope and pray won't take place. The Jewish State will not rely only on the Jews living in it, but on the Jewish people all over the world, on the many millions who want to settle in Palestine and who *must* settle there. There are no millions of Arabs who want to or have to come to Palestine in the same way.

This is why I think the formation of a Jewish navy and the construction of a Jewish port is so important. The sea is the bridge between the Jews in Palestine and the Diaspora — the millions of Jews all over the world. And we must prepare things so that in any hour of need we will be able to bring to Palestine, in our own ships, with our sailors, thousands of young people. And we must prepare these young people for all possible tasks in Palestine, even if they remain in the

Diaspora for the moment.

I am sure that setting up a Jewish State, even in part of the country, will make this possible. And so I do not have any conflict between my mind and my heart. Both of them tell me: Erect a Jewish State at once, even if it is not in the whole land. The rest will come in the course of time. It must come.

Show this letter to your mother and sisters.

London
October 7, 1937.

This morning I received your long letter written on September 29. It was on a plane which sank in the sea. But they saved the letter, even though it was wet, and put it in a new envelope *On His Majesty's Service* with my address on it. That's why it was delayed until today.

Although many things in your letter made me very sad, I was happier to read them than I have been for a long time. I was happy because you were telling me about your feelings and experiences. You don't know how thirsty I am for words of friendship from you. I don't understand why you felt bad in London and Zurich. I knew and sensed that you were unhappy. But I didn't know why, and you didn't tell me. I am grateful to you for writing to me about it now.

Life, Paula, life is difficult altogether. My life in particular is very hard. I have never complained, and I am not complaining now. I know what life is all about, and I know that others suffer even more than I do. All my life I have tried to do my work and to take my share as best I could, whether this was easy or difficult, safe or dangerous. But I am very lonely. All my life I have been alone, although I have many comrades and friends. Perhaps my nature is to blame. But the fact is that I am a lonely man, and sometimes I find this almost intolerable. I stand alone, and a heavy burden rests on me. Sometimes this burden becomes too heavy. Yet I carry it with love, and with all my power. When I am duty-bound to strengthen the party, encourage the comrades, bolster their confidence, I occasionally find myself eaten up

157

by bitter feelings which I show to no one. I do not think my comrades have ever heard any complaint from me. All the same, it is sometimes too hard to bear, and a terrible feeling of loneliness overcomes me as if I was living in a desert, buried inside its bare emptiness.

So every sign of love and friendship on your part is precious to me.

I won't write anything now about my membership of the Executive, as when I get home I'll explain it all to you. I don't agree with what you say about Chaim and Moshe, particularly about the latter . . . The things we hold dear are dear to him also, and he performs his task as well as he can. His ability is limited, as the ability of each of us is limited to some degree. He is not a man of vision; his thinking is not profound; he sometimes fails to comprehend complicated problems. He does not always see far enough, and he is unable to decide things which require considerable intellectual and moral courage. But he knows his job, he is talented and many-sided, he is devoted and loyal. And I think Moshe himself knows that he needs to be directed, and more or less accepts this.

Chaim, naturally, is a different kind of man. He is a great man, with great advantages and great drawbacks . . . But he must be taken as he is, because no one else can do what he does. We must preserve him, and must also watch over him. But he is essential for our movement, and I try to keep him from the kind of errors and failures of which he is unfortunately capable.

I am not in the least interested in how Chaim behaves towards me. I am not dependent on him, and I don't need any special relationship on his part. I see him as an important tool for our whole enterprise. And I am interested only in this enterprise, and in nothing else.

I'm leaving here next week. On October 16 I sail on the *Esperia* from Genoa, and in another fortnight I'll be at home.

Port Said
January 23, 1938.

The ship leaves here at 2 a.m. The moment I arrived at Kantara the ship went through the Suez Canal. And although I only took the train from Kantara three-quarters of an hour later, I arrived in Port Said two and a half hours before the ship, which berthed at 10.30 p.m. after coming from India. It is not at all like the Italian and French ships which sail the Mediterranean, but a huge ship rather like the great Atlantic liners. I have a special cabin, large and comfortable. And I think I'll be able to have a good rest during the next four days.

Nearly all the passengers are British. A few are Indian.

The papers here are still pre-occupied with the wedding of the Egyptian King. I won't hear any news from Palestine for the next five days, and I hope that nothing happens during this time.

Mediterranean Sea
January 27, 1938.

There is an acquaintance of mine on the ship — Redcliffe Salaman* from England, who is returning from a scientific conference in India. He was in Palestine four years ago, and is opposed to partition. He says there are other Jews on board, but they don't want people to know they are Jews. Good luck to them.

London
February 1, 1938.

My little Renana,

I am really sorry I won't be in Tel Aviv when the port is opened to passengers. A long time ago I spoke to the High

---

*Redcliffe Salaman, F.R.S. (1874-1955): Director of the Potato Virus Research Station at Cambridge; Governor of Hebrew University.

159

Commissioner about this, and he promised to let passengers travel to and from the city. When I come home I'll try to take a boat which sails to Tel Aviv.

Write and tell me what you saw and what you felt on the great day when the Tel Aviv port was opened.

I don't know how much longer I shall be in London. Weizmann will be here tomorrow, and perhaps by next week the political situation might be clearer.

Tomorrow night I might meet the new High Commissioner* who is coming to Palestine in March.

When I come home I'll bring the things you asked for. But why do you want artificial flowers?

Has Mother gone into hospital yet?

London
February 18, 1938.

I haven't heard a word from you since I left. You don't seem to realize how much this saddens me and hurts me. I learned only from Renana's letter that you are going into hospital. You didn't even write to me about this.

I left Palestine more worried about the way things are going than I've ever been before. All our work over the last fifty or sixty years, all our hopes for hundreds of years, for two thousand years, are in danger. The situation in Palestine is difficult, and is becoming worse every day. Unemployment is increasing, and the acts of terror show no sign of ending. The Government in London, we were told, is thinking of liquidating the Mandate. The Zionist movement is confused. The plight of the Jews in the Diaspora is dreadful. Yesterday Germany, today Rumania, tomorrow Austria and Poland. I left for London with a heavy heart. The work here is far from easy and demands complete concentration of mind and will and spiritual strength. Paula, I beg you to write to me. Don't cause me such sorrow.

Weizmann arrived here yesterday. The news he brought me is not too encouraging. But our cause is not lost. It was a bad mistake to leave London unattended during November and

*Sir Harold MacMichael, High Commissioner 1938-1944.

160

December. Brodetsky is not the man to handle top-level political activities and he doesn't spend all the time watching the situation. It will be difficult now to repair the damage done during these weeks.

Yesterday I met our new High Commissioner at dinner. I had a long talk with him, but not about the matters that concern us. He naturally doesn't want to express an opinion before he comes to Palestine. As a man he doesn't make a bad impression. But I don't think he's another Wauchope.

It was a pity I couldn't be in Palestine when Wauchope left. Although during these two years he gave us a lot of trouble, he also did a lot of good things, and he is not an enemy of ours.

London
February 23, 1938.

Yesterday I met the new High Commissioner again. The first time was at a dinner party a week ago. We talked a lot then, but not about politics. Yesterday I had my first political talk with him. He worked for years among the Arabs (in the Sudan), and speaks Arabic. Because he knows the Arabs so well I thought he might be against us. But my talk with him yesterday has largely erased this fear. He knows the Arabs and despises them, and also has a low opinion of their strength and importance. What he thinks of us — this is a different matter. He makes a pleasant personal impression, and in the course of these two meetings we 'became friends'.

We met yesterday for dinner at Amery's (the former Colonial Secretary). The others there were Jimmy Rothschild, Chaim, (Sir Archibald) Sinclair (leader of the Liberals), Clement Attlee (leader of the Labour Party), (Josiah) Wedgwood+ and (Herbert) Sidebotham+. I sent Moshe the diary in which I wrote down the entire conversation, and you'll probably receive a copy.

We have decided to call a meeting of the Actions Committee in London on March 8. So I'll probably return home in the middle of March, not later than the 20th.

I'm sorry I'm not in Tel Aviv today, when the new port is

161

opened to passenger traffic. I would have liked to say goodbye to Wauchope. Perhaps I will meet him here in London, when he returns completely to private life.

The Middle East situation is still unclear. Eden's resignation has caused great confusion in Britain, and this makes our work harder. Eden never received Chaim all the time he was in office. But before Chaim arrived in London this time he received an assurance that Eden would see him. And now suddenly he is no longer Foreign Secretary. The other Ministers are also busy because of the crisis. So it's all very difficult, and I want Chaim to stay here much longer than he originally intended to.

London
February 24, 1938.

I'm enclosing a copy of the letter sent to the Colonial Secretary this week. I wrote the letter, and Chaim signed it. It seems that the Government will soon take a decision on this matter. I hope we'll obtain something, even if it's not the whole of what we are asking. I consider the struggle for immigration the most important thing at the moment. I am in favour of a Jewish State, as I was before. But it's clear that this won't happen soon, and meanwhile immigration is the key issue.

London
March 1, 1938.

I received your letter written after you left hospital, and I need not tell you how much it hurt me to read what you wrote. After this it is difficult for me to remain here, and if it was not for the session of the Zionist Actions Committee in another fortnight I would return home at once. I cannot come back now. But the moment this meeting is over I'll return to Palestine.

Yesterday Stephen Wise, Louis Lipsky and Bernard

Joseph* arrived here. Joseph is going back to Palestine today, and he promised to give you regards from me. There has been no change in our political situation. You probably read in the papers that the new committee has been nominated, but it won't leave for Palestine before the end of April. The new High Commissioner is due to arrive the day after tomorrow, and whatever happens I don't think he'll be worse than those who had the job before him.

As I wrote to you, I've met him twice, and the impression he made upon me was not bad at all. I think we'll be able to work with him, if only the Colonial Office here in London don't create fresh problems for us.)From what I've heard about him, it seems that he is a dynamic and firm man. And I don't think he is an enemy of ours. Soon there will also be changes in the military administration. Wavell will be replaced by General Haining, who is a friend of ours. And with two new people like this at the head of the British administration, the atmosphere in Palestine should change a little for the better.

I hope that the initiative we have taken now will produce some results. But I am anxious about the economic situation in Palestine. Can we keep going until things start improving? Lack of work, lack of building, people unable to make a living — everything is getting worse, judging from the reports I receive. I'm afraid that as long as there is no decisive political change the situation won't improve. And we must try to speed up the final solution.

London
March 16, 1938.

I didn't write to you last week, because all my time was taken up by the session of the Zionist Actions Committee. In Palestine there was strong opposition to our holding this meeting, and particularly to choosing London as the venue. It is difficult for the leaders of the party and the community to leave the country at present: the security and economic

*Bernard (Dov) Joseph, (b. 1899): Legal Adviser to Jewish Agency Executive. Appointed Israel Military Governor of Jerusalem in 1948.

situation does not allow them to absent themselves now. Some people advanced another reason for opposing the meeting: they feared that the political debate over partition would flare up, and then the division within our movement would increase. Others were afraid that the Actions Committee would propose changes in the decisions taken by the Zionist Congress at Zurich, and that this could lead to a rift in the movement.

However, I stood firm and insisted that the meeting take place, and in London, although I was aware of all the arguments against it. There is growing confusion and uncertainty in the Zionist movement, particularly in Europe and America, and all sorts of rumours are flying about suggesting that the British Government is about to end its assistance to the Zionist cause. Those who want a Jewish State were afraid the Peel Plan was about to be dropped. Those who oppose the State feared the Zionist Executive was ready to make far-reaching concessions so that a small state would be established. And I felt it was necessary and timely to give the leaders of the Zionist movement in the various countries a true report about the situation, both the external situation and the internal one. We had to clarify our stand, and it was particularly important to meet our American comrades who could not come to Palestine or did not want to do so.

And there was another vital matter: our attitude during the difficult struggle over immigration, in which we will try to annul the political limitation on Jewish immigration and to return to the principle of immigration levels being fixed according to economic absorptive capacity. And every possible kind of pressure on the British Government had to be applied. We knew the Government was discussing this question and could take a decision at any moment. And we wanted to enlist the entire weight of the movement and to apply it in London.

But we were too late. The British Cabinet took the decision the very day the Actions Committee opened its session. We couldn't know this in advance. True, there was no guarantee that the Actions Committee's session would help in the battle over immigration. But it was our duty to do all we could to increase the pressure on the Government as soon as possible.

And there was a third thing: important political negotiations had taken place. Several points raised during these negotiations had changed, and we wanted the entire Zionist movement to know what was happening so that it could reach its own decision. I wanted to return to Palestine before the session, so that Moshe could come to London and report on developments in Palestine. But the comrades insisted firmly that I should take part in the Actions Committee meeting, and so Moshe had to stay at home.

Before the meeting opened I was stunned to hear that our comrades who had criticized the meeting — Berl, Tabenkin, Idelson (Bar-Yehuda)+ and others — had decided not to come. I wrote a long letter to Berl today about this, and am enclosing a copy for you.

Now, after the meeting has taken place, I see that I was right. It is a long time since we've had such a comradely and constructive meeting. Although the discussion did not produce any new ideas, it cleared the air. The anti-State members did not change their minds (although some people at the meeting did switch camps), but they came to realize that it is not such a simple issue, and that the Executive is not selling Zionism down the river and is not ready to make concessions freely. I have never seen such a warm atmosphere at an Actions Committee session. After the political debate, all the resolutions were adopted unanimously, and in his closing address Ussishkin expressed his satisfaction with the stand taken by Weizmann.

For me there was another purpose in calling the session. In recent months there have been rumours of Jewish-Arab negotiations, and several people (Magnes+, Hyamson+ and others) have indeed tried their hand at this. It was necessary to tell the others what the real facts were, once and for all, and to stop the activities of 'those who pursue peace', which are endangering our whole political stance. This could be done only at the Administrative Committee of the Jewish Agency, and this Committee could meet only in London. I wanted this Committee to forbid any negotiations without the agreement of the Executive. This resolution was approved unanimously by the Administrative Committee, after I had given it all the details of these talks. (I've written you a long and detailed letter about this).

Meanwhile Ormsby-Gore has made public his new letter on immigration and the decision it contains. We haven't got all we demanded, but we've obtained something.

1) The overall political maximum has been abolished for the present. So now there is no longer an upper ceiling for Jewish immigration.

2) The number of certificates reserved for people with capital (1,000 Palestine Pounds) has been increased. During the last eight months we received 900 of these certificates. Now we will be given 2,000 in the next six months.

3) The restriction on the immigration of students and young people has been lifted. On the other hand, the number of workers allowed in has been reduced. During the last eight months we received 2,200 permits for workers. Now we won't be able to get more than 1,000. But the reason, to our regret, is the high level of unemployment in Palestine.

It is clear from Ormsby-Gore's communication that the Government intends to carry out the partition plan in earnest. But we heard about this before the communication was made public. I don't know whether the Government will stand firm all along the line. But they assure us that it won't take as long as we thought it would earlier, when Ormsby-Gore's letter was released at the beginning of January.

Weizmann left for Paris today, and he will be in Palestine next week.

I have another two or three days' work here. Then I shall spend a day or two in Paris and should be home at the end of March.

The new committee will probably arrive in Palestine at the end of April, and will keep us busy until the summer.

Meanwhile there has been the great tragedy of Austria, and the whole world is full of gunpowder. Who knows if we are not facing a new world catastrophe, more terrible than the one in 1914. But we in Palestine cannot do anything to avert it, and we must prepare ourselves for the difficult days we ourselves shall have to face.

London
September 20, 1938.

Last night I took part in a talk with M.M.* for the first time. During his recent meeting with Chaim it was decided that the three of us should meet at M.M.'s farm in Essex on Saturday. But meanwhile Neville Chamberlain flew to Munich, and when he returned the Cabinet sat for days at a time, at first by itself and then with the French, ¡ and · finally on its own again. So the meeting was postponed until last night.

What has happened in the interim has not improved our position. The surrender of the two large democracies to the Nazi plague, the hand-over of Czechoslovakia, the resultant increase in Hitler's prestige — all these must leave a strong impression on the Arabs, and because of them Hitler's and Mussolini's agents in the Middle East will find their work easier.

Leon Blum put the situation in a nutshell:

'Chamberlain flew from London to discuss a fair and honourable arrangement, and returned from Berchtesgaden with an ultimatum from the Fuehrer in his pocket. The British Government gave in to the ultimatum, and the French Government fell into line. I don't yet know what Czechoslovakia's reply will be. But it is obvious that Hitler has defeated England and France. The danger of war might have passed. But in these circumstances I, who have never ceased fighting for peace, cannot feel any great joy, *and I am torn between the relief of a coward and a burning feeling of shame.*'

It's hard to predict how public opinion in Britain will react to the latest development. Blum's feelings are undoubtedly shared by the best people in Britain. But even if the Labour Party and the Liberals, and perhaps even Churchill's faction

*Malcolm MacDonald, the new Colonial Secretary.

with the Tory Party, protest — the deed has been done, and Czechoslovakia will be smashed. Hitler's prestige will rise even higher in Germany and the world. America will retreat into its shell and will recoil in disgust from the affairs of Europe. The Central European countries will hasten to make peace with the Nazis, and a new and terrible threat will face the Jews of Europe.

The talk last night took place in Chaim's home and lasted from nine to twelve. I arrived an hour earlier and had dinner with Baffy* at Chaim's place. Baffy did not take part in the discussion with M.M., although she stayed with Vera** in her room until after midnight. When we spoke about the events of today, Baffy burst into hysterical tears. She was utterly depressed and humiliated not only about the despicable hand-over of Czechoslovakia, but also hurt in an almost personal sense by the treachery of her friends, who had assured her only the day before that it was quite out of the question, and that if Neville were to surrender, heaven forbid, they would leave the Cabinet without a qualm. But no one left the Cabinet, and Baffy felt her friendship with them and her faith in them were hollow. When she had calmed down a little she cried out proudly: 'I'm not English!' (She is Scottish. But she forgot that our 'friend' is also not 'English' . . .)

M.M. opened our talk with Czechoslovakia. This time the Germans have a *case:* Sudetenland should belong to Germany . . . There are two opinions about Hitler. One says: Yesterday Austria, today Czechoslovakia, tomorrow Poland or Alsace, the day after tomorrow the Colonies — and eventually the whole world. The other says: Hitler is an intelligent and practical man, who wants to free the Rhine area and to annex Austria and Sudetenland, and nothing more. He, M.M., accepts the second view. The arrangement with Hitler ensures peace in the world.

Chaim asked him: Have you read *Mein Kampf?* (While I think to myself: If people like this decide the fate of the world, heaven help us!)

We moved on to the matters that concern us. (In my

*Blanche Dugdale (see glossary).
**Mrs. Weizmann.

168

opinion Czecholsovakia also has a great deal to do with us). I will try to sum up the conversation, in particular M.M.'s remarks, because it was a very poor example of how to conduct a discussion. Chaim spoke in a tired manner, without any inspiration, and not to the point, even though I had tried to prepare him beforehand, orally and in writing, and had given him an outline of the main points.

M.M. apologized for not being able to think about Palestine during the last few days. The lengthy Cabinet meetings and handling the Dominions (the Secretary for the Dominions, Lord Stanley, is out of London) had taken up all his time. For this reason he does not think he will be able to add anything new.

After studying the McMahon Correspondence* he has the feeling that the Arabs have not been given a fair deal. The promises contradict one another. It could be said that Palestine was promised to the Arabs. In any event, the Arabs had reason to think that this was their country.

He doesn't know what the committee will propose. Perhaps it had been a great mistake not to implement the Peel Commission's proposal right away. The delay caused the Arab resistance to grow and crystallize, and now it was more determined and embraced the entire Arab and Moslem world. The Moslems of India are firmly against partition. He is not interested in the opinion of the Palestinian Arabs. It would be possible not to take them into account. But their propaganda has been successful, and the opposition to partition is alarming. Hitler and Mussolini are conducting active propaganda campaigns in the Middle East, and if war breaks out the Arab and Moslem world could rise up against Britain, and the British Empire would be in danger.

'Aren't you to blame for not doing anything against this propaganda and for not explaining your attitude to your Arab allies?' Chaim asked.

*The Correspondence conducted in 1915-16 between Sir Henry McMahon, High Commissioner in Egypt, and Sharif Husain, of Mecca, on the terms upon which the Arabs would side with the Allies. In 1939, the Arab and British delegations of a joint Anglo-Arab Committee, set up to enquire into the interpretation of the Correspondence, failed to agree. The British delegation, led by the Lord Chancellor, maintained that 'on a proper construction of the Correspondence Palestine was in fact excluded' from the areas in which the Arab was to secure independence.

'Possibly. But this is the situation.'

He thinks we should look for another solution. A mistake has been made in the tempo of immigration. The number of people coming in was too high. The Arabs became frightened, and this fear should be removed. The rate of immigration should be slowed down — at least for a time. We will continue to hold the Mandate. The principle of economic absorptive capacity should be restored, formally speaking. But the former mistakes should be avoided, and we should agree to limit immigration in practice until a Jewish-Arab-British agreement is brought about.

'Why should the Arabs give their agreement,' I asked, 'especially after they see that the riots forced the British Government to declare that the Mandate could not be implemented? And when, although you accepted the Royal Commission's proposal for partition, the Arabs forced you to abandon this plan?'

'The Arabs of Palestine will not agree. I am not thinking of an agreement with them, but with Ibn Saud. He is the greatest Arab leader, with much moral and political power. Ibn Saud has tremendous influence in the Moslem world and in India, and he must be persuaded to reach an agreement and to reconcile himself to the National Home.'

'Why should Ibn Saud agree to this?'

'We will persuade him, and perhaps you can also reach an understanding with him,' he added, with a naivete which may or may not have been genuine.

Chaim pointed out that Ibn Saud's opposition is partly motivated by hatred for Abdullah, because he is afraid that partition would strengthen the Hashemite Emir. He, Ibn Saud, was pressing the British Government for political and territorial concessions on the border of Hejaz and Transjordan, and the British Government could no doubt easily compensate him in this way.

M.M. admitted that this conflict exists, but added that Ibn Saud is opposed to the establishment of a Jewish State in principle. Palestine is an Arab country, and he does not want to see part of an Arab territory transferred to a foreign people. If Ibn Saud declares a holy war, he could rock the Empire . . .

170

'And why should he agree to a National Home?'

'The National Home would be under a British Mandate. Naturally the National Home should be established slowly. The speed with which it is being done is what creates the problems. The original intention didn't take into account such a fast tempo. No one foresaw at that time how things would turn out in Germany and Austria. Even Smuts+ spoke about generations.'

'Only 400,000 Jews after 20 years — do you call that a fast tempo?'

'Yes. No one dreamed the development would be so quick.'

'Didn't the Royal Commission state that the intention behind the Balfour Declaration was the possibility of a Jewish State in the entire area of historical Palestine?' I asked.

'Yes. But no time was laid down. They thought this would be done during several generations. They didn't mean to make Palestine a refuge for immigrants.'

Chaim pointed out that even before the war the focal point of the Zionist Congresses had been the speeches by Max Nordau on the plight of the Jews in the Diaspora. The deterioration in the situation of Jewry today could hardly be a pretext for cutting down immigration.

M.M. seemed sure that he was comforting and reassuring us by saying that he wanted to see a large Jewish community in Palestine, and possibly even a majority and a Jewish State, but only if this was done slowly, without undue haste. At the moment, he said, it was important to calm things down in Palestine. The National Home did not depend on numbers. A large immigration would only shock the Arab world. Ibn Saud would not tolerate 50,000 Jews a year going to Palestine. We could not push him into the arms of Italy. If immigration were stepped up Ibn Saud would become alarmed.

'Was Ibn Saud alarmed in 1935?'

'No. But meanwhile there have been riots, and the Mufti has been conducting widespread propaganda. Ibn Saud is afraid not only of Palestine being flooded, but of the possibility that his own country might be invaded. We must allay the Arabs' fears.'

171

Chaim said: 'This means suffocating the National Home. And at this moment in time — when every day a fresh disaster hits the Jewish people.'

M.M. returned once more to his idea (he must have learned Hyamson's letter by heart!) that Palestine is not a home for refugees, that this wasn't the intention, that the Arabs have to be placated, etc. Samuel Hoare* was reading the report of the Royal Commission once more and could see the mistakes which had been made. The officials should be replaced.

'And perhaps it is the *system* which should be changed?' I suggested. 'Instead of delaying the building of the National Home and limiting immigration, we should speed up the immigration of large numbers of Jews within a short time, so as to remove from the Arabs' minds the idea that they can frighten us and destroy what we have done.'

'That is a declaration of war on the Arab world,' he answered me. 'We cannot keep a large army in Palestine. What happens in Palestine has strong repercussions in India, and all the Arab peoples will become our enemies.'

I pointed out to him that there is no need for a single English soldier to be sent to Palestine — and yet they would have an army of 100,000 men there. We could bring them from America, Poland and Palestine itself. All we needed from Britain was equipment and training.

'We can only talk about this in the event of war,' he replied.

'When war breaks out it will be too late, because our young men who live in Poland will be conscripted into the Polish army. We must prepare in time.'

He didn't reply to this.

Chaim commented on the fact that the province of Alexandretta had been removed from Syria without any protest by the Arab world. He also spoke about Iraq, Syria and Egypt, and said they interfere in the affairs of Palestine only because the British representatives do not react in the right way.

M.M. stood firm: 'It is essential to reach an agreement with Ibn Saud. If he became reconciled to the National Home, the

*Foreign Secretary 1935, First Lord of the Admiralty 1936-37, Home Secretary 1937-39.

the Arab rulers, in order to give them a status equal to you. There is a plan to have parity, non-dependence, so that it will not matter who is in the majority and who in the minority.'

He himself, M.M. said, could not decide anything at the moment. If the international situation became stable and he was freed from the anxiety of the Czechoslovakian crisis, he would concentrate on thinking about Palestine and would try to put his thoughts down on paper. In a few days' time we should meet again. He is very friendly with the Prime Minister. He hopes that if he reaches any conclusions he will be able to carry the P.M. with him. That was what happened on the Irish question. And if both of them agreed on something, he had no doubt that the Cabinet would concur. But at the moment he could not decide anything. (I remembered that when I met Ramsay MacDonald at Chequers seven or eight years ago he said the same thing, in almost identical words. And Malcolm had been present).

During the conversation M.M. received two phone calls from the Dominions Office. The second time they told him there was a reply from Prague. It was neither positive nor negative, but was more inclined towards the positive. At midnight he rose and went off. The two women came in, and the four of us went on talking until half-past one.

It seems to me that the situation is more or less clear: the Government has decided to place us in the hands of the Arabs. No State and no immigration. Malcolm has learned a lesson from 1930: not to use *formulas* that could harm us. Why should he announce that the Mandate has been annulled, or that a political limit has been placed on immigration? He can do these things without spelling them out in precise terms.

This surrender to the Arabs is in line with Britain's conduct on other world matters: Ethiopia, Spain, China, Czechoslovakia. If it is true, as M.M. wants us to believe, that they are afraid of the Arabs and the Moslems, does it mean that they have received an ultimatum from Hitler and Mussolini? Helping the Jews is not a profitable business nowadays. Hitler has broken the power of the Jews — and the hand-over of Czechoslovakia has finished the job. All the small nations of Europe, who despaired of the League of

175

Nations after the conquest of Ethiopia and the failure of sanctions, still pinned their hopes on the two large democracies. Now they are forced to lose faith in even this broken reed. Hitler will take over the whole of Europe. Thanks to Hitler, Mussolini will enjoy greater prestige in the Arab world. The Jews of Europe no longer have anyone to lean on. Anti-Semitism will increase, and England, this kind of England, will not want to quarrel with Hitler, Mussolini and the Arabs for our sake.

Chaim doesn't accept my pessimistic appraisal. But he doesn't seem to have understood the political significance of M.M.'s remarks in our earlier talks and particularly in the last one. It is difficult to guess whether this is a new development which is a by-product of the international situation in recent weeks, or a calculated policy, worked out during the last year or so, since Britain decided to aim at an agreement with Hitler and Mussolini. It's possible that the dispatch of the committee which studied partition was merely a smokescreen covering up a predetermined decision. Perhaps I am being too suspicious. But we cannot ignore the bitter truth that this is the present policy of the Colonial Secretary and it can be assumed that it is not his private opinion, but the opinion of his great friend who is at the helm.

Britain is now following the line of *real-politik,* like Hitler and Mussolini, without using their terminology. And we are the victims of the shift.

This afternoon I met Berl and David Hacohen+. I summed up our talk with M.M. and gave them my impressions. Then I asked Berl what we should do now, but I didn't agree with his answer. In his opinion there is only one thing we can do: summon the Actions Committee at once, tell them everything, and alert Jewry to the grave danger we are facing. When the Jewish people as a whole sees what lies ahead, it will find the strength to act.

I don't accept this advice, for the following reasons:

1) We can't tell the Zionist movement yet what the true situation is. Not so much because this would be incorrect protocol — the talks were private and confidential — but because they were not final and conclusive. From a political standpoint, they were only a monologue. M.M. was the only

one who really spoke. (It is true that Chaim did most of the talking during the last meeting. But most of his remarks were not to the point, and there was no *political* response to M.M.'s attitude. Even before this recent meeting I had a fairly clear idea of what M.M. was thinking, on the basis of Chaim's account — and I also knew how we should react to his statements. But the conduct of the discussion on our side was naturally in Chaim's hands, and I couldn't divert him to the required train of thought, despite the written notes I had given him before the meeting.)

2) We must first of all make our position clear to M.M. He must be made to realize that he cannot close our eyes with reassuring phrases. In our next discussion we must talk to him in plain language. We must tell him that the Jewish people are interested in one thing only: and this is *broad, widespread immigration,* which is the sole meaning and purpose of the National Home and the Mandate, and the only reason why we agreed to discuss the partition plan. Not immigration in the distant future, and not abstract formulas, but large-scale immigration *at once, now.* All the other proposals which are meant to replace immigration will merely hand the Yishuv over to the Arab terrorists and to the agents of Hitler and Mussolini in the Arab world.

From the talks held to date M.M. has no reason to think that this is our attitude. Of course there is no guarantee that making our stand crystal clear will change his view of the problem. But as long as he has not heard our reaction and replied to it, we cannot say honestly what the Government's final decision is going to be.

3) We might not be able to move the Government from its resolve. But the next four weeks will be fateful ones, and we should concentrate our efforts on influencing the Cabinet directly. The situation is too serious for us to intoxicate ourselves with pointless rhetoric. What will the Jewish people do now? I doubt very much whether *European* Jewry will want to attack Britain. The Jews of Poland, Rumania, Czechoslovakia (and Germany, I need hardly add) are so depressed and downtrodden by the anti-Semitic regimes under which they live that they will not be able to free themselves from the illusion that at least one Great Power is

177

friendly and will help them. But even if we assume that we can persuade the Jews of Poland, Rumania and so on to protest, the fact remains that protest and political war are only a means to an end — which is pressure on the Government. And we have to see how this pressure will pass through the various channels and reach the Government. Will Malcolm and Neville read an article in *Haint,* or will they hear the protest resolution adopted in Pinsk?

During these four weeks we must talk with the Government here in London. They know now that those who are talking with them are not just private individuals, but that they are speaking on behalf of a people whose plight and tragedy are far from imaginary.

London will be the nerve centre of the action during these four fateful weeks. In the first line of attack is the Cabinet. In the second line are our friends in Parliament and the press. They claim that they still do not know what the committee is thinking of doing. But in another two or three weeks they won't say this. Then we shall hear from them, and we shall tell them what is worrying us.

4) If we have centres of Jewish strength, then these are in Palestine and America. True, it is doubtful whether official America, i.e. Washington, will lift a finger to help us. It is also doubtful whether American Jewry will be ready to quarrel with officialdom at present. So America is a doubtful factor. But if all our efforts in London fail, we shall have to try to enlist whatever help we can in the United States.

Our main strength lies in Palestine, and in my opinion — which I've held for a long time — we might have to use the little power we control. The time for this has not yet come. For two reasons: 1) We are not yet facing the critical moment; 2) At present the main thing is to bolster our strength in the police force, in the army, in immigration as far as this is possible. The task of the hour is to increase our strength, not to use it.

So London is the focal point of our actions.

In our next talk with M.M. we must make another thing clear: that we will not tie ourselves to an agreement with Ibn Saud. Ibn Saud is the business of the British Government, as Mussolini is. We are talking with Arab leaders and politicians

178

from outside Palestine, and we will continue to do so in order to pave the way to a mutual understanding in Palestine. But we cannot accept Ibn Saud as a factor in Palestine. The British brought him in, and it is up to them to take him out again.

It is not our job to appease and soften him. It is not our duty, and it is beyond our power. This idea of a triple agreement — with Ibn Saud as the third rib — could become a hidden mine and a trap for us, and we should disown it at once as vigorously as we can.

The third matter we must take up with M.M. and his friends is the partition plan. As long as there is no official announcement saying that partition has finally been dropped, we should not make things easier for those who oppose the Jewish State.

The political picture in the world as a whole changes almost from day to day, and we must arm ourselves even more than before with two clear objectives: one for today and tomorrow (literally!), and one for the future. Not the *distant* future. No one knows what lies ahead for the world and for us. I can foresee global cataclysms which will turn the earth almost upside down. For me Zionism is the opposite of 'Eternal Israel'. Without brutal realism there can be no Zionist thinking. I am concerned only with the future which can be seen now. And this future is clear to me, despite my gloomy appraisal of the British Government's attitude to us. I see a situation in which England might go to war. I can't see any other chance, or any other way.

These two guiding objectives should be, in my opinion:

1) *For the present* — to increase our strength in Palestine: police, army, equipment, training — and immigration. And, as long as there is any chance of it — a Jewish State.

2) *For the future* — military co-operation with Britain in the Middle East.

Even if the partition plan is dropped in another two months, this does not put an end to it, in my opinion, and it could appear again in another six months or a year. Our experience with Britain should have taught us that there are very few *absolutely* final decisions.

I changed my room today. I remained on the same floor, and they gave me Room 573, with a window in the bathroom. I had both breakfast and lunch in my room. I bought some beef, tomatoes, cucumber, lettuce, eggs and cheese, and a few other things. I spent five shillings on food, and I think it should last me for three days. When I returned to the hotel last night from the station, I felt a terrible loneliness, as if everything was empty and hollow. I am used to being alone and to loneliness. But this time I feel displaced. Everything is drained out and silent. I wrote to Renana and to Geula and Amos. I poured out my heart to them, but this didn't make me feel any better.

There is no news from Palestine today. People here in England are rejoicing over the Munich agreement, which they think has averted a war. But I'm not happy about it. It's certainly good that there's no war. But this peace will cost us dear. Hitler has won a great victory, and his influence will increase all over the world. Nothing good will come out of this for the Jews and the workers.

How was the journey back? And whom did you see in Paris? Write to me before you leave for Marseilles.

Secret

I'm enclosing a copy of my letter to the Zionist Executive in Jerusalem. From it you will see how I see our situation today.

The dark days have gone, the European crisis is over, and the tragedy of Czechoslovakia has ended. The fear of war has been averted — for the moment. Hitler's army has entered Sudetenland, and Berlin is celebrating its great victory. In London also people applauded 'peace' and the makers of peace. So there *is* peace for the wicked! The official circles here are rejoicing and in a festive mood. They have averted a

Delegates to the Twenty-First Zionist Congress in Geneva receive news of the outbreak of World War II. Seated in the front row, left to right: Shertok (Sharett), Ben-Gurion, Weizmann, and Eliezer Kaplan.

Prime Minister Ben-Gurion signs the Declaration of Statehood - March 14, 1948. Moshe Shertok (Sharett) is on his right.

Ben-Gurion, aged eighty-three, speaking in London in 1969.

massacre of nations this time. Was there really a danger of war? Once the French and the British had decided to abandon Czechoslovakia, despite France's clear commitments and Britain's moral responsibility, I did not believe there would be war. True, Hitler ranted in his usual impudent manner after making England and France submit to him, and presented new demands which surprised and shocked Chamberlain. But it was fairly obvious to me that there would not be a war over these 'trifles', now that Czechoslovakia had been mangled.

A man who was in the middle of the crisis here in London all the time told me the shocking details about the despicable treachery towards Czechoslovakia by France and England. Naturally all of us are happy that war has not broken out. But this happiness is marred, because a heavy price has been paid for peace. The abandonment of Czechoslovakia and the surrender to Hitler point to a new shift in world politics, which has shown itself first in Britain and France. Confidence in the strong countries' commitments to the weaker countries has been completely upset. Hitler's international prestige has risen, and the nations of Central, Eastern and Southern Europe, and perhaps even Northern Europe, have no choice but to hitch themselves to the victor's waggon. France has been dealt a mortal blow, from which it may never recover. The League of Nations is dead. The Rome-Berlin axis will now split France from Britain.

Some people here think the British people will rebel against Chamberlain's new line. But I don't think so. Chamberlain played his cards cunningly. When people were angry about the agreement giving Sudetenland to Germany, he introduced the fear of war. They gave everyone gas masks, evacuated the children from London, dug shelters in Hyde Park day and night. They stirred up panic about London being bombed by Hitler's planes in a day or two. Then they suddenly declared it was peace, and there was a tremendous feeling of relief. No bombs, no destruction, no massacre, and the man in the street cheered 'the saviour of peace'. And the fate of Czechoslovakia, the future of Europe — all this was far, foreign, unreal. Peace is what you can feel with your hand. So now there is peace. And perhaps Britain can come

181

to terms with Germany. At whose expense? That's not important.

I've seen nothing in the press here about the plight of the refugees from Sudetenland: Jews, Germans, Czechs. Prague is full of refugees already. But who's looking after them, and who cares?

We Jews are not a factor in *these* world events. We cannot influence matters one way or the other. The British politicians have their own calculations, and we cannot do anything about them. The British Jews are scared. The English say the Jews wanted war. Mosley shouts it out loud, and certain semi-anti-Semites say it in a whisper. And no Jew has the courage to raise his voice and to say what he thinks, even in this free country.

But if we are not a factor in this situation, we are perhaps the first victim of this new shift. Soon not only the Jews of Czechoslovakia, but all the Jews of Europe, and perhaps also of Asia and America, will feel the effects of this victory by evil forces. Anti-Semitism will spread all over Europe. Those who seek friendship with the Nazis will cover up their atrocities, and perhaps even defend them. Political sympathy will lead to ideological bonds. And even if they won't accept all Hitler's doctrines, they will accept the gospel of anti-Semitism, which has existed since the creation of the world.

In addition to the worsening situation of the Jews in the Diaspora, I am afraid that the latest political events will also effect our position in Palestine. They handed Czechoslovakia over. Why shouldn't they do the same with us?

Mussolini has proclaimed himself the defender of Islam. In his Nuremberg speech Hitler shed crocodile tears over the plight of the Arabs. The Fascist Government does not trouble to conceal its vehement opposition to Zionism. Jewish Palestine constitutes a bulwark of the British Empire in the Eastern Mediterranean, which Mussolini considers 'our sea'. Hitler hates us in principle, and certainly doesn't want to increase the prestige of the German Jews. Both these factors are opposed to a Jewish State — the Italians because it is in Palestine, and the Germans because it would be Jewish. Perhaps those among us who are against partition will note that while they call for a Jewish country in the whole of Palestine, Italy and Germany are against a Jewish State in a part of the country.

I see the Jewish people facing unprecedented hardships in the near future. And Zionism will also undergo a trying ordeal. During the next four to six weeks we shall discover the British Government's intentions on Palestine. In any event, we shall know what the committee on partition recommends. The Government will find itself in a difficult spot if these recommendations are not too bad, and if we don't reject them right away. None of us knows yet what line the committee is taking. The Government tells us that it also doesn't know. You can believe this if you like. But I have the feeling that those in our ranks who oppose partition can sleep soundly. If the partition plan was not buried last winter in the negotiations with Mussolini, and then later in the talks with the Arab rulers, headed by Ibn Saud (whom the British now mention too frequently for my liking), then it can be assumed that the present committee will bury the plan, and the Government will come out of the entire episode with its hands clean. But I fear that not only is the Jewish State in danger, but immigration is also approaching a crisis.

I am speaking about facts. It may be that the Government has not yet determined its final stand: and British Cabinets never hurry to take up a *final* position, and have been known to change their minds if the circumstances change. But circumstances are not in our favour. If they change it will be even worse for us, and it would be best for us not to cherish any illusions, but to prepare for bad news. We will prepare for this eventuality not with impotence and a lack of spirit and defeatist sentiments, but with the courage and wisdom of desperate people who are fighting for their existence with their backs to the wall.

We must free ourselves from rhetoric and phrases which have outlived their day. Until now we could do only one thing in a crisis like this: shout. I personally have little faith in the value of shouting or screaming. This is not 1930 — not in Jewry and not in the world, not in Britain and not in Palestine.

In 1930, when Lord Passfield+ published his White Paper,

183

there was a minority Government in Britain, and many of its members were our friends. The leading men in the country were outside the Cabinet, and it suited them to protest against the actions of the weak, unloved Government. Simon*, Baldwin** and Hailsham*** protested against the White Paper, and Ramsay MacDonald+ wrote a letter which softened Passfield's hostile recommendations. But now Britain has a firm, popular Government, with an enormous majority in Parliament and considerable newly-acquired prestige. The people think that this Government saved Britain and the world from destruction. The mood in the country is 'realistic', and people's ears are closed to demands for justice. Old promises and commitments are no longer honoured. They are being re-interpreted. And those who are 're-interpreting' them are also those who made the commitment, not us. And there is no court of appeal, as some naive people among us still believe. There is no judge and no justice these days, and it's each man for himself!

We cannot rule out the possibility that they might abandon us, as they abandoned Ethiopia, China, Spain and now Czechoslovakia. I don't say we should despair, and we should certainly continue our struggle along the entire political front. But we shouldn't ignore the very worst possibility. And we should prepare ourselves in case it happens.

At present we are battling on two fronts: the security front in Palestine and the political front in Britain. As I write this I have before me the distressing news of nineteen fresh victims in Tiberias. Who knows how many more losses we shall have in the days to come? But I am not afraid of the outcome on this front. The riots caused grievous losses, and each and every one of us could have suffered the same fate. But because of them we also strengthened ourselves, and we can continue building up this strength if we act wisely and intelligently. We are virtually in a state of war, and in war

*Sir John Simon (1873-1954): Foreign Secretary, 1931-35; Home Secretary 1935-37; Chancellor of the Exchequer, 1937-40.
**Stanley Baldwin (1867-1947), British Conservative Prime Minister, 1923-24, 1924-29, 1935-37.
***Viscount Hailsham (1872-1950), Secretary of State for War 1931-35, Lord Chancellor 1935-38.

there are higher considerations. We have not lost any strategic position, and in fact our settlements are stronger militarily and agriculturally than they have ever been. We are conquering new outposts and reinforcing old ones. This is the only comfort we can offer to the harassed and persecuted Jewish people of our time.

I doubt very much whether the British will suppress the riots by force, although I don't rule out the possibility entirely. If they added more troops, recruited more Jews and showed more goodwill they could stop the disturbances. But I have no confidence in the British officials, either at district or at a lower level. And they won't be replaced. Even if they were, there is no guarantee that their successors would be any better.

But in my opinion the continuation of the riots is not the greatest danger. What I really fear is 'making peace' without using force, the way they made peace with Hitler, at the expense of Czechoslovakia. Wouldn't it be easy to buy peace in Palestine at our expense? I believe there is a real danger of this. No one can be certain that they won't make a deal with the Mufti in the near future. They might already have approached someone else: Ibn Saud, the Iraqi Government. There are Jews who are helping them do this. There are many seekers of 'peace' among the Jews. Hyamson and his friends continue to undermine our position behind our backs.

During the recent talks with Malcolm MacDonald we heard an echo of this mischief-making. He spoke about an Anglo-Arab-Jewish agreement. Excellent. Which of us would oppose this? But I am afraid that what he was talking about was an Anglo-Arab agreement which will be presented to us as a *fait accompli,* in the same way that the agreement between the Four Powers was handed to Czechoslovakia. Obviously we must, of course, avoid automatic comparisons. What happened in Central Europe doesn't have to happen in Palestine. But it could happen, and we mustn't close our eyes to the possibility.

How can we overcome this danger of being handed over to the Mufti or to the Arab Kings? Whom can we rely upon in the struggle for our very existence and our future in this country? Our 'friends' in the Government are broken reeds.

The Colonial Office is headed by a man who has helped us considerably in the past. And we will never be ungrateful for that.

He has helped us in his present post as well. We have been able to obtain additional arms and to recruit more Jews with his agreement, although not on his initiative. But in our last talk with him I heard new things and an ominous new tone. The talk about unfairness to the Arabs, the 'mistake' of large-scale immigration, the need to slow down the tempo, to reach an agreement with Ibn Saud — all these are extremely worrying and testify to new winds blowing through Government circles. And this is the best 'friend' we have in the Cabinet.

The Prime Minister is an advocate of 'realism', and is also not attached to long-standing arrangements and commitments. And he will decide. At present he is virtually the sole ruler of the Cabinet, almost a dictator.

Public opinion in Britain is concerned with its own problems. The new political shift will soon be reflected, I think, in the attitude to Zionism. The new-style British policy is to take into account established facts. And so they take into account force, violence, reality the way it is. In this climate those among us who oppose a Jewish State based on partition will find a ready audience. But I doubt whether the same audience will respond to a demand for a larger immigration.

If there is no Jewish State, this means there will be no Jewish immigration. So when Malcolm MacDonald hinted to us that there will not be a Jewish State now, he was in effect explaining that there could not be widespread Jewish immigration either.

Can we rely on help from America? In other words, official, non-Jewish America. This America tried to make a gesture 'in favour of the Jewish refugees from Europe', and did not mention the name Palestine. This America is now being pushed by the British policies towards an outlook of isolationism and a shying away from all external 'complications'. This America did not help the Czechs. Would it help us? Will it quarrel with England over us?

As far as we know, Roosevelt+ does not believe Palestine

186

should be a haven for Jewish immigrants. I talked a lot about this with Ben Cohen+, who is close to the seat of power. I spoke to him before the end of the recent European drama, and he was very sceptical about the chances of any American help.

The League of Nations? Since Munich, it does not exist, and there is no point in talking about it.

I don't believe the spirit which produced Munich will last for ever. The 'peace' with Hitler will not be eternal. But meanwhile deception and corrupt thinking are in the air. And Zionism is not located somewhere outside time and place. The Jewish people lived with their belief in 'Eternal Israel' for 2,000 years — *in the Diaspora*. These 2,000 years are an argument not only in favour of Zionism, but also against it. During 2,000 years we did *not* build the country, did *not* return to it, did *not* have a foothold in our homeland.

I believe in the days of the Messiah. The wicked will not triumph for ever. Hitler and Chamberlain are not immortal, and the justice which is now being trampled underfoot will reappear. But not now, not soon. So we must prepare ourselves to live through the evil time which is coming.

If they betray us — it's not yet certain that they will, so we must remember the 'if' — we might remain alone and bereft of all external assistance, apart from the Jewish world.

But in this grave situation, with the terrible danger hanging over us, we must not have any internal illusions either.

I divide the Jewish people into four camps: a) Zionists; b) Sympathizers; c) Indifferent people; d) Enemies. Most of the Jewish people belong to the two middle categories. The number of Zionists in the Diaspora — let us not deceive ourselves — is very small. The Jewish haters of Zion are playing no small part in the struggle against the Jewish State, together with the Mufti and the Arab kings, the anti-Semites in Britain, the anti-British in Italy and the Nazis in Germany.

Let us say the Jews in Poland organize a protest meeting in a large hall in Warsaw. Will the echo of this protest reach the English people and its rulers? And will it make a difference even if it does? The Englishman knows that in the great Empire there is a black spot called Palestine, where his soldiers and policemen are being killed because of the Jews.

And if England decides, after two or three years of real fighting, that it is necessary to 'come to terms' with the rebels, will it pay any attention to the protests of a Zionist meeting in Warsaw?

I doubt whether even a protest rally in New York will have much impact. Protests like this are necessary in themselves, for the sake of the movement. But as political ammunition they don't have any particular value and exert little influence on the outside.

The time we are living in is one of *power politics*. Moral values no longer have any force. The ears of the leaders are closed, and all they can hear is the sound of the cannons. And the Jews of the Diaspora have no cannons.

If, heaven forbid, we are betrayed like the Czechs, there is only one prop we can rely on: *the Jewish community of Palestine itself.*

And this is why it is so vital and urgent to strengthen this community. If it is decreed that we are to be left to the Mufti's mercies, then only the Yishuv can save us. Because only the Yishuv can oppose this decree — and not with protest meetings or resolutions.

To prepare the Yishuv for this stand — that is, in my opinion, the burning Zionist task of the moment.

In order to do so we must enlist the loyal Zionists, who, as I noted, are regrettably only a small minority of the Jewish people. We must prepare men, means, land, equipment. This should be the focal point of all our activity.

It goes without saying that we should continue to do all we can to avert the evil decree by negotiating with the Government and by influencing public opinion in Britain, America and Geneva. We must carry on with our normal political and settlement work. We must avoid hysterical panic and defeatism. The whole situation could change tomorrow, so we must not despair. But at the same time we should prepare for the worst, and we should tell the heads of the Zionist movement in the world how grave the danger is and how much help we need so urgently.

To Geula, Amos and Renana — my dear children,

Today I sent Mother a copy of my letter to the Zionist Executive, in which I tried to analyze our situation in the light of the political position in the world and in Jewry. I would like you to read this letter. I only hinted at my main conclusion, because what I refer to is being enacted now and we don't talk about it, and I assume you're intelligent enough to take this hint.

My analysis of the situation is fairly pessimistic. But in my opinion it is true to the facts. The worst thing in the world is to behave like an ostrich, to hide our heads in the sand. This will not drive away the danger. Intellectual and moral cowardice is no better than physical cowardice.

I trust the difficult time I foresee will not come about and that my gloomy prophecy will turn out to be wrong. We are doing everything possible now to see that it will be wrong. Today, for example, we spoke from our office in London by telephone to three different parts of the world: South Africa, North America and Eastern Europe. We phoned Johannesburg, New York and Warsaw, warned our comrades there about the danger and asked them to help us urgently. Here in Britain we are enlisting the help of all our political friends in Parliament, the Government and the press.

In addition to these activities in England, we are trying to obtain help from other sources. First of all, the President of the United States of America. Today we spoke by telephone to the heads of American Zionism — Stephen Wise and Louis Lipsky — and they told us they have already contacted the White House in Washington.

We asked Johannesburg to contact General Smuts, one of the few people left who drew up the Balfour Declaration and who has supported us all these years.

Yesterday the High Commissioner for Palestine arrived in London with one of his officials. This official is no friend of ours, and he has the power to do us great harm. The High Commissioner is also none too sympathetic, and I don't think he will say much in our favour.

Arab pressure is increasing all the time. Today they are opening a conference of the Arab countries in aid of the Palestine Arabs, and I'm afraid that tomorrow the press here will be full of reports of this conference from Cairo. The British Government knows very well that Nazi agents are active in Egypt, Palestine, Iraq, Syria and other Arab countries. Although I don't believe that the Palestine question really touches the Arabs of Iraq or Egypt, the bond of religion and language and culture is powerful. And every ambitious Arab politician wants to appear as the saviour of the Palestine Arabs. Who knows what will win the day — the promises given to us by Britain, the justice and enlightenment of our achievements in Palestine and the dreadful plight of the Jews in the Diaspora, on the one hand, or the bombs and mines of the Arab gangs, the threats and influence of the Arab countries, and the growing anti-Semitism in the world, on the other.

In another week or two the committee set up to examine partition will submit its report (which is probably almost completed already). There are three possibilities:

1) The committee could find that the partition plan is neither 'practical' nor 'just'.

2) It could propose a partition plan which we could not accept. If we reject it then no one will support it, because the Arabs are opposed to any partition scheme (outwardly, at any rate), and I don't think the British Government will implement any kind of partition which is opposed by both the Jews and the Arabs.

3) The committee will propose a partition plan which could be accepted. It will probably change the recommendations made by the Peel Commission in 1937, which in my opinion went deeper into the Zionist *idea* than any other British commission. But changing the Peel plan is not necessarily a bad thing. The changes the new committee proposes might not all be against us, and if what is good in them outweighs what is bad, we should discuss the proposal.

But this third possibility is slight, I fear. The Cabinet has no wish to set up a Jewish State at present, and it is quite possible that in two or three weeks' time we may find that either the committee, the British Government or we ourselves

190

have ruled out the idea of partition.

What then?

Here there are two dangers:

1) The Government can in effect cease attempting to find any solution. The present situation will continue — and this means the Government will hesitate and vacillate and try to sit on the fence. And meanwhile there will not be any immigration, the economic situation will become worse, the despair in our camp will increase, and both the Yishuv and the Zionist movement will suffer.

Such a situation could not last long, for the Arabs will not remain quiet. They want independent rule, an Arab Government. And here I come to the second danger:

2) Britain could negotiate with the Arabs about founding an Arab State. For convenience's sake they would not call it an Arab State, but 'Independent Palestine'. But it would be the same thing. To make Palestine independent now means in effect setting up an Arab State, because the Arabs are two-thirds of the population. This is the greatest danger, because it would mean stopping immigration, paralyzing Jewish settlement and handing over the existing Jewish community to the Arabs.

In my opinion there is no immediate danger of this, although many people in Britain are thinking along these lines, and some of them might be in the Cabinet. If the Government should try to establish an Arab State, this must lead to partition, as long as the Jews of Palestine do not give in.

There was a time when the main strength of Zionism rested in the Jewish people, in the Diaspora. The Yishuv in Palestine was a political object, not yet a subject. If the Jews in the Diaspora had been more determined, our position in Palestine could have been much stronger. One million Jews could have been there, and not 400,000. In that case the riots would have broken out earlier, but they would not have been so strong, because the present disturbances are fed not only by Arab opposition, but also by such external factors as Italy, Germany, the possibility of war and so on.

The Zionist movement has only had a clear and definite programme for the last seven years, since we, the pioneering

Labour movement, took over the running of political affairs in Jerusalem. And over half the Yishuv entered the country during this period. But more could have been done, if we had been given more means. The Zionist movement was better at talking than at acting.

But now the Yishuv has become the main motivating force in Zionism; 400,000 people are an important factor in such a small country, especially as we must take into account not only the quantity but also the quality. In the principal cities — Jerusalem, Tel Aviv, Haifa — we are a majority. We control most of the citrus groves and almost all the industry. One harbour is entirely ours, and the second one — Haifa — is becoming more and more Jewish. We have a sizeable part of the best land in the country, in the valleys. The electricity supply and the Dead Sea are in Jewish hands. Our military strength has increased, and about 10,000 of our men have been recruited by the Government. We have a trade union which is perhaps unmatched by any other country. There is still some internal dissension, which greatly weakens us; but this can be overcome by firm and wise leadership.

If only the Yishuv, which is potentially so strong, stands firm and has the determination to act against any plot to set up an Arab State — to act not with demonstrations, but with *concrete deeds, without being afraid of anything,* I am absolutely certain we can foil this plot. Sooner or later an independent Jewish State will be established. We ourselves shall create it — and Britain will be forced to recognize it. Public opinion in Britain and America will oppose any attempt to suppress us by force and to turn us over to the Arabs by sending in the troops.

For these reasons I think our immediate and central task at this time should be to prepare, organize and *equip* the Yishuv so that it can face the decisive battle which might be coming. We must prepare *in spirit and in matter.* The Jewish youth in Palestine will perhaps play the main role in the near future. And this youth includes not only the eighteen to twenty-year-olds, but also people aged fifty and over. And I too don't consider myself too old to be among the youth, even though I will be fifty-two in four days' time. Remember what I have said.

At this crucial moment we must bear in mind this simple truth: in the Diaspora our history is made by others. In Palestine — by ourselves. And whatever others scheme and foreigners do, if we are able *to create history* even in the worst possible conditions, they will not be able to overcome us.

I am not among those who think that if the committee comes out against a Jewish State being established now, the State will not come about. The British and the Arabs will not solve the Palestine problem *on their own*. We also have something to say about it. The only thing that could defeat us would be our own surrender, fear and weakness.

And if our politicians, practical men of affairs and intellectuals panic and give in — then the youth of all ages, those who are young in spirit, will lift high the torch of rebellion and fight. I believe implicitly in both these kinds of youth. They will not disappoint the hopes of the people. And so I am not pessimistic, despite my pessimistic appraisal of the situation. And I am more afraid of a non-solution than of a bad solution.

I spoke about two possible dangers. There might be a third one: an attempt to force us to reach an agreement with the Arabs.

A Jewish-Arab agreement is actually an ideal solution, and very desirable. And during my whole term of office on the Executive I have aimed at such an agreement and also looked for ways to attain it. I tried to talk with Arab leaders and to find a path to mutual understanding. But at this time, after thirty months of rioting and murders, when we have lost hundreds of dead and wounded, and the Arabs have lost thousands, when Arab hatred of us has grown sharper, and the extremist Arabs, our mortal enemies, have the upper hand over the terrified Arabs of Palestine, it's hard to see the Arabs agreeing to any conditions which we could accept.

In the circumstances I think it is only possible to reach an agreement with the Arabs after we have established a Jewish State (or something similar to it). Only if the Arabs see that we are a force, that we are not entirely abandoned by the Mandatory Government, that they cannot ignore our existence, *and that we have something to offer them,* will the background for a Jewish-Arab agreement be created. This is one of the reasons why I am in favour of a Jewish State in part of the country. Because I do not consider this State the final objective of Zionism, but only the means of attaining it. When we have a State like this we will be able to talk with the Arabs about creating an Arab federation which would include Palestine, provided we could settle freely in all parts of the country and our State would be independent in all the things which are important to us.

Unless we have a State I don't think the Arabs will agree to a good-sized Jewish immigration, because they know this means a Jewish majority in the whole of Palestine within a few years. On the other hand, we cannot agree to accept a low rate of immigration, which would condemn us to remain a perpetual minority. I expressed this feeling the day before yesterday in a statement published by the Jewish Agency:

> 'The Jewish people remain ready to co-operate with the Arabs for the general welfare of the country. But they can consider neither the imposition of minority status nor any arbitrary limitation of their inalienable right to return to their homeland.'

The greatest danger at the moment is that the British Government may decide to continue the Mandate but cut Jewish immigration. This would be the easiest solution for the Government, and the worst for us. But if this happens I rely on the Arabs to 'help' us.

This will probably surprise you. Why should the Arabs help us? But strange things happen in history, and sometimes one side in a conflict helps the other without meaning to. For example, the Revisionists assisted the Arab gangs and the Mufti several times, not because they intended to but because they thought they were fighting them. So they killed innocent Arabs and by doing this increased the Arab terrorist attacks and helped the Arabs to unite.

In the same way the Mufti and his friends are helping us by their actions, *which are intended to harm us*. With the 'help' of the Mufti (who called a strike in Jaffa harbour) we won a port in Tel Aviv; with the 'help' of the Mufti and the Arab gangs the Government was forced to train and arm our boys. So I hope that with the 'help' of the Mufti we shall be able to put an end to the Mandatory regime, which is restricting our immigration.

How will this happen? The Arabs will continue to fight the British Mandate, because what they really want is independent rule. The British will not be able to withstand this struggle for long. And if London gives Palestine home rule, then everything will depend on our attitude. If we don't agree and don't accept what would be virtually an Arab State, then it will not come about, and they will be forced to return to the idea of partition. This is why I say that I rely on the 'help' of the Arabs.

And once more I say: what happens in Palestine depends more than anything else on our youth. This is why I have written all these things to you.

Write to me and tell me what you think — and whether you are ready, and whether in your opinion your friends will be ready, when the time comes.

And you, Amos, write to me about your impressions of your trip to Egypt, what you saw there and what you learned.

London
October 10, 1938.

Please give the enclosed letter to David Remez after you've read it yourself.

There's nothing new to report at the moment. We are bringing all our friends here and in America into play so that they can help us.

I sent Geula a long letter for her, Amos and Renana — and naturally also for you — in which I outline the possible political developments.

London
October 18, 1938.

After you left here the situation changed a little for the better — for the moment, at any rate. There is less danger

195

.1ow that the British Government will abandon us to the Arabs, the way it abandoned the Czechs. The fear of an immediate war has also passed, and Britain is no longer so worried about the Arabs joining its enemies. This time our call to our friends in America was answered, and they did some important work: they alerted the press, activated the leading politicians and the Church, rushed off telegrams to Chamberlain, and brought Roosevelt into play as well. This American pressure was effective, and it blocked any action by those who hate us. A friend of mine in the War Office said to us: Ten days ago people thought the Government would abandon the Jews, but the American actions changed the situation.

This doesn't mean they will give us a state now. Malcolm told Chaim yesterday that he's seen a draft of the committee's report, and found it better than he had expected. He hasn't yet seen the 'final conclusion'—I distrust that phrase — and next week he may be getting the committee's recommendations and will give them to us. But it's practically certain that partition will be dropped for the moment.

They won't give us immigration either. Some three weeks ago there was a danger that immigration would be stopped entirely; this was before Chamberlain flew to Munich and before it became certain that there would not be a war. The Government had already prepared a declaration banning Jewish immigration, with a view to acquiring the Arabs' friendship for Britain if war broke out. But when the danger of war passed this statement was also annulled, and Malcolm promised us that there is no question of stopping immigration completely.

It seems clear, however, that they will reduce immigration in the near future. As I wrote to the children, there is a danger that they might try to persuade us to come to terms with the Arabs. At present the Government has in fact no clear policy. It does not want to return to the policy which existed before the riots. And it has no new policy. So it will attempt a policy of 'peace'. Peace is an excellent thing. But at the moment I don't see any chance of an agreement between the Arabs and ourselves which could bring about peace.

196

Today the British press is full of stories about the Arab gangs' conquest of the Old City of Jerusalem. Who knows what will happen next . . . Here they assure us that in a few weeks' time they will subdue the Arab bands. But what is actually happening in Palestine bodes no good for us. The civil administration is undoubtedly hostile to our cause. There is perhaps one high-ranking man who is not against us and who, in fact, would like us to succeed, and that is Tegart*. But we can't tell whether he will be able to withstand the wall of enmity and indifference erected by the others.

Chaim went to Paris today, and won't return until the weekend. Next week both of us are meeting Malcolm, and perhaps he will tell us then what the committee has proposed.

We decided yesterday to summon the Zionist Actions Committee for November 25-26, in London. I intend coming home for six to ten days before this meeting. Eliahu and Moshe have fallen into a quicksand. They arranged an agreement with the Revisionists** which I opposed and which many comrades did not know about. I could not prevent this from London. But they promised not to make it final until I'm there.

I am thinking of flying with Imperial Airways at the end of next week, on October 28 or 29. Then I would return on November 6 or 7. I'll make a final decision when Chaim returns from Paris.

London
October 21, 1938.

Dear children,
What has happened to you? Since Mother left I haven't

*Sir Charles Tegart (1881-1946): Adviser to the Palestine Government on police organization, 1937-39.
**The agreement between the Hagana (the 'official' underground army of the Jewish community) and the Irgun Zvai Leumi (the Revisionists' Military Organization), reached on September 19, 1938. The Irgun bound itself to accept the Hagana's orders, but was allowed to keep separate units. Ben-Gurion opposed the agreement as long as the Revisionists did not accept the political decisions taken by the Zionist Organization.

197

received a single word from any of you. There have been no answers to any of my letters. Didn't you receive them? And it was holiday time, so you weren't at school. I am very worried.

When I wrote to Mother a few days ago I was thinking of flying home for a few days. But recent events here have changed my plans once again. At its meeting the day before yesterday the British Cabinet appointed a sub-committee to handle the Palestine question and to prepare guidelines for the Government's policies. On November 1 Parliament reopens, and it will discuss the Palestine question. During the coming weeks we shall be holding intensive negotiations with the Government, and I won't be able to leave London during this time.

London
October 25, 1938.

Secret

This morning I met Lord Lloyd* in his office, at the British Council. Two days ago he published an article in the *Sunday Chronicle* under the title 'A dream that has become a nightmare'. He begins with Dr Weizmann's meeting with Balfour ('A British philosopher-statesman') before the war, which led to the Balfour Declaration. But Balfour dreamed of a Jewish National Home which the Arabs would accept, while today there is civil war in Palestine. And the tragedy is that the Arabs are fighting not only against the Jews but against the British, and all the Arab countries which are friendly to Britain are complaining about Britain's policies and the way it suppresses the Arabs in Palestine. Further, the entire Moslem world from the Atlantic Ocean to India is showing hostility to Britain.

This situation cannot continue, Lloyd writes. Suppression alone will not bring about peace. The Arabs are afraid of Jewish donination. Several Zionists want a State in part of the country. But the Arabs are afraid that the Jews will have

*High Commissioner for Egypt and the Sudan, 1925-29. Colonial Secretary in Churchill's Government, 1940.

an army and arms, and that they will take over the rest of Palestine in the course of time.

There is pressure on the British Government from both the Arab world and the Jewish world. The time has come, Lloyd says, for the Government to refuse to surrender to either side and to lay down its policy once and for all: *the Arabs should be given assurances that they will always remain a majority,* while in compensation the Jews should be given the right to settle in Transjordan. Neither side will be satisfied, but they *will be forced* to put up with this solution.

I asked him to meet me before the article appeared. Meanwhile Colonel Kisch met Hyamson, and the latter told him that Lord Lloyd wants to invite Chaim Weizmann, Lord Reading, Nuri Said and Jamal Husseini for an unofficial talk. The Arabs trust Lord Lloyd, and consider him a fair and honest man.

He received me in his office (he is the Director of the British Council). I opened by complimenting him for his stand on Czechoslovakia.

'Do you agree with me?' he asked.

'Have you read my speech? I told the Government that this was nothing but a bluff by the Germans. They wouldn't have gone to war; they couldn't wage a war. I have no spies, and in any case I wouldn't speak in public about information gathered from spies. I heard from an important general in the German General Staff that their whole army is against a war, and that the German army couldn't last more than three weeks. And they told Hitler this clearly. But Hitler didn't agree with them, because he thought he could bluff the British Government. I went to the Foreign Secretary and told him what I had heard from the German general, and cautioned him not to be misled by the bluff. The German army knows that if Prague stands firm and France comes to its aid, Britain will be forced sooner or later to join in the war. And Germany could not stand up to France, Russia and Britain. But those "fools" wouldn't listen to me, and were trapped by the bluff.'

I said to him that I had heard the same thing from military circles when I had been in Paris. He remarked: 'You really have good sources of information.'

I said: 'I'm afraid that they are now going to do to us what they did to the Czechs.'

He answered at once: 'I'll tell you frankly what I think. I wrote an article two days ago . . .'

I interrupted him: 'I've read that article.'

'It was a bad article,' he apologized. 'I didn't put down everything I think. I wrote it quickly. They phoned me on Saturday evening, and I phoned in the text almost at once. I'll be frank with you. During the world war they gave the Arabs and the Jews conflicting assurances. *We sold the same horse twice.* Now we are facing both the Arab and the Jewish worlds. The Arabs are being stirred up by our enemies, and they will threaten our position in the Middle East unless we meet the demands of the Palestine Arabs. And on the other hand World Jewry, with all its economic and political strength and its influence in various countries, is rising up against us. Weizmann said to me: You betrayed Ethiopia, China, Iran and Czechoslovakia. You will betray us too. But we will put the whole world against you.'

'I don't know what the Government intends to do,' Lloyd went on. 'You know what I think of it. But I tell you what I think honestly and frankly. The Arabs cannot be driven out of Palestine. We should not be afraid of either Arabs or the Jews. I am not a Zionist nor a pro-Zionist. I am also not pro-Arab. We must act justly. The Arabs must remain a majority. They should be assured that they will have a majority. You should be given a "Vatican City". Not in the Old City of Jerusalem, but outside it. A symbol for all the Jewish people. I am a Christian, and I understand your feelings about Zion. I am sorry I didn't include this in my article. Your "Vatican City" will give the whole Jewish people spiritual satisfaction.

'There is also opposition on the part of the Moslems in India. But I don't think they are really interested in Palestine. I know India. Palestine doesn't touch them. They are concerned only with their affairs in India. But there is an Arab world, and we should ensure an Arab majority in Palestine, not because we are afraid of them but because it is right. If the problem is solved in this way, you could settle in Transjordan. The Emir Abdullah wants you. Our experts say
200

that the desert tribes in Transjordan want you. This would be the most practical and correct solution, in my opinion.'

I said to him:

'Allow me also to speak to you frankly. The British Government has declared more than once that Palestine was not included in these promises, and McMahon himself has confirmed this. But from my own personal knowledge I must tell you that there is no basis for talking about the expulsion of the Arabs. Our settlements have not expelled Arabs, but have attracted them into the country — to my great regret. We have not expelled Arabs and we will not do so.

'You can impose on us what you wish. I will not threaten you. Dr Weizmann is a genius, and he can say things which I would not allow myself to say. The Jewish people has no navy and no army, and you are a great and mighty empire. But if you decree that we are to be a minority — you should at least know that there is no justice here. I can tell you one thing: you will never be able to place us under Arab rule. Even if you send to Palestine more troops than you have there now, the Jews of Palestine will never accept Arab rule. We have suffered all over the world. In Palestine we will not suffer a foreign government, and I don't consider the Mandatory rule a foreign one in any way. You will not be able to force us with all the strength of the British Empire.

'You offer us a "Vatican City", and I appreciate the fact that you stress our religious link with Palestine. You feel this because you are a Christian. But I fear that there is one thing you do not feel, because no Englishman has ever felt it, and this thing is the chief motivating force behind our movement: *homelessness*. Palestine is our home. All over the world the nations do to us what they will. Palestine is our homeland, and there we want to feel at home. A "Vatican City" is not a home for a people. And in any case it would be destroyed by the Arab Government. We have the example of the Assyrians in Iraq.'

Lord Lloyd's face became stern, and he made a nervous gesture.

I said: 'Forgive me for quoting this example. Perhaps I shouldn't have done so. But you can take one thing from me: we will not be strangers in Palestine, and we will not submit

201

to any Arab rule.'

'And so you think a Jewish State is necessary?' he asked.

'Yes,' I replied, 'a Jewish State is necessary. But a Jewish State isn't everything. We need a large and strong Jewish State. Otherwise it will not be able to exist, and it would not have any value for the Jewish people and the British Empire. I am not British, I am a Jew first and foremost. But as a Jew I consider our fate tied to Britain. We are an oriental people, but we have lived in the West for hundreds of years. Now we are returning home with a Western culture, and our link with the West is vital to us. And we cannot see any link more desirable than the link with the British Empire. I wish I could say that the reverse was also true. And a strong Jewish Palestine could be an important fulcrum for Britain in that part of the world.'

Here he interrupted me: 'On this point I have my doubts.'

I said: 'I'll ask you an indiscreet question: don't you trust us?'

He replied: 'I trust Weizmann. I know he is loyal. I trust you. I don't know why. But leaders can be replaced. You won't always be at the helm. The Palestinian coast of the Mediterranean is a *vital* part of the Empire. The Jews who will control this coast will be foreign Jews, from Poland and other countries, who have no British sentiments and who don't understand the British institutions. I am speaking frankly. I think that if they hold this vital spot, *they will blackmail the British Empire.*'

I said to him: 'I am not surprised to hear you say that. Because you haven't had an opportunity to get to know our people as a whole, and the Jews of Palestine in particular. I know my people, and I will tell you what I think. You can accept what I say or not. Zionism has always placed its hopes in England. Even before the World War the founder of our movement, an Austrian Jew, Dr Herzl, looked to Britain, and the first Zionist body ever established — the Jewish Colonial Trust — was founded here in London.'

'What was his name again?' he asked.

'Dr Herzl. And this was no coincidence. During the war the Jewish workers of Palestine volunteered for the British army, even though they were still Turkish subjects. I myself was expelled from Palestine by the Turks at the beginning of the war, and I returned to Palestine with 4,000 Jews serving in the British army. Almost all of them were Polish Jews. American citizens were not allowed to volunteer, otherwise I could have brought 100,000 to Palestine.

'Our return to Palestine does not mean simply moving from one country to another. When in Palestine our people change their whole structure, their entire mentality, their way of life. We are bringing people from the cities to the villages. Our people are going back to do work that Jews have never done before. We are putting down roots in the homeland and becoming a new people with a sense of a homeland. There would be no point to all our efforts in Palestine without this transformation. Before the war all the Jewish youth were revolutionaries. Their inclination was to destroy the régime which oppressed them. I went to Palestine when I was still a boy. I was also a revolutionary before I went to Palestine.'

'And you still are,' he said with a smile.

'More than ever today,' I replied. 'Our young people have gone from destructive channels to constructive ones. In Palestine they are building up a country. There we have done things which are more important for us than an attitude to England. But as far as what interests you is concerned — my people have acquired some sense of sovereignty. And they know that, with all our constant criticism of the Government, which is unfortunately justified in most cases —'

Here L. interrupted me: 'I am not arguing with you . . .'

'They know how valuable our ties with Britain are. Not out of gratitude — this is not a factor in politics — but out of national interest. A strong Jewish Palestine would be a bastion of strength for Britain in the Mediterranean.'

'Well,' he remarked 'I see you think there has to be a Jewish State, and a strong one. You may be right. I was against partition. However, what I am proposing is in effect a partition, although I won't call it that. A strong Jewish State should be partly in Western Palestine and partly in Transjordan. This solution is impractical, unless we widen the picture. What you want is possible only if we bring the neighbouring Arab countries into the plan. A Jewish State

203

can only exist with an Arab federation.'

I said: 'I personally accept this idea. All these years we have thought this the real solution, and I also talked with Arabs along these lines several years ago.'

'What I am thinking of,' he said to me, 'is a federation comprising Palestine, Transjordan and Syria. We would have to persuade France to agree to this.'

I said: 'I'm afraid that France won't agree. For two reasons: 1) Such a federation would allow Britain to control Syria; 2) It would be an act against Turkey, and France wants friendship with Turkey.'

'So do we, ' he remarked. 'Perhaps we could compensate France with a colony in Africa, like Gambia.'

'I doubt whether France would make an exchange of this sort. They have traditional ties with Syria, and particularly with Lebanon.'

'Perhaps we could add only Hauran and Damascus,' he suggested to me.

I said: 'We would certainly agree. Hauran is part of Palestine. But the French won't do it.'

'Without the French,' he replied, 'This naturally can't be done. So what could the federation consist of?'

I replied: 'It could be Palestine, Transjordan and Iraq.'

He said: 'This would be impossible without the southern countries: Yemen and the Hadramaut.'

I said: 'I doubt very much whether even the Arabs want to be joined to Ibn Saud. He is an autocratic ruler, a Wahabi and a man of the desert. The Hashemites certainly won't agree.'

Lloyd replied: 'Perhaps the Arabs talk differently with you. As far as I know, the Arabs want unity with Ibn Saud.'

I said: 'In your presence I'm afraid to discuss Arab politics. You are an expert. But I have lived in Palestine for thirty-two years, and I know what the Arabs say to me. Only a little while ago, at the recent Cairo conference, Jamal Husseini criticized Ibn Saud vehemently.'

'Perhaps,' he remarked. 'And so what you want is a strong Jewish State and an Arab federation? You may be right. I have a proposal: Let's meet together with Weizmann.'

He looked in his diary, telephoned at once to Great Russell Street and asked for Weizmann. But he had already left the office. L. told Miss May* that he was inviting Weizmann to dinner together with me on Friday (October 28).

'This time there will only be the three of us. We'll discuss the matter. I'll bring a map with me. Then I'll arrange for you to meet several Arabs. The Arabs trust me. I am not pro-Arab, and I talk with them as frankly and openly as I have been talking with you. I say to them that they must not think we shall deny our commitments to the Jews. They know I'm an honest man. We'll see if anything comes out of it.'

I said 'Excellent,' and we parted.

When I returned to the office I immediately asked Orde Wingate+ to come and see me. I summarized our conversation for him and told him that Lloyd doubted our loyalty to Britain. I asked Wingate to go and see Lloyd without saying he had been sent by me, and to tell him about his experience with the Jews and about our boys in the Hagana.

Wingate promised to do this, although he was a little surprised. I told him that Lloyd headed the British Council, and suggested that he, Wingate, should say he was a British officer serving in Palestine who was interested in spreading British culture.

Wingate remembered that he had met L. once, in Egypt.

London
October 27, 1938.

Dear Children,

I still haven't heard anything from you, and I am very worried and concerned. I can't understand it. Why do you do this to me, at a time when I have so many other things to worry about?

For me and all of us in London the last days have been ones of relief and at the same time anxiety.

If you read the material I've been sending to Mother almost every day you will know what is happening. Here I will just add a few personal and political comments.

One of the most interesting talks I've had here recently

*Dorris May, secretary to Dr Weizmann.

was with Lord Lloyd. He was the High Commissioner in Egypt, and before that he served in India and the Arab countries. He belongs to the right wing of the Conservative Party, what people here call the 'diehards.' He is a thorough imperialist and a proud Englishman.

A year or two ago he visited Palestine, and I met him at the King David Hotel. We had a long talk about the situation, the riots, Wauchope, the Government. I found before me a different man from the one I had imagined from newspaper descriptions. Instead of a cold, proud, closed and sarcastic person I found a tolerant, pleasant, frank and intelligent man. We didn't see eye to eye on political matters. It is difficult to imagine a greater contrast than between an English lord, one of the Conservative pillars of the Empire, and a spokesman of the Palestinian Labour movement and the Zionist Organization. But we became friends during that talk, and when we parted Lloyd asked me to come and see him if I was ever in London.

Since then I have met him here several times, and we had some rather hurried and random talks. I knew that he is much more interested in Palestine now than he used to be, and that he is active — against us. He also published an article against us in one of the weekly papers. He has great influence among the Arabs, and they rely on him. He is not an anti-Semite, but says frankly that he is anti-Zionist.

I decided to meet him and to see what I could do. He arranged to meet me the day before yesterday. I sent the contents of our talk to Mother today. It is in English, and it's worth reading. I left his office very satisfied with our talk. I removed from his mind (for the moment, at any rate) the idea that we could be made into a permanent minority in Palestine, and I also brought him closer to the idea of the Jewish State. Tomorrow I am meeting him again with Weizmann and a British officer, one of our most devoted friends in Palestine, who happens to be in London at present. We'll see what comes out of tomorrow's talk.

I had another important talk, also the day before yesterday, when Weizmann and I went to see the Colonial Secretary. He is very different from Lord Lloyd in almost every way. He is the son of Ramsay MacDonald, who founded the British Labour Party and was its leader until his death a few years ago. The son, Malcolm, was raised on socialist ideals. His father always supported Zionism, and many of our people met him. Even before the son became a Minister he helped us considerably.

He did a great thing for us after the publication of Lord Passfield's White Paper in 1930. This White Paper caused us considerable harm, and the Cabinet appointed a sub-committee to negotiate with us and to amend the harm done. The result was the publication of a letter* from the Prime Minister to Weizmann, which has become known as the MacDonald Letter. The life and soul of these negotiations was the Prime Minister's son. It would be difficult to over-estimate the value of the help he gave us at that difficult time.

I met him a year after that at Chequers, the summer home of the Prime Ministers in Britain. This was during the 17th Zionist Congress, in 1931, when relations between us and the Mandatory Government were extremely bad (Sir John Chancellor was then the High Commissioner). I flew from Basle to London on the invitation of the Prime Minister, Ramsay MacDonald. It was a Friday or a Saturday.

The plane broke down on the way, and we were forced to return to Paris in order to repair the engine. So we were two hours late. Professor Namier+ flew with me. The Prime Minister waited for us in vain. From London we sent a telegram to Chequers explaining the reason for our delay and saying that we would come there next morning (we had been supposed to arrive in the evening and to stay there overnight).

In the morning we went to Chequers by car. It is an old castle set in woods and marvellous lawns, about two hours drive from London. Ramsay MacDonald and his son Malcolm met us at the gate. We had a long talk, lasting about four hours, on the great problems facing Zionism. During this conversation Ramsay informed me that he had appointed a new High Commissioner (Arthur Wauchope) with whom he was sure we'd be satisfied. I had a very friendly talk with Malcolm as well. He arranged my journey back to Basle, and

*Dated February 13, 1931.

207

asked the British Minister in Paris to meet me at Calais and to speed up my passage through France, as I had no French visa.

Since then I have met Malcolm several times. When his father was Prime Minister Malcolm was made Minister, and three years ago he became Colonial Secretary. In the autumn of 1935 I met him in London together with Wauchope, and again we spoke about our fundamental problems: increasing immigration, buying land, especially in the Negev, helping industry and so on. Malcolm showed an extremely friendly attitude to our concerns. But he didn't stay long at the Colonial Office, and was replaced by Thomas*. A few months ago Malcolm was made Colonial Secretary again, in place of Ormsby-Gore (who was also a friend of ours).

Over the years Malcolm's friendship for Zionism has cooled a little, but he is still one of our few friends in the British Cabinet. He is not very powerful, because he has not got a strong party behind him, and he is wholly dependent on the Prime Minister, Neville Chamberlain. But he has a certain amount of influence on the Prime Minister, and we should not make light of his friendship. He has just saved immigration for us, and he didn't allow them to turn the country over to the Arabs. He supported the arming of the Jews, and I hope he will continue to support us: it will not be as much as we would like, of course. After all, he is a non-Jew, and he looks after his post and does not want to quarrel too much with the Arabs because of his assistance to us.

I can't write to you about our talk with Malcolm. You will find a summary of it in one of my recent letters to Mother. Although I left that meeting (which was held in Weizmann's home) filled with anxiety about the future, I still felt a certain relief. We had not been completely abandoned, and someone was listening to what we said. The riots will, I hope, be suppressed, but not as quickly as we would like and not completely. But we shan't have to continue suffering the anarchy spread by the Arab bands. Also the Mufti will not be able to come back so soon.

True, Malcolm's words are much better than his deeds. But his deeds could be worse than they are, and good words are

*J.H. Thomas (1874-1949): Secretary of State for the Colonies, 1935-36.

also preferable to bad ones. In any event, he is not an enemy, and that is also no small thing nowadays. We haven't got many friends, and everyone is important, even if he helps only a little.

This Malcolm is still young, about thirty-seven and a bachelor. I doubt whether he would have become a Minister if he had not been the Prime Minister's son. He is not a great speaker and has no special talent. But he is perfectly capable of being a Minister like many of his colleagues, who are also not brilliant or outstanding personalities. He is a decent and fair man, tactful and with much common sense. Not much of the socialism he learned from his father in his youth has remained. But he is not a reactionary, and is certainly not anti-Semitic.

He is remarkably simple and unpretentious. I remember once attending a banquet with him. Wauchope was also there. At the end of the banquet I went out of the hall, and one of my friends was waiting with his car. It was raining outside. When I was about to get into the car I saw a shortish, young man walking about in the rain with a briefcase in his hand, looking for a taxi. This was the Colonial Secretary, Malcolm MacDonald. This Minister of the British Empire didn't have a car.

Well, I've told you a little bit.

On October 11, in about another fortnight, the Zionist Actions Committee is meeting here in London. After this meeting I'll return home.

London
October 29, 1938.

I'm enclosing the report of the second talk with Lord Lloyd. He has now become an advocate of the Jewish State, and Wingate and I are working out the map. I don't know if anything will come of it. Lloyd and Wingate are both over-optimistic. They don't see any difficulty. What they are ready to offer us today goes far beyond what the Peel Commission proposed. I doubt whether the Cabinet would

209

accept their point of view. Malcolm might. But everything depends on Chamberlain, and I'm afraid he won't take such a bold step. The civil service in Palestine would also oppose it.

Lloyd's plan could be implemented only if the Cabinet placed the whole matter in the hands of the new High Commissioner, and if that High Commissioner was Lloyd himself. But the real practical value of these talks is that I turned Lloyd from an opponent of the idea of a Jewish State into a supporter. This man has enormous influence in the Arab world, and in England as well.

London
December 22, 1938.

From my letter to Renana you'll already know that the journey wasn't very easy this time. Wind, snow, cold, all the way from Corsica to London. In London itself it's snowing all the time, although it's not as cold now as when I arrived.

I didn't find Dov Hos here, because on the day I arrived in Marseilles he sailed from there. But I spoke to him on the telephone. Eliahu is here, also Moshe and Tsippora (Shertok). She is returning to Palestine soon. Chaim went to Holland and France yesterday, and won't be back in London until the first week in January.

At the moment it looks as if the 'talks' won't start before the end of January, and I'll probably stay in America a little longer, perhaps a fortnight. I cabled you yesterday to say that I'm leaving on Saturday, December 24, on the *Franconia*, and I'll reach New York on January 1.

Yesterday Dr Nahum Goldmann returned here from America, and the report he gave showed once again that we have to act in America. I am pleased now that I decided to go there.

The situation in Europe has become serious again, and once more people are talking about the possibility of a war before long. It is said that Germany's economic position is very poor, and Hitler wants to declare war on England before the latter arms itself any more.

If war does break out, our situation will be very difficult. Britain will have to make concessions to the Arabs, so that they don't go over to its enemies. And we shan't be able to do anything against Britain, because our whole existence and future would then rest on a British victory.

Franconia
January 1, 1939.

I've been on board for nine days. We left Southampton the Saturday before last, on December 24, and now 1938 has gone and a new year had begun, and I'm still on the waters. But I'm pleased it's such a long journey. It's the first time for quite a few years that I've had such a complete rest. I don't know any of the passengers, and I don't need to talk to anybody.

So I really thought I could arrive in New York without having to open my mouth the whole way. But the day before yesterday one of the passengers 'discovered' me. He is a well-known painter from Czechoslovakia by the name of Sterk, a Zionist who spent a few years in Palestine. He found my name in the passenger list and came to me to ask if he could paint my portrait.

It was rather cold on the ship, and I couldn't walk on deck as much as I usually do. So I did a lot of reading, more than I have for a long time. Today I finished the memoirs of Foch, the French general in the last war. A fascinating book, from which I learned several important things.

We'll reach New York tomorrow. I don't know how long I'll be able to stay in America. Before I left London we thought that the Jewish-Arab 'talks' wouldn't start before the end of January. This meant I could stay in America for about a fortnight. But there might easily be a change in this schedule; I've heard nothing while on board ship, either from London or New York. Perhaps tomorrow I'll have some news.

I am here *en route* from Washington to New York. Yesterday in Washington I met the French Minister, Brandeis and Ben Cohen. Since I saw Brandeis last, about eighteen months ago, he has become old. He hears with difficulty, and his face has become wrinkled. But he still speaks with the energy and enthusiasm of a young man, and when he talks you forget completely that you are listening to an old man of eighty-two. This time it emerged that we both agree on all the outstanding problems. I found Brandeis very optimistic — a little too optimistic. Ben Cohen, whom I saw after Brandeis, poured some cold water on his enthusiasm. But I think Cohen, on the other hand, is too pessimistic about the situation here in America.

Yesterday was a great day for American Jewry: as you probably know already, Felix Frankfurter was appointed to the Supreme Court. When I arrived in New York last Monday Hexter met me at the ship, and the first thing he told me was that Frankfurter's candidacy was out of the running, not only because they didn't want to create a precedent of having two Jews on the bench at the same time, but also for geographical reasons: there is no Justice of the Supreme Court from the West. New England is already represented by Brandeis, and as Frankfurter is also from New England he won't be nominated.

But when I went into the French Consulate in Washington yesterday, I saw a paper which said: 'It is rumoured that Frankfurter will be nominated to the Supreme Court.' And when I left the Consulate the papers were already reporting his appointment. I could hardly believe my eyes. From the French Consulate I went to Brandeis, and he told me that Roosevelt had decided against Frankfurter several months before, and that he, Brandeis, was sure he had appointed him now as a demonstration against Hitler. (Only the day before Roosevelt had delivered a strong speech in Congress against the dictators.)

I immediately sent Frankfurter this telegram:

'Affectionate congratulations. Our people everywhere

will proudly bless your deserved nomination to supreme responsibility.'

New York
January 8, 1939.

I returned from Philadelphia the day before yesterday. There I had a long talk with Cyrus Adler+, head of the non-Zionists in the United States, about the conference we want to hold in America immediately after the coming 'talks' in London. At the beginning of the meeting Adler was full of fire and fury, and was particularly angry about Weizmann. But eventually he calmed down and softened, and I parted from him on friendly terms.

Sir Ronald Storrs+ is here from London. He is going to lecture in four American cities. One of his lectures will be on Palestine. He is no fool, and he knows that opposing the Jews is not popular here in America. The moment he arrived he gave an interview to the press which was almost totally in favour of Zionism.

At the moment I am not sorry I came to America, although I haven't yet done what I set out to achieve. I am very satisfied with the talk with Brandeis, and the meeting with Adler was also not bad at all. But the Zionist movement in America is not yet up to the required level, especially today when so much depends upon American Jewry and American Zionism. They don't yet realize over here that we are living in a time of great dangers and also great possibilities, a difficult and cruel period in which what was enouth yesterday is no longer enough today.

I still have no definite news about the 'talks' in London. But it's clear that they won't start before February. So I'll probably stay here until January 21.

213

I've been busy with meetings — the non-Zionists, Hadassah, all the Zionist parties and the Labour Zionists. In between all these I had to spend a few hours at the dentist to have an abscess lanced and a tooth removed.

Once more I've realized how much the Zionist movement in America suffers from the fact that our people come here only to collect money, and do not spend enough time and energy strengthening the organization itself. The Zionist movement here needs help and guidance from outside more than the movement in any other country. It's important that one of our leading people be sent here for several years just to work with the movement.

Tomorrow ·I am meeting all the Zionist parties in connection with the national conference we want to hold after the London 'talks.' Then I will see the Labour Zionist leaders, and on Saturday the non-Zionists. So I think I should be able to leave America at the end of next week.

I returned this afternoon from Washington, from the convention of the United Palestine Appeal. The convention opened the day before yesterday, but I was busy here with the non-Zionists, who were causing me a bit of trouble. So I arrived in Washington yesterday.

This time I took part in the convention against my will. ι had decided not to appear in public during this visit, and I have been able to elude the press so that the general public did not even know I was in the United States. But the Executive in Jerusalem urged me to take part in the convention, and our colleagues here also insisted. So I was forced to go to Washington against my will. This is the first fund-raising convention I have ever attended in the United States.

It was a good convention. There were about 800 delegates

from all over the country. At first I wasn't billed as a speaker, and then they decided I should be the sole speaker at the dinner which would close the convention.

As usually happens over here, there were several speakers at the dinner who announced that they would not say anything 'because all of you want to hear our guest speaker,' and then went on to make a speech. The chairman, Dr Goldmann, who also announced that he wouldn't speak, spoke before every single speech and afterwards as well. So by the time my turn came the audience was tired, and many people had left to catch their trains home.

I faced a difficult problem — the language of my speech. Almost the whole convention took place in English. Only two or three people spoke in Yiddish. I have never until now addressed a large gathering in English. But this time I decided to make the leap — and so I spoke in English. Naturally this didn't make it any easier for me.

In general I dislike talking to a crowd which comes to hear speeches the way they would go to the cinema, although many of them undoubtedly are really interested in what is being said. Some speeches at the convention were greeted with great enthusiasm, although this was often superficial. But I wouldn't wish any man to undergo the experience of talking to an American audience which is sitting around the dinner table in evening dress and has already heard twenty hours of declamations and rhetorical foreworks. I can't understand why the professional orators in America can't tell their listeners something. After the speech is finished you scarcely know what the man said, even though while he was talking you enjoyed the skilful style and the musical voice and the artistic flow of words. But there is no content. To get up and explain serious things in a serious way to this audience is neither easy nor pleasant. And when I had finished and could sit down I feld a great relief, as if I had been saved from the gallows.

To my amazement, I had no difficulty at all in speaking English fluently, apart from one word I needed and couldn't find at that particular moment. I just couldn't think of the right word, and only remembered it when I was speaking about something else. But I passed this first test, at any rate from the language aspect. I told the crowd what I wanted to say, and the audience, although it was already tired listened attentively. I saw for myself that it is possible to talk even to the American public in a serious way, without rhetoric and bombast. During the whole day I think I was the only speaker who didn't relate jokes and stories, but tried to speak to the point, and the audience heard me with great interest.

Yosef Baratz spoke the evening before me. I wasn't in Washington then, but I heard that he was a great success and made a considerable impact, again not through oratorical tricks but by his simplicity and the inner truth of his words.

I will soon finish my work here. Almost all the matters which brought me here have been settled, to the extent that they can be settled in such a short time, and I am getting ready to leave. I still have several meetings in New York during the next three days, and at the end of the week I shall be able to return to London.

I received a telegram from London the day before yesterday saying that the 'talks'* might start on January 30, and asking me to return to London for prior consultations. If I am able to take a ship on Saturday (January 21) I will do so. In any event, I will leave New York not later than the 22nd, on the *Aquitania*. I'll send you a cable before I leave.

London
February 4, 1939.

This morning I went with Moshe and Arthur Lourie+ to Chaim's house to tell him what I thought of the negotiations.

Moshe told me that Rabbi Berlin+ had asked Chaim about the results of the negotiations. When Chaim told him that they would give us 30,000 immigrants a year, Rabbi Berlin said: If you can obtain this, the Jewish people will bless you. Chaim was impressed by this reply, and now he is thinking of demanding 30,000.

When I heard this story I shuddered. There is quite enough pressure already from the non-Zionists and the Government.

*The London Conference, held at St. James's Palace.

And if Chaim starts the negotiations with this kind of negative thinking — we are lost. I asked Chaim yesterday to give me half an hour this morning so that I can have a talk with him.

When I met him I told him that the political circumstances surrounding the talks are not in our favour, and added that I think we shall have a rough time: the long-continued terrorism, the support for Hitler in the world, the danger of war, the weakness of the British Government — all these make our task very difficult. But we must take into account not only the negotiations and their immediate consequences, but also the chances we have of succeeding later, when the conditions change. The British Government's decision will not be final, and the world constellation will not always be against us.

We must always reckon with the needs of the Zionist movement. We cannot rely on the non-Zionists, because when we receive a bad blow they will leave us to ourselves. The American non-Zionists have already virtually pulled out. We must now devote more time and energy to the future of the Zionist movement. Apart from the Yishuv in Palestine, this is our only prop for the future. The Zionist movement will not criticize us or weaken if we encounter a setback this time — as long as this is not our fault. So in entering these 'talks' we must think not only of the needs of the moment, but also of long-range implications.

We have to determine our attitude to the Arabs and to the Government. I'll start with the Arabs. There is virtually no chance of an agreement with them. They see themselves as victors, and they really have won a victory. They use terrorist methods, and then they are invited to negotiate with the Government. They enlisted the help of the Arab Kings, and Britain summoned them to London and gave them what is virtually official status in Palestine. The world situation is playing into their hands. The Jewish State has been dropped. And so why should they surrender their extreme demands and make an agreement with us?

Despite all this, we should make every possible attempt to negotiate with them, and if there is any chance of it — to come to terms. We owe this to ourselves, we owe this to the

217

Government, we owe this to our future relations with the Arabs. We should not be held responsible for the failure of the Government's attempt to bring us together. The whole world should know that we have not missed this opportunity. But it is almost certain even before the talks open that there will not be an agreement, and then the Government will enforce its policy.

We know more or less what this will be. It might be worse than we think at present, and there is a hint of this in *The Times* this morning (after M.M.'s talk with the press yesterday). But this British decree will not be eternal, and if we don't agree to it and insist on what we are entitled to we can foil it. So this time we must not give way on our fundamental rights, and particularly on immigration. Any bargaining by us over the annual rate of permitted immigration would be a fatal error. I say this because:

1) Any figure we give would become a maximum, and this would make it easier for the Government to reduce it. For their part, the Arabs will demand the total cessation of immigration, and will not give in on this point.

2) If we bargain over figures we would in effect retreat from the principle of economic absorptive capacity, which has been accepted by the Government and could be defended before world public opinion.

If it were possible to come to terms with the Arabs over a desirable number of immigrants, it would be worth sacrificing an abstract principle. Peace and an agreement with the Arabs would be adequate compensation. But unless there is an agreement, any number, even a low one, which the Government fixes would anger the Arabs, and the troubles would continue. Why, then, should we depart from the legal and political basis of our struggle?

Chaim said that he agreed with me. If we want a figure of 30,000 immigrants a year we have to demand 60,000.

I said to him that this time as well we should take the attitude he adopted before the Royal Commission: a large immigration, and a rapid increase in the Jewish population, as the only possible solution. Chaim said he is ready to include what he said at the penultimate session of the Royal Commission, and to repeat it during his opening speech to

218

the London Conference.

I added that there was another important thing we had to stress this time which hadn't been discussed by the Royal Commission, and this was the defence of the Yishuv. This should be one of our central demands: the existence of sizeable Jewish defence forces during orderly times, and also a Jewish army which could be trained and ready in the event of war.

Chaim replied that he agreed wholeheartedly with this.

The conference will be a stern test of our resolve.

London
February 6, 1939.

This morning we received a copy of the welcoming speech which Neville [Chamberlain] will make at the official meeting tomorrow. It is naturally built along 'appeasement' lines, and contains only two political points: a) an appraisal of the Yishuv's stand at the present time, and b) a demand that we recognize 'reality'.

This second point should be answered at once. We should declare that our achievements in Palestine have been the fruit of a bitter reality, and the Jewish people have never faced a reality as arduous as they do today.

The first point also calls for a reply on behalf of the ishuv. At the meeting of the Executive I proposed that after Weizmann's reply Ben-Zvi should speak on behalf of Palestinian Jewry, if he manages to arrive by tomorrow morning. (He has been held up in Paris by fog).

In the evening I drafted a reply for Ben-Zvi:

'On behalf of the Jewish community of Palestine I thank you, sir, from the bottom of my heart for your appreciative words about us. The Yishuv's conduct during the difficult test of the last three years has been dictated by the ideals of peace, justice and brotherhood expressed by our prophets and by our people's invincible desire to rebuild the debris of its land even under a hail of bullets.

'Although most of the Jewish settlers in Palestine are new

219

to the country, the Yishuv is the oldest Jewish community in the world. Despite the repeated destructions of our homeland by Babylon, Greece, Rome, Persia and other foreign conquerors throughout history, the remnant of Jewry has clung to its country and maintained the connection between the people of Israel and the Land of Israel and the Jews' hopes of returning to Zion. And these hopes have been realized. During all the generations Jews have flocked to their homeland from all the countries of the Diaspora. And when Allenby's army conquered Palestine* his troops included a Jewish Legion from the Land of Israel, who fought side by side with Jewish Legionnaires from Britain and the United States.

'I can promise you, in the name of the Jewish community in Palestine, that we will continue in all circumstances to devote our energies to building up the country, and that in the same way we will continue to fortify and preserve peace and justice in our land, in the spirit of our prophetic heritage.'

Wise will be the third speaker on our side. In his reply he will stress America's partnership in the policy of the National Home, and also American Jewry's expectation that Britain will stand by its commitments.

I don't place must hope on these talks. But we should not stay away from them.

London
February 7, 1939.

Ben-Zvi and Mossinson+ arrived at last — at ten o'clock this morning. The whole delegation will be here tonight or tomorrow morning. So the opening reception was not attended by the entire panel (Zionists and non-Zionists). It was a festive occasion, dignified and formal.

The Arabs left St. James's before we arrived. They entered and left through another gate (the Friary Court entrance), while we used the Ambassadors' Gate.

At the gate we were met by officials of the Colonial Office

*In December, 1917.

220

and the Foreign Office. Inside were Malcolm, Lord Halifax+, R.A. Butler and others. A crowd of journalists and photographers thronged around the entrance. First they brought us into Queen Anne's Room, where Chamberlain received us. After short talks with most members of our delegation we all went into the large conference hall, the Picture Room. Four tables were placed in the centre of this room to form a square. The Government sat at one table: Chamberlain, Malcolm, Halifax, Butler, Lord Dufferin, Sir Lancelot Oliphant, Sir Cosmo Parkinson. At the table facing the Government sat Weizmann, with the members of the Zionist Executive next to him.

After we were seated and had been photographed, Chamberlain opened the proceedings. His speech to our delegation was a repetition of the speech to the Arab delegation, apart from two passages which were added specially for us, in place of one passage which was addressed particularly to the Arabs. The real political content of his speech lay in this passage:

'Your people no less than ours have cherished traditions and a history which goes far back into the past. But, while not unmindful of what lies behind us, let us concentrate on the realities of the present situation, giving due weight to all essential facts and endeavouring to appreciate each other's point of view.'

In reply to these words of Chamberlain's, Weizmann said inter alia:

'We meet you at a dark hour in our history: it is no exaggeration to say that the hopes and prayers of millions of Jews, scattered throughout the world, are now centred, with unshaken confidence in British good faith, on these deliberations. We believe that all our work in Palestine has been the result of a grim necessity to face realities, and I would submit that no reality today is more bitter than that which the Jewish people is called upon to face . . .'

Ben-Zvi delivered the speech I wrote for him, in Hebrew. Lourie then read the English translation. Stephen Wise's speech, which followed, sounded much better than it had seemed on paper. All this part of the session was dignified

221

and serious.

The speeches took up less time than had been allocated to them. After they were over we talked with some members of the Government. Chaim spoke with Neville, and Halifax came over to me. He expressed his regret at never having visited Palestine, although he had always wanted to see it. Lady Halifax, however, had visited Palestine about four years earlier.

He asked about several details in my life, and also about the nature of the Labour movement in Palestine. I explained to him that he should not think of our movement in terms of the British workers' movement, because our party and the lives of our members revolved around the idea which had led us to become workers: that only through creative labour could we identify with the Land of Israel and 'earn' it.

He understood and appreciated this concept. Chaim came up and asked him whether he would be present the next day, when he (Chaim) would present the Jewish case. Halifax promised to be present.

Malcolm told us that the Nashashibi delegation had not taken part in the reception, because the other delegates did not want them to attend the conference. But he is trying to make peace between them.

Outside the photographers swarmed around us again. In the evening I learned that Malcolm had tried the whole day to reconcile the Arab factions, but couldn't. As a result the talks with the Arabs, which were scheduled for this evening, have been postponed, and the Jewish case will therefore be heard first, as it turns out.

This will certainly prevent Musa Alami+ and others from meeting me . . .

The rift in the Arab camp is the main story in today's papers.

At night Berl, Locker, Ben-Zvi, Moshe, Eliahu and I met to discuss the situation. Our discussion didn't make me much wiser.

The talks with the British have just begun.

Yesterday I sent you *The Times,* which had a full report of our first meeting with the Government, and also some pictures. I haven't had time to write to you in detail about the 'talks', because since I returned from America things have been hectic. First of all we had to decide on the composition of the Jewish delegation, and this wasn't easy. From every side came proposals and demands, and if we had fulfilled them all we would have ended up with a delegation of nearly a hundred people. Then we had our hands full deciding the arrangements with the Government. And of course there were meetings of the Zionist Executive and endless consultations on our platform, our demands, our tactics.

This afternoon things eased off a little and I find myself with some spare time. So I'll try to outline my views on the various questions involved in these talks.

Several of my colleagues, both in the Executive and in the party, were against our taking part in the talks. Their main reason for abstaining was the Government's refusal to allow into Palestine 10,000 Jewish children from Germany. I handled this matter before I came home last time. I saw Malcolm about it twice, and also wrote him a strong letter just before I left for Palestine. But it was clear to me that we couldn't absent ourselves from the 'talks' for this reason. The Government did not say it would never allow the children to enter, but only that it could not allow this *before* the talks, because if the immigration situation was changed just before the conference the Arabs would not attend. The Government said it was ready to discuss the children's immigration at the beginning of the 'talks'.

I argued that if we did not take part in the conference this would only hurt us, because we would place a dangerous weapon in the hands of our enemies, who would be able to say that the Jews did not want a mutual understanding with the Arabs. We would also make it easier for the Government to pass harsh decrees against us. London would say: For three years, we waged war against the Arabs because of the Jews. We put the entire Arab world against us. And when we wanted to make peace so that Palestine could return to normal and life could carry on quietly, the Jews refused to come, although all these years they've been telling us their hand is stretched out for peace. You can't do anything with these Jews . . .

We also had to take into account the impression our non-participation would have made on public opinion in Britain and America. Many of our friends would not have understood us. In America I did not find a single person who thought we should stay away from the conference. And I am certain that public opinion would have held us largely responsible. We need this public opinion, because our struggle is not over yet, and it will not be over so soon either.

A better reason for not taking part in the 'talks' was the invitation issued to the Arab Kings. By issuing this invitation the British Government has in effect changed the status of the Mandate. What has Ibn Saud or the King of Iraq or the King of Yemen to do with Palestine? We fought the participation of the kings. I sent you a copy of the letter I wrote to Malcolm on November 1, in which I referred to this. But the intervention of the Arab Kings is a political fact. They have been intervening in the affairs of Palestine for the last three years. They have embassies in London, and they speak with the British Government and apply pressure to it even without a special conference. So it is difficult for us to refuse to attend the conference because the Government is negotiating with the Arab Kings, especially when the talks themselves are being held separately*.

I don't expect anything favourable to result from the talks themselves. It is virtually certain that we will not reach an agreement with the Arabs. And why should they make an agreement with us? They are in a strong position. The terrorism in Palestine is continuing, and the Government cannot stop it. Hitler and Mussolini, whose prestige has increased so much, are helping the Arabs, not because they love them but because they hate the British and the Jews. There is fear of another war, and the Arabs are able to threaten Britain by saying that they will join its enemies if

*The Arab representatives had refused to meet the Jewish Agency Zionist Delegation officially.

war does break out, unless it changes its course in Palestine.

The Mufti is not in London and is not taking part in the talks. But the whole of the Arab delegation gets instructions from him, and the Arabs here do nothing before he is consulted. The Mufti considers himself the victor in this situation. He has frightened off all his opponents or killed them; he has frightened the British Government and he has blocked the plan for the Jewish State. And it's unthinkable that he should suddenly surrender his great ambition of controlling Palestine and reach a compromise with the Jews.

And because there won't be a Jewish-Arab agreement, there also won't be a Jewish-British one. *This* British Government — and I'm afraid every other British Government would have done the same — does not want to antagonize the entire Arab world, especially as the danger of a new world war is grave and very real, even after Hitler's 'peaceful' speech last week.

The British Government thinks to itself: If war does break out, we are certain of the Jewish stand. This war would not be like the last one. Then Britain, France and Russia, on the one hand, faced Germany and Austria on the other. The Jews in Germany and Austria had equal rights, and in Russia there were anti-Jewish pogroms. Many Jews in the world, even outside Germany, were on the side of Germany because they hated Russia. If war does break our now, it will be between Britain and France, the friends of the Jewish people, and Italy and Germany — and no Jew in the world can possibly want the latter to win. So the Jews must be for Britain, whatever the conditions and even if it makes life difficult for us in Palestine.

This doesn't apply to the Arabs. Britain has to buy them, because they could join Hitler. And so Britain has to put up with the Arabs — *now at any rate* — to ensure their friendship, at our expense, naturally.

This is the objective situation, which we cannot change. And I have no doubt at all that we will emerge from the London 'talks' worse off than before — without a Jewish-Arab agreement and with new decrees against us. All the same, we have to face up to this new challenge, because we have a lot to lose. This will not be the last battle.

225

Whatever is arranged, even if it harms us for the moment, will be only temporary. We should prepare now for the next battle, so as to avoid mistakes which will weaken us when it comes, as it will.

So we should try to come to terms with the Arabs and to do everything possible to attain a Jewish-Arab agreement. It must be made clear to the British, the Jews and the Arabs that it is not our fault that there is no agreement (and I am virtually certain that there won't be one, despite all our efforts!). If we miss this opportunity not only the British but also many Jews, both Zionists and non-Zionists, will accuse us of not trying hard enough.

I am working in this direction now and trying to talk with Arabs. I don't know if anything will result from this, because at the present moment the Arabs don't want to meet me and even the Arabs I know already are afraid, although they would like to talk to me. But there might be some discussions with the Arabs, particularly after the British Government declares that it does not intend setting up an Arab State in Palestine. And I think they will hear this from the Government, sooner or later.

At the moment we are talking only with the Government. Yesterday was the first working session, and Chaim delivered a lecture. The beginning and end were good, especially the end. There were some rather weak passages in the middle, but the overall impression was positive. Tomorrow morning the Government is going to give us an 'examination'. Malcolm will ask us questions, and these questions might give us some clue about the Government's intentions.

Please let me know if some books arrived for me after I left for London: French books from Paris and English ones from London. Some of the books were sent to Jerusalem.

London
February 10, 1939.

At this morning's session with the Government the onslaught began. First we heard the Arab arguments, and then
226

we were given a momentary glimpse of the Government's own thinking.

Malcolm opened the session. He announced that he would not cover the whole subject and would not yet give the Government's attitude in detail, because he wanted a free discussion. But, he said, he would comment on Weizmann's remarks. Malcolm has been busy trying to sort out the differences between one Arab group and another, and so his speech was not as well-phrased as it might have been. But he was clear and precise, because he has been thinking about these things for several months.

He said he naturally has great sympathy for the Jewish case, and could have spoken at length about the threat of persecution in Central Europe. He could have spoken about the binding commitments given to the Jews. He could have spoken about the splendid achievements of the Jews in Palestine. But he wanted to place other considerations before us — to talk about the situation from the standpoint of the Arabs. This did not mean that the Government is pro-Arab or pro-Jewish. It is pro-Mandate, and it wants to see both sides of the question.

Weizmann spoke about the tragedy of a minority people and the need for a State belonging to the Jews. There was a certain amount of truth in this, and if Palestine was empty it would be a simple matter. But there is another nation in Palestine, over a million people, who have been living there for many generations. This is their country. He does not consider they have no political rights. If these million people had been Scots or Germans the world would have hastened to recognize their rights. Should the Arabs' rights be ignored only because they are weak, and because their rebellion could easily be crushed?

Promises were made to the Jews. The British didn't want to back out of these promises. But they were *vague* — intentionally so, because the people who gave these assurances said: Let's promise them and see what comes out of it. They assumed two things, neither of which happened in practice:

1) That the Arabs would agree or at least acquiesce; in fact, the Arabs opposed the promises to the Jews, and this

227

opposition grew as time went on.

2) That there was not such a large number of Arabs involved. Meanwhile the Arab population increased considerably.

The Arab opposition was genuine, Malcolm went on. The rebellion is not confined to a minority or to bandits. The enmity towards the Jews has grown, despite the benefits conferred by their enterprise in Palestine. The present revolt was being conducted entirely by Arabs from Palestine. We should also take into account the opposition by Arabs outside Palestine. Legally speaking, the Arab countries had no rights in Palestine. But a political question cannot be settled by legal considerations.

The promises to the Jews were vague. Lloyd George spoke as he did because he took it for granted that the Jews and Arabs would not be far removed from one another. Put yourselves in the Arabs' shoes, Malcolm said. You argue: If there were a Jewish majority there would be a Jewish State. And because there is now an Arab majority — it should be an Arab State.

We are bound by the terms of the Mandate to set up institutions of self-government, he said. There is at present an Arab majority in Palestine. Chaim Weizmann said the assurances to the Arabs have been fulfilled — so why should the assurances to the Jews not be implemented? Giving Iraq independence does not satisfy the Arabs of Palestine. On the contrary, it steps up their demand for a similar independence. We must recognize the force of the other side's arguments.

Chaim Weizmann asked whether the British were going to deny their commitments and follow a policy of expediency. The Arab world is in a turmoil. The Moslem world is in a turmoil. Can we ignore these factors? We must be realistic. When the Moslem world is hostile to Britain it is a serious matter. We can't overlook these hard facts. If we sink, Malcolm said, you will sink even deeper.

You might say: this is expediency. But you would be wrong. We must act according to a principle. We are acting according to the Mandate, and we have a commitment to both sides. The Arabs resent our policy and claim that we are overlooking their basic natural rights. We don't think so. But

228

this is what the Arabs claim.

He asked if we wanted to reply, and added that they would allow us to consult among ourselves. Then he and all his colleagues left the room.

Stephen Wise and the other Americans strongly opposed giving an immediate reply to Malcolm. The Colonial Secretary had made a statement of great significance, and we should study every word and prepare a carefully-formulated reply. But I for my part firmly opposed leaving the session without a reply by us. What Malcolm had said wasn't new, and they, my colleagues, could hardly claim to have been stunned by the Government statement.

Chaim put the question to the vote, and the majority voted in favour of an immediate reply. But Chaim wasn't prepared to make this reply, someone else also didn't want to, and so it fell to me. Before I had a chance to prepare anything the members of the Government came back into the room, and Chaim announced that I would reply. I said more or less the following (according to the notes made by the Government):

The Colonial Secretary has spoken as if the debate is between the Arabs and the Jews. This is an erroneous approach. In our opinion, this is a debate between the Jewish people and the other nations of the world. If it were not a world problem the Jewish delegation would not be sitting here to discuss it with His Majesty's Government. This is not the British Government, but the holder of the Mandate given to it by fifty nations.

The Colonial Secretary asked us to put ourselves in the Arabs' shoes. This demand would be in place if the Arabs would do the same and put themselves in the Jews' shoes. But they are not ready to do this in any way. They don't even want to sit together with us.

The Colonial Secretary claimed that the people who drew up the Balfour Declaration didn't know what was happening in Palestine, and thought it was an empty country. But the British Government and public opinion in Britain knew perhaps more about Palestine than anyone else, because they explored the country extensively from the 19th century onwards.

229

The Jewish people's link with the Land of Israel didn't begin with the Balfour Declaration or the British Mandate. These merely recognized an existing historical fact — the historic link between the Jewish people and Palestine. The Mandate accepted that we were in Palestine by right and not by favour. Everyone who knows anything about the history of Palestine and of the Jewish people knows that we were there many hundreds of years before the Arabs. Sixteen million Jews living today consider Palestine their national home.

It is true that neither the Balfour Declaration nor the Mandate said expressly that a Jewish State would be established in Palestine. They could not force the Jews to settle there. But this was their intention: that if the Jews wanted to, they would set up a state. In fact, the references in the Balfour Declaration and the Mandate to guarding the religious and civil rights of the non-Jewish communities in Palestine prove that they know it was not an empty land, and it was obvious that a Jewish State would guard these rights.

The Colonial Secretary argued that the Arabs' agreement, or at least their acquiescence, is essential if the Declaration and the Mandate are to be implemented. But this condition of Arab agreement or acquiescence does not appear in either the Balfour Declaration or the Mandate. The nations of the world, through the League of Nations, recognized the prior rights of the Jewish people, as long as the religious and civil rights of the other inhabitants are preserved.

The Colonial Secretary also claimed that the Balfour Declaration implied that when Palestine is ready for self-government the side which has a majority should rule the country. But wasn't there an Arab majority when the Balfour Declaration was granted? And doesn't the Colonial Secretary know that if there is not yet a Jewish majority in the country, this is the responsibility of the Mandatory Government, which has limited Jewish immigration artificially?

The basic assumption of the Balfour Declaration was that the existing Jewish community in Palestine was only a small part of the community we would build up there, if the country was developed as we were able to develop it. This

230

assumption was correct then, and it is still correct today. The most convincing proof of this assumption is the growth of the Arab and Jewish communities since then. It is not a question of the 900,000 Arabs or the 400,000 Jews who live in the country today, but of the size of the present Jewish community and the millions of Jews who could come there, and who want to come there. And the Jewish community is increasing not by displacing inhabitants, but by developing the latent potential of the country, as only the Jews can.

The Jewish people understand perhaps more than any other people what it is like to be without a country. But the Arab people are almost entirely concentrated in the Arab countries, and they rule themselves. Palestine is one of the countries the Arabs conquered. But the historical inhabitants of the country are the Jews, and throughout the hundreds of years of their exile the Jews have always considered Palestine their only homeland. The nations of the world thought the same way when they gave Britain the provisional Mandate over Palestine until the Balfour Declaration could be implemented in full.

If the Arabs of Palestine see themselves — and rightly so — as part of the Arab nation, they should realize that Arab aspirations are being fully met, even if Palestine, which occupies less than one per cent of the Arab countries, becomes a Jewish State.

The terms of the British Mandate refer to 'reconstituting' the Jewish people's National Home in Palestine, and note the Mandatory Government's responsibility for doing this. It follows from this that the Mandatory Government's first and central function is to create the political, administrative and economic conditions which will ensure the founding of a Jewish State. Only afterwards would come the development of institutions of self-government, which would preserve the religious and civil rights of all the inhabitants of the country, whatever their race or religion.

When I finished speaking, Dr Weizmann asked Malcolm MacDonald: 'Was the founding of a Jewish National Home in Palestine not a question of *restitution*? Didn't the Mandate speak of *reconstituting*?'

Malcolm replied: 'Naturally the Jews have special rights.

But these are rights of Jews, and not of the whole Jewish people.'

After a short discussion it was decided that the debate would be continued at the second session.

London
February 11, 1939

Today we prepared a summary of Chaim's opening speech for the press, now that the papers have published the Arab case (this morning). We'll hand the summary to the London papers on Monday, and it will appear on Tuesday morning.

From the Arabs we've learned that:

1) They won't budge an inch from their demands.

2) Ragheb Nashashibi and his colleagues have not yet decided whether to join the general Arab delegation. The final decision will be taken only after Yakub Faraj* comes to London.

We heard from other sources that M.M. promised the Arabs that they will receive concessions.

Matters are drawing to a head — in London, at any rate.

The focal point of activity will soon move to Palestine and to the United States.

London
February 13, 1939.

It's almost impossible to describe how busy I am over here. Apart from the talks with the Government, my routine day almost always includes: 1) A meeting of the Executive; 2) A meeting of the Jewish delegation; 3) A talk with Stephen Wise and the other Americans; 4) A talk with the Palestinian delegation; 5) Discussions at the Political Department on the general situation, apart from endless current business. When I finished my day's work yesterday I was dizzy with exhaustion, and so I can't write to you now about the way

*Vice-Chairman Arab Christian Society. Member of the Arab Higher Committee.

things are going. This afternoon there is another session with the Government, and we are busy preparing the speeches which will be made today by Wise, Shertok and Chaim.

Ask Kaplan to show you the speech I made on Friday, and also a copy of my journal from America, in which I summed up my recent visit. I don't want to write about this to Tel Aviv, for reasons you will appreciate.

Today, tomorrow and the day afterwards will be very busy ones. Perhaps I'll have a little spare time at the end of the week, and then I'll write to you again about the situation as I see it.

London
March 6, 1939.

I haven't written to you for the last three weeks. All this time I haven't taken hold of a pen. I couldn't write. And now I am unable to describe what these three weeks have been like.

I've already in my life been in some most unusual situations. I remember when I was arrested for the first time, by a Russian policeman in Warsaw in 1903 or 1904, when I was still a boy, and in my town people were convinced (naturally, without any foundation) that they would hang me. I was in prison for about a fortnight, for the first time in my life, and I was tense because of the unknown factors that confronted me.

I recall a week of tension of a different kind — at Sejera, in Galilee, when one Passover a Jewish passer-by killed an Arab in self-defence. I also remember another very tense episode, when I was arrested in Jerusalem during the World War, after an order had been issued by the Turks against the Zionists, and many of my friends and well-to-do citizens of Jerusalem began to shrink away from me in fear. Eventually we (Ben-Zvi and I) were arrested and placed in a Turkish jail. Only one man, apart from the members of the party, dared to come and see us in prison, and this happened to be a Sephardi Jew named Entebbi (he also was deported later on). And until we were sentenced to deportation from the

233

country we had no idea what our fate would be.

I can bring to mind several difficult and nerve-wracking days in America, from the days of the Jewish Legion, the first riots in Palestine, the time of Tel Hai, the pogrom in Jerusalem, and many others. But in all these I have never been through anything like these last three weeks.

The London conference is not over yet, although I think it is coming to an end. But I can't describe it or sum it up now, and I can find time to write to you only because I am spending the third day in a row in my room. (I caught a slight cold, and have to stay in bed).

Not only can't I describe my state of mind during these last three weeks, but also I can't put down the facts in a letter, because I'm not sure you'll be the first to read this letter. Kaplan told me he will see you receive a copy of the journals from the conference, and when I come home (and I hope this will be soon) you'll be able to read all the material I shall bring with me — all the private talks with the heads of the British Government and all the minutes of the official sessions. This material still doesn't convey a faithful, comprehensive and living picture of everything that happens here, because the cold paper and silent letters cannot bring the human drama directly to life. The minutes are also shortened and more like summaries. But all the same these documents will give you some idea of the unequal struggle, the David versus Goliath situation, which was waged here in St James's Palace between the spokesmen of a poor, homeless, hopeless people and His Majesty's Government, the rulers of the mightiest empire on earth.

The struggle is not ended. But its results can already be predicted. The London conference will end, of course, without any agreement. There will not be a Jewish-Arab agreement; there will be no Jewish-British agreement; there won't even be an Arab-British agreement. True, the Arabs have received the main concession from the British — a promise of independence, the independence of Palestine, which means in effect Arab independence. But this promise is not absolute, and it is tied in with various conditions, and it's clear to me that the Palestinian Arabs who take their cue from the Mufti won't agree to these conditions.

The Government is demanding that the Arabs agree to certain guarantees providing for 'the Jewish National Home' within an 'Independent Palestine'. I cannot imagine that the Mufti will agree to guarantee a Jewish National Home. And why should he? He will no doubt say to himself: If I agree to guarantees now, this will mean I am granting something I have refused to do all these years, and I would still receive nothing in return. The Government is promising me independence in the future. Who knows whether it will keep its promise or not? Meanwhile I would have to recognize the Jewish National Home. And this recognition would be a fact. Why then should I agree to it?

So it is clear to me that the conference will close without an agreement, although the Arab countries (who are the main factor in these talks, as far as the British Government is concerned) will leave London with a certain degree of satisfaction if the Government stands by its promise of 'independence' for Palestine.

We undoubtedly face difficult days in Palestine, after the failure of these talks. But I see no reason for panic and despair. If we can only avoid making any mistakes ourselves; if we can remain determined and consistently hold the position we have taken until now, and refuse to take part in any action, institution or other attempt to erect an 'independent' (Arab!) State in Palestine, and if it is established, not to recognize it and to fight it tooth and nail; if we remain united here and in Jerusalem and insist on obtaining what we are entitled to under the Mandate, or the only thing which can replace it — a Jewish State, then neither the British nor the Arabs will be able to put an end to our hopes in this country. The British will not hand us over to the Mufti against our will, and the Mufti is not strong enough to dominate us on his own. I explained this several times during the talks with the British Government.

If we do face any danger, this is only from within: from Jews hesitating, becoming confused, giving in. Only we Jews could allow the British and the Arabs to turn Palestine into an Arab State. And I consider our main political task during the coming months to be the organization of the internal front. The Zionist movement must know what it wants and

235

what lies ahead of it. In my talks here with the people who are closest to me I see with sorrow and amazement that even the best among them do not see the situation clearly, and the path ahead is blurred. This is the greatest danger I can see at this moment.

I am completely opposed to all talk of arranging strikes and demonstrations. All these proposals are signs of impotence. And we are far from impotent. If there is a plot to turn Palestine into an Arab country — and there *is* such a plot — *we are powerful enough to foil it.* In the first stage we will resist passively: but in the second stage we will take action. The Arab State will not come about if we oppose it firmly enough.

We don't need strikes. These harm *us* and no one else. And why should we harm ourselves? No, we shouldn't strike unless it contributes directly to the final aim. The only essential strike action we should take now is to refuse to take part in the bodies which are preparing the Arab State. Five months ago I wrote a long letter to the children in which I discussed this in detail. I have been aware of the danger for some time, and I said that if we don't make the mistake that Czechoslovakia made, we won't suffer the fate of the Czechs.

There is a chance that the talks might end this week, and unless something unexpected comes up I hope to come home as soon as possible. In any event, I will definitely be home for Passover.

London
March 16, 1939.

The Anglo-Jewish conference ended today. The Jewish delegation assembled in our office at 3 p.m. this afternoon and decided unanimously that we could not accept the Government's proposals as a basis for an agreement, and that the delegation was therefore dissolved. And that was the end of the London talks — as far as we are concerned.

There can be little doubt that tomorrow the Arabs will also inform the Government that they reject the proposals.

They asked the Government for two days to think them over. As a matter of fact, the Arab countries were inclined to accept the proposals, but the Palestinian Arabs were vehemently opposed to them, and in my opinion rightly. Although these proposals take almost everything away from us, they give the Arabs nothing, and it is obvious that the Arabs will also turn them down.

What the Government recommends is, briefly:

1) That Jewish immigration should stop after five years, and should only continue if the Arabs don't oppose it.

During these five years not more than 75,000 Jews would be allowed to immigrate; 25,000 of these would be refugees (mainly children and relatives), who would be allowed to enter immediately, once the High Commissioner has ascertained that there are sufficient means to absorb them. In theory it would be possible to bring all these refugees in during this year, or even over a few months. On the other hand, a maximum of 10,000 settlers would be allowed in each year, if the country's absorptive capacity permitted this. In examining this capacity the Government would be advised by both Arabs and Jews.

The illegal immigrants who are in Palestine already (the Government estimates their number at 40,000) would be allowed to remain, but the Government would take measures to prevent illegal immigration in the future. If anyone came in without a permit, and he couldn't be deported, he would be deducted from the number of immigrants allowed for the year.

2) That the High Commissioner would be empowered to forbid the purchase of land by Jews. He would determine in which areas Jews would be completely forbidden to acquire land, in which areas they could buy some land, and in which areas land purchase would be unrestricted.

3) That the ultimate aim of the Government is the establishment of a Palestinian State which would be neither Jewish nor Arab. It might be a federal State. The State would not be established at once, and the process might take ten years. But in the near future an advisory council would be formed, two thirds of whose members would be Arabs and one-third Jews. Arabs and Jews would also be appointed to

237

an executive council. In the course of time this council would become a legislative assembly. The State would be set up only when the Government is satisfied that the two peoples are working together.

This is more or less the plan presented to us and the Arabs yesterday. And of course we rejected it.

When the ornamental details are stripped from the plan, what remains are the following stark facts:

a) The Jews would always remain a minority, not more than a third of the population.

b) There would be no Jewish immigration without Arab consent.

c) Without Jewish consent there would not be an 'independent' State.

In this way the British Government has taken away from each side what it most desires.

The Jews want immigration – so the Arabs are given the power to veto immigration.

The Arabs want 'independence' – so the Jews are given the power to veto independence.

This programme is bound to anger both sides and to incite the Arabs against the Jews. For now the British will say to the Arabs: You wanted independence. Well, we have given it to you, but the Jews are holding it up. And to the Jews they will say: You wanted immigration. Get the Arabs' approval and you will have it!

It would be impossible to find a plan better calculated to deepen the abyss between the two peoples. The Government claims that the purpose of the new plan is to force both sides to co-operate. But in fact it can only increase the opposition between the Jews and the Arabs. Each side will now be able to hinder the other's development. A more evil, stupid and shortsighted policy cannot be imagined. And I am absolutely certain this policy cannot be carried out for long.

For the moment we have received a heavy, almost mortal blow. The Government has in effect annulled the Balfour Declaration, and has declared for the first time that we must remain a minority in Palestine. But I see no reason for panic or low spirits. The new plan is so absurd that I am not afraid it will be put into practice. We shall have some difficulties.

238

But we shall overcome them, if meanwhile a world war doesn't break out.

However, our struggle here in London during the last six weeks has not been in vain. For the first time in the history of Zionism and in the history of the Jewish people after the Roman conquest we faced a serious combat with a mighty power and did not rely only on pleading, requests for mercy or appeals for justice. For the first time we used a new argument: our own strength in Palestine. At first the British thought we were speaking rhetorically. But when they saw we spoke the truth, they became angry.

When we told the Government firmly and with an inner confidence that they could not set up an Arab State in Palestine and that the Arabs could not rule Palestine against our will, they could hardly believe their ears. I told Halifax and Malcolm that we did not need any guarantees and that the Jewish minority in Palestine could look after itself. And they were surprised.

When they understood that we were right and that we could indeed prevent an Arab State being formed, they said: Since you can prevent the Arabs' 'independence,' we'll give the Arabs the right to prevent your immigration ... But this 'punishment' will not frighten us. The 'independent' Palestinian State will not arise, unless the Yishuv betrays itself and the Jewish people.

We have also taught the Arabs something. We had two meetings with the representatives of the Arab countries (Iraq, Egypt and Saudi Arabia), one on February 23 and the other on March 7. The chief spokesman on the Arab side at both meetings was the Egyptian delegate, Ali Maher Pasha. The first time he spoke about the Jews in Palestine as if they were Jews living in Egypt and Iraq, and promised us equal rights ... The second time he did not think of talking that way. By then he understood that the Jews of Palestine are not like the Jews in Egypt and Iraq. And although we have not yet persuaded the Arab countries to support Zionism, they now understand Zionism better than they did before, and they also respect it more.

The non-Zionist Jewish aristocrats of England also learned something during these talks. For the first time Lord

Bearsted, Lord Reading, Lionel Cohen and their friends heard Jews talking with the rulers of the world firmly, in a proud manner, with confidence, stubbornness and a feeling of strength. And although perhaps they did not always agree in their heart of hearts with what we said, they were forced to enjoy it and to rejoice that we were proud and dignified. I'm sure that they are secretly proud that there is one place on the globe where the Jews are a force. All these years they have considered the Yishuv a kind of community of paupers who have to be supported. This time they saw a new kind of Yishuv: a source of Jewish strength. And now they have respect for the Yishuv, and will listen to it.

If only for these things the talks were worthwhile, even though they cost us blood and nerves and anxiety. I don't think I would have been able to continue the terrible tension of those six weeks for another week or two. And although we lost this battle, our political and strategic strength has not been reduced but, on the contrary, has increased. I am sure we will go on fighting and will win in the end.

What is important now is that the Yishuv must not panic or weaken, must not lose its head or do anything foolish. The Jewish people must stand by it and must give all the material and moral help it needs for a difficult and lengthy war, because it is still a long way to the final victory.

Before returning to Palestine I must rest for a few days. But the coming week will still be a busy one, because we have to prepare for a debate in Parliament in another ten to fourteen days. But I will be home for Passover.

To Paula, Geula, Amos and Renana — my dear and beloved ones,

Tonight I received the news that my father had died. I heard the news far away, alone over here — without being able to stand by his bedside during his last moments, without being able to see him before he left us. And when I come home he will not be there.

I know how much he wanted to see me, especially now, when he feared that his last hour had come. I am sorry, very sorry indeed, not to have seen him again. For from my eleventh year onwards, after my mother died, he was a father to me and also a mother. He gave me much — and from great love. And we had so much in common — even though I belonged to another generation, and was different from him in some things.

From him I obtained my love for the Jewish people, the Land of Israel, the Hebrew language. In our small house in Plonsk, at the end of the town, next to the deserted garden and the garden belonging to the Polish priest, the Lovers of Zion members used to meet when I was a child; and when Herzl's Zionist movement came into being, our home became the focal point of the Zionist in our town.

After the Kishinev pogrom* we young boys in Plonsk secretly founded a self-defence group and acquired some arms. I was the head of the group, and I hid the arms in our house. My father knew about this, but he didn't interfere with me, although he knew full well the danger to him and his position in the town if the guns were discovered. On the contrary, he was proud of what his son was doing.

When I added socialism to my Zionism, my father didn't agree with me, but he did not oppose me and did not try to bring me back to 'the straight and narrow path'. True, he did not want me to spend so much time on public activity at my age. His ideal was that I should become a student and finish university. And he was sorry when I told him I had decided to emigrate to Palestine in order to become a worker. This

*April 1963; 47 Jews were killed and 92 severly wounded.

decision of mine was a grave disappointment for him, because he had hoped that I would become a famous scholar. But he did not interfer with me; on the contrary, he gave me the necessary means so that I could go to Palestine, and arranged the journey for me.

The letters he received from me from Palestine were very precious to him. And only after he heard from one of the people in Plonsk who went back there after being in Palestine that I was ill and hungry and that my clothes were torn, did he write to me that I should come 'home'. But when I explained to him that this was out of the question, he accepted it — although he tried to send me money; but when I asked him to stop doing this, he did.

Then it became the dream of his life to come to Eretz Yisrael — he and all the family. But meanwhile the First World War broke out. I was expelled from Palestine by Jamal Pasha, and wandered to America. And only after the war did his dream come true, and he and all his other children came to Palestine, one at a time.

He was a rare father, full of love. He was a good and faithful Jew. He was an honest and good-hearted man, with compassion for others and an open heart. When I come home I shall not see him again. And this makes me sad.

GLOSSARY

Note: This Glossary is intended to assist the reader of Ben-Gurion's letters to understand the many references to personalities which occur in this book. It makes no pretence to be either exhaustive or comprehensive.

ABDULLAH IBN HUSSEIN (1882-1951): Son of King Hussein of Hejaz. Took part in the 1916 Arab revolt against the Turks of Transjordan, 1921; King of Transjordan, 1946, and later of Jordan.

ADLER, CYRUS (1863-1940): President of the American Jewish Committee, and co-Chairman of Jewish Agency for Palestine, 1929.

ALAMI, MUSA EL (b. 1897): Junior Legal Adviser to the Palestine Government, 1923; Private Secretary to the High Commissioner, and Government Advocate, 1933. Left Government service to take up political activities on behalf of the Palestinian Arabs.

AMERY, LEOPOLD (1873-1955): Parliamentary Under-Secretary for the Colonies, 1919-21; Secretary of State for the Colonies, 1924-29.

ARANNE, ZALMAN (1889-1970): Director of the Histadrut's school for Trade Union leaders, 1936-47; Israel Minister of Education and Culture, 1955-60, and from 1963 to 1969.

245

ARLOSOROFF, CHAIM (1899-1933): Editor of the Mapai monthly journal *Ahdut ha-Avodah,* 1930; head of political department of Jewish Agency, 1931. Assassinated in Tel Aviv, 1933.

BAR-ILAN (BERLIN), RABBI MEIR (1881-1949): For many years President of Mizrachi movement in the United States; founded Mizrachi daily paper *Hatzofeh* (published in Tel Aviv).

BAR-YEHUDA, (IDELSON) ISRAEL (1895-1965): Prominent figure in Palestine Labour movement. Served twice as Israel Minister of Communications.

BEN-ZVI, YITZHAK (1884-1963): Pioneer of Poalei Zion movement in Russia before settling in Palestine in 1907; among the founders of *Ahdut ha-Avodah,* of the Histadrut and of Mapai. President of *Vaad Leumi* (Jewish National Council) from 1931 to 1948. Succeeded Chaim Weizmann as President of Israel in December 1952.

BERLIN, RABBI MEIR — see Bar-Ilan.

BLUM, LEON (1872-1950): Leader of French Socialist Party from 1919 and Premier of the Popular Front Government of 1936-37. Served on the Jewish Agency Council.

BOROCHOV, DOV BER (1881-1917): Among the founders of Poalei Zion, and secretary of World Conference of Poalei Zion.

BRANDEIS, LOUIS DEMBITZ (1856-1941): Justice of the United States Supreme Court, 1916-39. President of Zionist Organization of America, 1918-21, and of World Zionist Organization, 1920-21, resigned after differences with Weizmann.

BRODETSKY, SELIG (1888-1954): Professor of Applied Mathematics at Leeds University, 1920-49. Member of Jewish Agency Executive from 1928. President of Board of Deputies of British Jews, 1939-49. President of Hebrew University, 1949.

CHAMBERLAIN, NEVILLE (1896-1940): British Chancellor of the Exchequer, 1931-37; Prime Minister, 1937-39.

CHURCHILL, WINSTON (1874-1965): British Prime Minister, 1940-45 and 1951-55; Colonial Secretary, 1921-22. Opposed Passfield White Paper, 1930, Partition Plan, 1937, and White Paper of 1939.

COHEN, BEN VICTOR (b. 1894): Lawyer and American Government official. Director of Palestine Economic Corporation and a trustee of Palestine Endowment Fund.

D'AVIGDOR-GOLDSMID, SIR OSMOND ELIM (1877-1940): President of Anglo-Jewish Association, 1921-26; President of Board of Deputies of British Jews 1926-33.

DOBKIN, ELIAHU (b. 1898): Co-founder of World Hechalutz Organization. Head of Youth and Hechalutz, Jewish Agency, 1948-68.

DUGDALE, BLANCHE (Mrs. E.T.C. Dugdale) (1881-1948): Niece and biographer of Arthur James Balfour. Member of the British Delegation to the League of Nations Assembly in 1931 and associate of Dr Weizmann and his colleagues.

EDER, DR. M.D. (1865-1936): Member of Zionist Commission in Palestine, 1918. Served on Zionist Executive, 1920-21 and 1926-28.

ELATH, (EPSTEIN) ELIAHU (b. 1903): Headed Middle East division of Jewish Agency, 1934-45, and its Washington political department, 1945-48. Israel's first Ambassador to United States, 1948-50; Ambassador to Britain, 1950-59. President of Hebrew University, 1962-68.

EPSTEIN, ELIAHU — see Elath.

247

ETTINGER, AKIVA YAAKOW (1872-1945): Agronomist. Played an important part in developing new villages in Palestine.

FEISAL IBN HUSSEIN (1885-1953): King of Iraq from 1921. Took a leading part with T.E. Lawrence in the Arab revolt against Turkey, 1916-18.

FRANKFURTER, FELIX (1882-1965): Justice of United States Supreme Court from 1939. Legal adviser to Zionist delegation at the Paris Peace Conference, 1919. Collaborated closely with Weizmann in his negotiations with Feisal.

GOLDMANN, NAHUM (b. 1894): Represented Jewish Agency at the League of Nations, 1935-39. Joint Chairman of Jewish Agency, 1949. President of World Jewish Congress Executive and its president from 1953. President of World Zionist Organization, 1955 to 1968. Negotiated the reparations agreement with W. Germany in 1952.

GOLOMB, ELIAHU (1893-1945): One of the creators of *Haganah* (the Jewish defence forces) and its striking force, *Palmach.*

GREENWOOD, ARTHUR (1880-1954): Deputy leader of the Labour Party, 1935.

GROSSMAN, MEIR (1888-1964): A collaborator of Jabotinsky in founding the Jewish Legion during World War I and subsequently a leader of the Revisionist and Jewish State parties. Member of Jewish Agency Executive, 1948-1961.

GRUENBAUM, YITZHAK (1879-1970): Leading figure in Polish Zionism. Elected to Jewish Agency Executive in 1933 and settled in Palestine. Minister of the Interior, 1948-49.

HACOHEN, DAVID (b. 1898): Founder of the Histadrut contracting company, Solel Boneh. A Mapai representative in the Knesset from 1949. Israel Minister to Burma, 1953-55.

HALIFAX, LORD (1881-1959): Secretary of State for War, 1935; Leader of the House of Lords, 1935-38 and 1940; Secretary of State for Foreign Affairs, 1938-40.

HARZFELD, ABRAHAM (b. 1888): A Palestinian colonization expert. Member of Zionist Actions Committee from 1921. Helped to gain support for Zionism from United States Labour leaders.

HERZL, THEODOR (1840-1904): The founder of political Zionism. Convened the First Zionist Congress in Basle, 1897, and founded the World Zionist Organization of which he served as President until his death. The best Life of Herzl is by A. Bein (East & West Library. London).

HEXTER, DR. MAURICE (b. 1891): President of National Conference of the Jewish Social Service, 1925-26; member of Jewish Agency Executive, 1929-38.

HOOFIEN, ELIEZER SIEGFRIED (1881-1957): Joint General Manager of the Anglo-Palestine Bank, 1919 and General Manager, 1924. Chairman of the Board of Directors of Bank Leumi le-Israel, 1951.

HOS, DOV (1894-1940): Deputy Mayor of Tel Aviv, 1935-49.

HUSSEINI, HAJ MOHAMMED AMIN EL (b. 1893): Grand Mufti of Jerusalem. President of the Supreme Moslem Council, 1922; President of the Arab Higher Committee, 1936. Fled the country in 1937 after the Arab Committee was declared an unlawful organization, and spent the Second World War years in Germany.

HYAMSON, ALBERT MONTEFIORE (1875-1954): Director of British Mandatory Government's department of immigration in Palestine, 1921-34.

IDELSON, ISRAEL — see Bar-Yehuda.

JABOTINSKY, VLADIMIR (ZEEV) (1880-1940):

Journalist, orator and right-wing Zionist leader. Helped to establish the Jewish Legion during World War I. Member of Zionist Executive, 1921-23. Founder-leader of the Revisionist Party, 1925, and the New Zionist Organization, 1935.

KAPLAN, ELIEZER (1891-1952): Prominent in the Labour Zionist movement in Europe, and from 1923 in Palestine. Member of Jewish Agency Executive from 1933, and headed its finance department. Minister of Finance, 1948.

KAPLANSKY, SHLOMO (1884-1950): After settling in Palestine in 1924 headed the Zionist Executive's settlement department in London. Director of Haifa Technion from 1932.

KATZENELSON, BERL (1887-1944): One of the founders of the Histadrut and Mapai. Born in White Russia, went to Palestine in 1901 quickly becoming a leading personality and ideologist in the Labour movement. Edited several Labour journals including *Davar*.

LIPSKY, LOUIS (1876-1963): A close associate of Weizmann. President of Zionist Organization of America, 1925-30; Vice-President of American Jewish Congress, 1934. Co-founder of World Jewish Congress.

LLOYD GEORGE, DAVID (1863-1945): British Liberal statesman. Chancellor of the Exchequer, 1908-15; Secretary of State for War, 1916; Prime Minister, 1916-22.

LOCKER, BERL (b. 1887): Prominent in Poalei Zion movement in Poland. Settled in Palestine in 1936 and served on Jewish Agency Executive, 1931-56, being its Jerusalem chairman, 1947-50.

LOURIE, ARTHUR (b. 1903): Political Secretary of Jewish Agency for Palestine in London, 1933; Israel Ambassador to the United Kingdom, 1960-65.

MACDONALD, MALCOLM (b. 1901): Son of Ramsay MacDonald. Secretary of State for the Colonies, 1935 and 1938-40.

MACDONALD, RAMSAY (1866-1937): British Socialist Prime Minister, 1929-35.

MACK, JULIAN (1866-1943): United States jurist. First president of American Jewish Congress, 1917, and President of Zionist Organization of America, 1919-21.

MAGNES, JUDAH LEON (1877-1948): United States Reform Rabbi and first president of the Hebrew University. Prominent in promoting the cause of Arab-Jewish understanding.

MOSSINSON, BENZION (1878-1942): Member of Zionist Actions Committee and of the *Vaad Leumi*. Chairman of Confederation of General Zionists in Palestine until 1935.

NAIDITCH, ISAAC (1868-1950): Member of Zionist Actions Committee in Paris for many years.

NAMIER, PROFESSOR SIR L.B. (1888-1960): Historian. Political Secretary of Jewish Agency for Palestine, 1929-31; Political Adviser to the Jewish Agency Executive in London, 1931-45; Professor of Modern History, University of Manchester 1931-53.

NASHASHIBI, RAGHEB BEY (b. 1880): Mayor of Jerusalem, 1920-35; Chairman of Arab National Defence Party, 1937.

ORMSBY-GORE, WILLIAM, later Lord Harlech (1885-1964): British liaison officer attached to Zionist Commission, 1918; Secretary for the Colonies, 1937.

PASSFIELD, LORD (Sidney James Webb) (1859-1947): Secretary of State for Dominion Affairs and for the Colonies, 1929-30.

PERSKY, DANIEL (1887-1962): American Hebraist. Born Minsk, Russia. Went to United States in 1908. His first book, *Spoken Hebrew*, was published in 1920.

REMEZ, DAVID (1886-1951): Secretary-General of Histadrut, 1926-36; Minister of Communications, 1948-50; Minister of Education, 1950-51.

ROOSEVELT, FRANKLIN D. (1882-1945): Governor of the State of New York, 1929-33; President of the United States from 1933 until his death.

ROTHSCHILD, JAMES DE (1878-1957): Son of Baron Edmond de Rothschild. President of Palestine Jewish Colonization Association (PICA); Governor of Hebrew University; member of British Palestine Parliamentary Group.

RUBASHOV, ZALMAN — see Shazar.

RUPPIN, ARTHUR (1876-1942): A leading Zionist, economist, sociologist and author. Went to Palestine in 1908. Deported by Turks in 1916, returned in 1919. Director of Zionist Executive's colonization department in Jerusalem, 1921.

RUTENBERG, PINCHAS (1879-1942): Engineer. Obtained a concession from the British Mandatory government for a hydro-electric project at the Yarmuk and Jordan rivers. Founded the Palestine Electric Company.

SACHER, HARRY (b. 1881): Journalist, lawyer, businessman and philanthropist. Leader writer on the *Manchester Guardian*, 1915-19; practised at the Palestine Bar, 1919-30. Member of Zionist Executive, 1927-31, and author of *Israel, the Establishment of a State* (1952) and *Zionist Portraits and other Essays* (1959).

SAID, NURI AS— (1888-1958): Fought in Desert Campaign with T.E. Lawrence. Prime Minister of Iraq fourteen times between 1930 and 1958.

SAMUEL, HERBERT LOUIS, 1st VISCOUNT (1870-1963): First professing Jew to become a member of a British Cabinet; held office in the Liberal Government of 1905-16 and in the National Government, 1931-32. Helped prepare the way for the Balfour Declaration. First High Commissioner for Palestine, 1920-25; leader of the Liberal Party in the House of Commons, 1931-35, and in the House of Lords, 1944-55.

SCHWARZBART, ISAAC IGNACY (1888-1961): Elected to the Seym (Polish Parliament) in 1938. Member of the Polish Government in exile, 1940-45. Founder of World Union of General Zionists.

SHARETT, (SHERTOK) MOSHE (1894-1965): Succeeded Chaim Arlosoroff as head of Jewish Agency's political department, 1933. Israel Foreign Minister, 1948-55. Prime Minister, 1953-55. Resigned from the Cabinet in 1956 as a result of differences with Ben-Gurion.

SHAZAR, (RUBASHOV) ZALMAN (b. 1889): Settled in Palestine in 1924 and a Mapai representative in the Knesset, 1949-57. Minister of Education and Culture, 1949-51. Succeeded Ben-Zvi as President of the State of Israel, 1963 .

SHERTOK, MOSHE — see Sharett.

SIDEBOTHAM, HERBERT (1872-1940): Prominent British political journalist. Closely associated with the Manchester group of Zionists (Weizmann, Israel Sieff, Simon Marks and Harry Sacher) during World War I and until his death. Author of *Great Britain and Palestine* (1937) and other works.

SMUTS, FIELD-MARSHAL, JAN CHRISTIAN (1870-1950): South African Prime Minister, 1919-24. Member of British Imperial War Cabinet, 1917-18.

SOKOLOW, NAHUM (1860-1936): General Secretary of World Zionist Organization, 1905-09. In 1914 moved from Berlin to London where, with Dr Chaim Weizmann, he became a key figure in the negotiations leading to the Balfour Declaration in 1917. Chairman of Zionist Executive, 1921-31; President of Zionist Organization and Jewish Agency, 1931-35.

SPRINZAK, YOSEF (1885-1959): One of the founders of the Histadrut and Mapai. A Mapai representative and Speaker of the Knesset from 1949.

STORRS, SIR RONALD (1881-1955): British military Governor of Jerusalem, 1917-20; civil Governor of Jerusalem and Judaea, 1920-26.

STRICKER, ROBERT (1879-1944): President of the Austrian Jewish National Council, 1919-20. Following a rift in the Revisionist movement, founded the Jewish State party in 1933 with Meir Grossman.

SZOLD, HENRIETTA (1860-1945): Secretary of the Jewish Publication Society of America, 1892-1916. Founded *Hadassah,* the Women's Zionist Organization in America in 1912. In 1918, responsible for the despatch of the American Zionist Medical Unit to Palestine. First woman to become a member of Zionist Executive, 1927. After the Nazi rise to power, became the leader of Youth Aliyah.

SZOLD, ROBERT (b. 1889): President of Zionist Organization of America, 1920-31.

USSISHKIN, MENAHEM MENDEL (1863-1941): Delegate to the First Zionist Congress, 1897. Chairman of Jewish National Fund, 1923-41.

WARBURG, FELIX (1871-1937): Banker and philanthropist. Chairman of administrative committee of Jewish Agency when it was formed in 1929. Chairman of American Joint Distribution Committee, 1914-32.

WAUCHOPE, GENERAL SIR ARTHUR GRENFELL
254

(1874-1947): High Commissioner and Commander-in-Chief of Palestine and Transjordan, 1931-38.

WEDGWOOD, JOSIAH (later Lord) (1872-1943): Close friend of Weizmann; Vice-Chairman of the Labour Party, 1921-24. Author of *The Seventh Dominion*.

WEIZMANN, CHAIM (1874-1952): Born in Pinsk. Lecturer in biological chemistry at Manchester University, 1904. Director of the British Admiralty Chemical Laboratories, 1916. During World War I, Chairman of London Committee of the Zionist Organization and largely responsible for obtaining the Balfour Declaration in 1917. Led the Zionist delegation to the Peace Conference, 1919. President of World Zionist Organization, 1920. Lost leadership in 1931 but regained it in 1936. Resigned from the presidency in 1946. First President of the State of Israel, 1948. Bibliog.: *Trial and Error* (London H. Hamilton, 1949).

WINGATE, MAJOR-GENERAL ORDE CHARLES (1903-44): While serving in Palestine during the Arab riots of 1936-39 he organized formations of Jewish volunteers, known as the Special Night Squads. Commander of Special Force (Chindits), in Burma Campaign, 1943.

WISE, STEPHEN SAMUEL (1874-1949): American Reform Rabbi. A close friend of President Wilson, he played a significant role at the time of the Balfour Declaration. Founder and first secretary of Federation of American Zionists which developed into the Zionist Organization of America. Also founded American Jewish Congress and was its President, 1925-29 and 1935-49.

ZAKAI, DAVID (b. 1886): Associate Editor of *Davar;* Secretary of Histadrut Executive, 1920-25.

INDEX